EMERGENT DHARMA

ASIAN AMERICAN FEMINIST BUDDHISTS ON PRACTICE, IDENTITY, AND RESISTANCE

EDITED BY

SHARON A. SUH, PHD

North Atlantic Books
Huichin, unceded Ohlone land
Berkeley, California

North Atlantic Books
Huichin, unceded Ohlone land
2526 Martin Luther King Jr Way
Berkeley, CA 94704 USA
www.northatlanticbooks.com

Cover art © Aine Ging via Shutterstock
Cover design by Jess Morphew
Book design by Happenstance Type-O-Rama

Printed in the United States of America

Emergent Dharma: Asian American Feminist Buddhists on Practice, Identity, and Resistance is sponsored and published by North Atlantic Books, an educational nonprofit that collaborates with partners to develop cross-cultural perspectives; nurture holistic views of art, science, the humanities, and healing; and seed personal and global transformation by publishing work on the relationship of body, spirit, and nature.

North Atlantic Books's publications are distributed to the US trade and internationally by Penguin Random House Publisher Services. For further information, visit our website at www .northatlanticbooks.com.

The authorized representative in the EU for product safety and compliance is Eucomply OÜ, Pärnu mnt 139b-14, 11317 Tallinn, Estonia, hello@eucompliancepartner.com, +33757690241.

Library of Congress Cataloging-in-Publication Data

Names: Suh, Sharon A. editor
Title: Emergent dharma : Asian American Buddhist feminists on practice,
    identity, and resistance / edited by Sharon A. Suh, Ph.D.
Description: Berkeley, CA : North Atlantic Books, [2025] | Includes
    bibliographical references and index. | Summary: "An essential critique
    of American Buddhism-11 Asian American women reclaim a vibrant feminist
    Dharma against whitewashing, patriarchy, and model-minority
    stereotypes"-- Provided by publisher.
Identifiers: LCCN 2025016552 (print) | LCCN 2025016553 (ebook) | ISBN
    9798889842330 paperback | ISBN 9798889842347 epub
Subjects: LCSH: Women in Buddhism--United States | Buddhism and
    culture--United States | Women--Religious aspects--Buddhism |
    Feminism--Religious aspects--Buddhism
Classification: LCC BQ4570.W6 E44 2025 (print) | LCC BQ4570.W6 (ebook)
LC record available at https://lccn.loc.gov/2025016552
LC ebook record available at https://lccn.loc.gov/2025016553

1 2 3 4 5 6 7 8 9 VERSA 30 29 28 27 26 25

For all the bad Buddhists
and the feminist killjoys—

this book is for all of us.

ACKNOWLEDGMENTS

After you complete a book, one of the most wonderful things that happens is that you get the opportunity to sit back, take a deep breath, and remember how you got here in the first place. As with all my book projects, this one took a lot of coffee, a lot of silence, a lot of alone time, a lot of bribing my dog to let me write just a little more before going to play fetch, and a lot of good fortune.

This book came about through the processes of emergence and convergence I shared with multiple friends and colleagues over the years; their generosity and wisdom have shaped the stories featured here. Most of these amazing interlocutors whom I am so fortunate to call friends probably had no idea how helpful they would be: That one brief conversation we had in the vast hallway of the AAR (American Academy of Religion) conference; or that time when we sat in a hotel lobby crammed in two to a seat at the AAAS (Association for Asian American Studies) conference; or that time we sat around a gas firepit on our hotel patio at yet another APARRI (Asian Pacific American Religions Research Initiative) gathering laughing our heads off; or that time when we passed around one single red lipstick tube to see how it looked different on each of us (this was during the pre-Covid era!) seeded this book project.

Emergent Dharma is really the fruition of countless seeds planted by my many *kalyanamitra*, or good spiritual friends. They have shaped my thinking and feeling since I was a graduate student in Buddhist Studies wondering what an Asian American feminist Buddhist was doing in a field of study that seemed to only validate Euro-American scholarship produced by white men. It was during this time that my first graduate advisor shrugged his shoulders when I told him I wanted to study Buddhism and gender. He disdainfully remarked, "Gender? What issues of gender?" This advisor was also the first to notice that I had gotten engaged during my doctoral program, to which he then remarked, "Congratulations! Well, I guess that's it then." After I had parted ways with him and moved to Los Angeles to conduct fieldwork at a Korean American Buddhist temple, I found another advisor who simply stopped taking my calls (back when we used the landline). But while in LA, I immersed myself in a community of Korean Buddhist immigrant practitioners. I taught their children and learned about what parts of Buddhism they applied to make sense of their daily lives and which parts had little to no role in their practice—surprisingly, meditation was not a big part. At this point, I knew I wanted to study Asian and Asian American Buddhism and Buddhists while paying attention to the intersections of gender, race, and class; it was evident that my new advisor had no idea what to do with me, so we also parted ways.

In retrospect, breaking with these two advisors was for the best because shortly thereafter, Professor Diana Eck stepped up to be my dissertation advisor and she did the one thing that the others had not—she trusted my instincts and expressed confidence in my ability to pursue an area of research in which she was not an expert. She wanted *me* to be the expert, and I am forever grateful for her guidance in helping me listen to and follow my gut.

It was during my time doing fieldwork in LA and while I was working at a museum that I received an invitation to travel to the University of California, Santa Barbara, to attend the first-ever meeting of mostly Asian American graduate students and faculty who understood intersectionality far before it became a part of our daily parlance. This group eventually became the Asian Pacific American Religions Research Initiative (APARRI). It has been over twenty-five years since that inaugural meeting of APARRI, an organization of scholars dedicated to the study of Asian Pacific American religions. I am confident that all of my work has been shaped and made better by this vibrant group of scholars, mentors, teachers, and students who recognize the value of flocking together and supporting one another through whatever iterations our work may take. When I decided that I wanted to not only teach and write about Buddhism, but also to become a mindful eating teacher, a trauma-informed mindfulness practitioner, and a yoga instructor, the APARRI network invited me to offer workshops at the annual conferences. These generative scholars obviously know how important embodiment and mindfulness are to supporting the resilience that we need during difficult times.

My friends at APARRI helped form me into the scholar-teacher-practitioner that I am today because they intuitively knew that the different branches of my studies and practices were more integrated than I realized at the time. I have recently decided to go back to graduate school to begin a clinical mental health counseling program for reasons that are both obvious to me and that also remain somewhat mysterious. But what I do know is that this incredible network of people will help me see the significance of what I am doing, even if I can't yet see it.

So, thank you to all my APARRI friends—your friendship, collegiality, and wisdom are simply unparalleled. I am grateful to all of you. For this particular book, let me shout out some of the infamous APARRIstas and friends of APARRI who are featured in this book—Chenxing Han, Funie Hsu/Chhî, Jane Naomi Iwamura, Thanda Aung, Nalika Gajaweera, and Mushim Patricia Ikeda. Some of you have known each other since the 90s, others are newer to APARRI, and the organization gets better and better because of all of your contributions. To Mihiri Tillakaratne, Gina Masequesmay, Syd Yang, and Naomi Kasumi, I intend to invite you into the mix, then give it a stir, and see what emerges! I also want to give a big shout-out to other *kalyamitra* and friends who have shaped my thinking and being in the world in countless ways—Joe Cheah, Carolyn Chen, Khyati Joshi, Himanee Gupta—really, the list is countless. Suffice it to say, at each APARRI gathering, someone says something that works like a shot of adrenaline to get my brain thinking bigger, more expansive, and better thoughts. To all, a big giant bow with hands in *gassho*.

I also want to extend my deep appreciation to Mark Unno, whose support and guidance have been immeasurable. Mark invited me to deliver the annual Taitetsu Unno Memorial Lecture at the Institute of Buddhist Studies (IBS) in Berkeley in April 2024, which was a great honor not only because of my deep, abiding respect and admiration for his father's writing, but also because it was at this lecture that I offered the first public discussion of *Emergent Dharma*. Special thanks also to Scott Mitchell, IBS president, for supporting my talk; to Tammy Ho, for sewing the button back onto my dress that popped off ten minutes before my talk; and to the compassionate faculty member who combed through his desk drawers to find a needle and thread. I am indeed supported by multiple webs of interconnected compassionate beings.

My thanks also go to the Patricia Wismer Professorship for Gender and Diversity Studies that I have had the great fortune of holding for the two years it has taken this book project to move from a thought seed to its current form. I also want to express my deep gratitude to Sakyadhita, an international association of Buddhist women, and one of its original founders, Venerable Karma Lekshe Tsomo, who is an icon of deep wisdom, tireless energy, and support for all Buddhist women across time and place. She has always seen something in me that I have not seen and has helped me grow in my capacity as a scholar of Buddhism and women, as well as in my role as president of Sakyadhita. I aspire one day to have a fraction of her reach, compassion, wisdom, and clarity.

Another deep bow of gratitude goes to Senior Acquisitions and Production Editor Gillian Hamel of North Atlantic Books, who immediately saw the value in this anthology and has been a wise, compassionate, and patient guide through the entire process of writing and publication. North Atlantic Books has always been a goal as a publisher for me due to its dedication to social justice, its representation of unheard and unseen voices, and its being on the cutting edge of all things that push the envelope to make our world a better place.

To the two people in my life who have made me a better person with each day they have been on this earth—Emily and Olivia. Being your mother is the greatest gift of healing and love that I ever could have imagined for myself. And to my father, who passed away over ten years ago: You have seen me through all my books minus this one, and I miss your comments and feedback. This is my first edited volume, and I know that my contributions would have been even better if you had been able to jot down your thoughts and questions in the margins of the draft with your office pen. And as the running joke goes, Dad—*one day*, I will write that popular textbook on Buddhism, just not today.

CONTENTS

PREFACE

This book traces its origins to a roundtable that I convened at the American Academy of Religion (AAR) in 2019 entitled "Buddhism and American Belonging: Gender, Race, and Intersectionality." I had long lamented the lack of attention or interest in the experiences of Asian American Buddhists in both academic circles and popular meditation centers in the US. Like I have with many of the favorite events I have organized, including the compilation of this current volume, for this roundtable, I cast a wide net, inviting some of the most exciting, compassionate, brilliant, and delightful Buddhist scholars and practitioners I knew; I eagerly awaited their response. When the group finally began our discussion at the AAR, the roundtable consisted of many of the authors featured in *Emergent Dharma: Asian American Feminist Buddhists on Practice, Identity, and Resistance.* In our roundtable, they all provided such a powerful punch and a critical intervention against the erasure of Asian Americans in Buddhist Studies, one that laid bare the politics of race that had shaped our own experiences, that audience members gave us a resounding standing ovation. This stuff does not usually happen at typical stuffy academic conferences, and I knew in that moment that we had a hit a nerve—we simply needed to continue sharing our experiences of exclusion while simultaneously centering our own forms of Buddhist practice and identity, in order to resist the totalizing efforts of white supremacist capitalist patriarchy that still tarnish academia and meditation centers today.

Panelists at this conference explored the themes of Buddhism and American Belonging with the explicit purpose of naming and thinking beyond Buddhism and whiteness to address the following questions—Whose Buddhism counts as "real" tradition in the academy? Whose America do we envision in the study of Buddhism and America? What steps do we need to take to disrupt views of Buddhism that are continually beleaguered by the heavy inheritance of whiteness? As the roundtable went on, each speaker brought their own experience and intellect to thinking through the legacies of whiteness that continue to delimit the flourishing of Buddhism in contemporary US culture and the academy. This panel took a collaborative, co-creative, and collective model of skillful response to racial injustices and whiteness with an eye toward the yearning for belonging and unbelonging.

The collective joy that this roundtable created was palpable for speakers and audience members alike. We knew we wanted to continue these conversations not only for the sake of the field of Buddhist studies, but also because we finally felt that we had created a community of cutting-edge Asian American Buddhists who were tired of being overlooked, exoticized, minoritized, or critiqued. We wanted to shift our marginal positions in the academy and in meditation centers by centering our own experiences. What we perhaps underestimated was the delight and fun we would have when we joined forces as an emergent, on-the-spot sangha, or community; we wanted to keep up the momentum. Flash forward to 2021 when we were in the midst of the Covid-19 pandemic while still reeling from the racist murder of George Floyd. The world was on fire with a virus that led to a global shutdown and collective trauma that we are still trying to get a handle on. Asians and Asian Americans were being pushed in front of subways, sucker-punched on the street, stabbed in their workplaces, and taunted in grocery stores. We were on edge as we once again became the icon of otherness and symbol of a contagion to be eradicated. We were isolated, demoralized, traumatized, and fearful just walking outside by ourselves. Despite the mask mandates, we were never more visible, and for all the wrong reasons.

In an effort to recover our sense of self-worth, strength, and resilience, members of the original 2019 roundtable decided to create an online sangha where we could join together as Asian American Buddhist practitioners seeking community to break through some of the loneliness and heightened anxiety we felt. Thus, in 2021, we created a monthly online Zoom sangha replete with chanting, meditation, and talk-story with a core of Buddhist practitioners—we became the ones we had been looking for all along. We became a supportive presence and lifeline as and for Buddhist practitioners and scholars while sharing a racialized suffering that continued to assault our sense of well-being. Thankfully, the members of this online sangha brought with them their compassion, their wisdom, their humor, *and* their joy. This gathering of mostly female-identified practitioners, one transmasculine non-binary practitioner, and one male-identified Buddhist scholar and priest continued the momentum we had at the roundtable in 2019; this essential community began to hold us in hope, to shore us up, and to provide a spiritual sustenance that had relinquished the kind of formality that would be a barrier to our bonding. We needed each other and we showed up for each other for the good part of a year.

Fast forward to today and the publication of this anthology in Winter 2025. Now, in the early days of Trump's second presidency, we are faced with the slashing of social support networks that protect the most vulnerable in this country. We are witnessing the second term of a president committed to rolling back any efforts at true diversity, equity, and inclusivity. And once again, we need each other more than ever. *Emergent Dharma: Asian American Feminist Buddhists on Practice, Identity, and Resistance* is the latest iteration of this ever-emerging and evolving sangha that transcends time and place. We envision the book as both a sangha and a sutra of sorts that weave us together with the spiritual resources we need to sustain ourselves as we move forward despite all efforts to push us back and down. Once again, when I began this project, I put out a call and awaited a response from many of the Asian American feminist Buddhists whose wisdom, commitment, creativity, compassion, and joy I have long admired and desperately need to cultivate resilience and resourcefulness. To my delight and relief, these folks showed up to reveal the beauty, tenderness, suffering, and healing that the Buddhadharma can offer. It is my great hope that you will benefit from their intimate stories and reflect upon them as a form of care.

May this book serve as a support, a companion, a response, and an invitation to join us in this collective effort toward liberation.

INTRODUCTION

Emergent Dharma: Asian American Feminist Buddhists on Practice, Identity, and Resistance is the first anthology of its kind to surface how Asian American feminists have been doing, being, and seeing Buddhism in generative ways outside of the stereotypes of what it means to be Buddhist in the United States. Despite the prevalence of images equating Buddhism primarily with meditation, the authors featured in *Emergent Dharma* reveal their often-ambivalent relationships with meditation and how they favor alternative modes of practice. They also reveal a more complex picture of Asian American religiosity and spirituality—for being, seeing, and doing Buddhism has not always come easily. Some embraced Buddhism after intentionally turning away from their inherited religious tradition, or they came to Buddhism somewhat later in life. For others, Buddhism is both a source of ambivalence and inspiration. Counter to the prevailing notion that Asian American Buddhists simply adhere to their familial religious rituals and beliefs, the narratives featured here reflect a more complicated picture of disavowal, yearning, ingratitude, and transformation with and through Buddhism. Although this anthology centers feminist perspectives, the contributors include individuals of varied gender identities who engage with Buddhism in ways that challenge dominant narratives. The Asian American authors of *Emergent Dharma* also give the lie to the stereotype that they are somehow less authentic practitioners of the Dharma if they are not engaged in seated meditation, which has become iconic of an American Buddhism narrowly defined by Euro-American white convert practitioners.

Each chapter in this volume expands the contours of Buddhism and intentionally blurs the boundaries between what has heretofore been deemed "authentic" or "real" Buddhism by sharing how Buddhism is perceived, received, and practiced differently by Asian Americans. In this anthology, readers are introduced to a side of Buddhism that has been kept from public view. Readers will discover an "ungrateful" daughter who pushes up against the filial debt to her mother; a Buddhist attending to nonhuman species as an act of compassion; a mother visiting gravesites as part of a Buddhist ethics of care; a queer, bad-Buddhist auntie troubling temple life; a Zen teacher engaging the Dharma through talk-story and poetry; a Buddhist donating blood as a form of giving while cultivating a critical affinity to her tradition; an artist healing from an abortion through Buddhist-inspired art; academics cultivating feminist Buddhist killjoy identities to survive academia; a trans-masculine nonbinary Buddhist practitioner healing from an eating disorder through meditation; and a twice-divorced mother learning to accept her rage and cultivate self-love.

By exposing lesser-known ways of practicing Buddhism, each author dismantles the model-minority stereotypes of Asian American women as being compliant, silent, rule-following, passive practitioners. It is our hope that readers will be inspired by the distinctly liberatory feminist spirit that serves as a thread throughout this volume. In highlighting their stories, *Emergent Dharma* serves as a critical intervention in the overlapping fields of American Buddhism, Western Buddhism, and Buddhist Studies. It endeavors to clarify that Asian Americans not only practice Buddhism differently, but that a flourishing world of Buddhism is out there, beyond seated meditation aimed at relieving individual and collective suffering. This anthology makes plain what and who have been suppressed in the construction of American Buddhism and dismantles racialized categories that measure Asian American Buddhist women as other, overly devotional, less authentic practitioners of the Buddhadharma.

Emergent Dharma draws inspiration and its title from the work of adrienne maree brown, author of *Emergent Strategy: Shaping Change, Changing Worlds*. brown draws upon the visionary work of activists such as Grace Lee Boggs to advocate for a collaborative, co-creative, and collective model of skillful response to social injustice. Emergent strategy prefers "critical connections over critical mass," and emphasizes the deep significance of relationships that underpin complex systems.[1] One of the core principles of emergent strategy that strikes the most resonant chord for us relates to complicating normative knowledge production about Buddhism and mainstream manifestations of American Buddhism. In this anthology, we argue that creatively and constructively re-imagining, re-imaging, and re-visioning Buddhism and Buddhists and intentionally inviting Asian American Buddhists to narrate their own relationships to Buddhism generates a far more complex and exciting glimpse into the lived plurality of American Buddhism. In so doing, *Emergent Dharma* critically reveals how racism, racialization, white privilege, patriarchy, and heteronormativity have shaped the reception and construction of Buddhism in the West and the limited conceits of what constitutes real Buddhism. We are not inauthentic or illegitimate Buddhists if we do not practice meditation; Buddhism has always been multivalent and multimodal. Limiting the tradition to meditation as the primary means of liberation is simply misguided, and doing so hinders the networks of support that we have relied on as a refuge during uncertain times such as these. Like the jeweled net of Indra, this volume has emerged to sustain us through our collective and individual struggles; a key component of this support has been our insistence on cultivating joy as a form of care. Many of the authors featured in *Emergent Dharma* have known each other for almost three decades; we've filled these years with shared meals and coffee breaks during conferences, and we've gotten together to conjure up book panels over full-hearted belly laughs. Some are newer to the net, which is strengthened and expanded by their contributions.

Despite rich and sustaining relationships to Buddhism, not a single author in this volume centers meditation as the sole form of their practice. Rather than continuing to worry about whether we meditate enough and if we are good enough Buddhists, this anthology gathers several distinctive voices to collectively explore the following questions—How might we identify Asian American Buddhism? What makes it distinctive? How does Asian American Buddhism relate to American Buddhism? How does focusing on Asian American Buddhist spiritual lives change what counts as Buddhist practice? What do Buddhism, American Buddhism, and Asian American Buddhism look like when grounded in an Asian American feminist approach? Weaving together these stories in a single volume also constitutes a constructive Buddhist practice of sangha, or community building, where Asian American Buddhist practices and identities are not viewed as watered down versions of some purported "real" Buddhism. This book envisions an opportunity to collectively create an Asian American Buddhist sangha in written form that invites readers to pause and see if and where they may find themselves reflected in these narratives. We hope that this text will expand perceptions of American Buddhism by breaking through the limits of what is considered legitimate practice and by offering a refuge to the many Asian American Buddhists who have often struggled to find Buddhist spiritual homes that resonate with their experiences.

The authors highlighted here actively examine whether Asian American Buddhism is a religious, spiritual, cultural, or political designation and conclude that it is all of these, but like all things in Buddhism, it is also fluid and ever-changing. Instead of advocating for a monolithic category of Asian American Buddhism, we focus on Asian American feminist Buddhist spiritual lives and reveal that our Buddhism is how we do life itself—how we embrace the complexities of the everyday and let them function as a potent training ground for liberating self and others.

A note on the emergent methodological approach of this book: The authors have been invited to contribute creative original works that reflect their own experiences and relationships to Buddhism; these have been neither easy nor automatic for them. After participating in Sakyadhita's 2023 conference in Seoul as the organization's president, I returned to the US and was inspired to create an intentional community of feminist Buddhists because I realized how isolated I had been during the pandemic. Sharing time, space, and meals with over two thousand Buddhist women at this conference was the tonic, salve, and catalyst I needed to cultivate this sangha energy back home. Upon landing in Seattle, I typed up the following email message that I immediately rushed off to as many Asian American feminist Buddhists as I knew:

July 7, 2003

Dear Friends,

I hope that the summer finds you well! I am just back from an incredible two weeks in Korea at the Sakyadhita International Association of Buddhist Women conference and inspired to get moving on a book project I have been dreaming about that I believe we really need. I have always been inspired by the prophetic voices of Black Buddhist teachers and the collections and single-authored books that explore how Buddhism and the Dharma have served many Buddhists in cultivating strength and resilience in the face of deep racial trauma. I am thinking of Black & Buddhist and Radical Dharma as exemplary models of what I have in mind.

As you may know, this is an area that I have been exploring quite a bit over the past five years and I have always lamented that we did not have enough Asian American Buddhist voices addressing the intersections of sexuality, race, and gender. I am also deeply inspired by the work of Sara Ahmed and have often referred to myself as an Asian American feminist Buddhist killjoy in predominantly white spaces.

Given the intensity of violence against Asian Americans during the pandemic, it seems the time is right. So—here is my ask and my invitation: Would you be interested in writing an essay from a personal perspective on the relationship between Buddhist practices and identities and the racialization and experiences of anti-Asian and Asian American violence?

I would like to edit this groundbreaking effort and include an essay of my own. I am asking each of you because you are all Asian American feminist killjoys in my view, and it would be my delight and honor to include your voices in the volume.

I do not have a proposal yet. I do not have a press in mind (open to any and all suggestions). What I do have is a deep and abiding desire to offer such a resource to the public.

If you can think of someone else that I should invite, please do let me know!!! If you know of anyone else currently working on such a project, please let me know as well!

With gratitude,

Sharon

Imagine my delight and surprise when everyone I asked said yes (except for one potential author who was simply too busy researching their own book).

brown serves us a powerful reminder when she says that convergence is key to buoyancy when we are at risk of drowning in an ocean of suffering; this anthology is our Asian American feminist Buddhist women's response to her critically important question: "How do we turn our collective full-bodied intelligence toward collaboration, if that is the way we will survive?"[2] *Emergent Dharma* is premised upon recognizing that creative resilience rests upon emergent strategies of adaptation and organic growth, and as brown eloquently puts it, "[there] is an art to flocking; staying separate enough not to crowd each other, aligned enough to maintain a shared direction, and cohesive enough to always move toward each other."[3] In so doing, the authors highlighted in this volume share their individual experiences to re-imagine and co-create a broader sense of sangha and collective healing; we need it now more than ever in the early days of the second iteration of the forty-seventh president's second administration.

This anthology emerges as the physical threats of the Covid-19 pandemic slowly wane; yet, though the virus may have become more routinized in our physical bodies, its social effects have left indelible marks on the body politic. The conditions of the virus brought into stark relief the continuing racist ideology that implies Asian Americans embody social, political, and economic contagion. The pandemic also revealed the predominance of anti-Asian violence, particularly against women, which remains breathtaking in its scope and virulence. This gathering of Asian American feminist Buddhists, one of the first of its kind in book form, emerges as a resource and refuge from which we share the collective grief and healing from racial trauma that is often overlooked when experienced by Asian Americans who are either hyperinvisible or hypervisible in America's racial politics.

Each author makes clear their habits of resistance against white supremacist capitalist patriarchy. During the Covid-19 pandemic and its wake, Asian Americans bore the brunt of racist violence, so much so that many of the authors featured in this volume feared for their own lives. It was not just Covid-19 but this violence that led many, particularly Asian American women, to protectively sequester themselves. We've also designed *Emergent Dharma* to challenge the painful silence surrounding these attacks and the fear we experience when we once again become targets of and seemingly easy scapegoats for the white nationalism that has spilled out as increasingly normalized venomous vitriol. The traumatic experiences resulting from anti-Asian and anti–Asian American violence continue to leave their marks on and in our bodies. It is our hope and intention that the shared narratives will offer a balm for these violent psychic and physical attacks and will assure others who have suffered that they are not alone. We recognize that Buddhist teachings can be applied to further suffering through exclusionary practices *and* provide healing from racial trauma.

As an anthology, *Emergent Dharma* is inspired by this term's roots: *anthos*, or flower, and *logia*, or collection or gathering. Thus, when we anthologize our voices, we gather flowers to conspire and create a refuge and *anthera*, or medicine extracted from a flower. *Emergent Dharma* is a collective blooming of individual voices that, when taken together, contribute to making Asian American Buddhism a field of possibility and creative potential that sustains and nurtures Buddhist ways of being, seeing, and doing. We hope it is a healing salve for the suffering experienced by Asian Americans. Like a sutra that weaves the different teachings of the Buddha into a whole, this volume sutures together individual voices to create a larger text to retrieve, redress, re-vision, re-image, and re-imagine not only Asian American Buddhism, but also American Buddhism, and Buddhism itself.

Emergent Dharma anthologizes and authorizes us as witnesses to our own Buddhist spiritual lives, particularly because, in the larger field of American Buddhism, we are often considered unreliable narrators of what it means to be authentic Buddhists. To *anthologize ourselves* means that we believe ourselves to be reliable narrators of what it means to be, see, and do as Asian American Buddhist practitioners. We are not all seasoned Buddhist priests who have spent countless hours in meditation; instead, we narrate our Buddhist lives differently, and often under the radar. Although Asian American Buddhists are often behind the scenes and out of the limelight, this does not mean that our practices are not potent; rather, they have been allowed to grow outside the purview of American Buddhism, and their roots are deep.

brown's approach to emergent strategy as an iterative method aligns and resonates clearly with the Buddha's invitation to explore the teachings. The

Buddha's Dharma talks were invitational in nature as he uttered the words, *Ehi Passika,* meaning "Come, and see for yourself," which connotes an exploratory spirit of inquiry. Coming and seeing for ourselves encourages us to approach the Dharma with a beginner's mind that allows us to creatively apply the teachings to everyday life. The authors here have done just that—they have responded to the invitation, and the results offer an invaluable insight into the contours and nuances of Asian American feminist Buddhist spiritual lives, however secular their orientation. Recognizing that our spiritual lives may be more secular than "religious" resonates with many of us who are not always the pious, devout temple-goers that many convert Buddhists may believe we are.

When we allow the spiritual and secular to coexist creatively, we gain a more expansive understanding of our own experiences of Buddhism, our relationship to the religion, and how each of us creatively assesses and applies the Buddhadharma to our everyday lives. Many of the authors' chapters indicate an ambivalence toward institutionalized Buddhist traditions, particularly when they are mired in nationalist violence and rhetoric, and they also feel drawn toward the dharmic lessons themselves. The chapters in this book also reveal the complexity of inheriting a Buddhist tradition and wishing to disavow parts of it while simultaneously engaging in Buddhist practices with white convert and BIPOC Buddhists who may romanticize Buddhism. It is for these reasons that we invite you to explore the struggles, nuances, and challenges of our spiritual lives and what it's like to practice as Asian American Buddhists in the United States.

Each of our stories, artwork, poetry, dialogues, and narrative essays, functions independently to offer a glimpse into our lived experiences. However, when taken together, they reveal and provide nuance to what has previously been hidden from the popular reception and perception of Buddhism and expand upon practices and beliefs that have heretofore been ignored or dismissed.

Each chapter contains both unique and widely known practices—unique in that they have not been readily discussed or addressed in larger convert Buddhist circles and widely known to and normative for many Asian American Buddhist practitioners. The collective and creative wisdom that emerges when we cast a wide net inspired by the Buddhist invitational Ehi Passika approach is a re-visioning, re-imagining, and re-imaging of Asian American

Buddhist spirituality as an emergent Dharma that creates a new vision of community. Each chapter contributes to an ever-growing Asian American Buddhist sutra that readers can approach; we hope you will discern what Asian American feminist Buddhists do and how they think, and also what they use as a generative and creative catalyst to reconsider their own Buddhist practices and spirituality.

Asian American Feminism and Buddhism

In writing our essays, we, the authors of *Emergent Buddhism*, make clear our commitments to feminism as a way of life and to feminist theory as a creative tool for our individual and collective liberation; thus, we understand the goals of feminism and Buddhism to be interconnected. As a collaborative response to injustice, this anthology signals that, at the outset, we need each other to act as a refuge, sanctuary, fuel, and nourishment so we can gather strength to dismantle the epistemic and physical violence against all minoritized communities that we experience and witness, for we are neither postracial nor postfeminist. Here we draw upon the wisdom of feminist cultural critic bell hooks, who saw feminism as a multipronged effort and argued that "Feminism as a movement to end sexist oppression directs our attention to systems of domination and the inter-relatedness of sex, race, and class oppression."[4] Throughout her all-too-brief life, hooks made clear that feminism needed to be intersectional to disrupt and dismantle imperial white supremacist capitalist patriarchy. In an interview with philosopher George Yancy, hooks explains:

> We can't begin to understand the nature of domination if we don't understand how these systems connect with one another. Significantly, this phrase [white supremacist capitalist patriarchy] has always moved me because it doesn't value one system over another. For so many years in the feminist movement, women were saying that gender is the only aspect of identity that really matters, that domination only came into the world because of rape. Then we had so many race-oriented folks who were saying, "Race is the most important thing. We don't even need to be talking about class or gender." So for me, that phrase always reminds me of a global context, of the context of class,

of empire, of capitalism, of racism and of patriarchy. Those things are all linked—an interlocking system.[5]

Emergent Dharma reveals how a feminist Buddhist's way of being, world-view, and practice can serve as a liberatory education to awaken and inspire us to dismantle racialized systems that categorize our bodies as exotic, different, and easily expendable in public and political life. It is also the very practice, philosophy, and way of being that gives us hope and offers us a framework for understanding, analyzing, feeling, and healing our suffering.

In *remembered rapture: the writer at work*, hooks shares how writing became a significant recuperative strategy to heal her brokenheartedness—"It was the sanctuary, the safe place" from which she could heal.[6] Her vision of the written word inspired *Emergent Dharma*'s creation as a sanctuary, refuge, and sangha in textual form. Like the Buddha's teachings, which were inscribed on palm leaves to create and bind a community of practitioners together, the chapters in this volume are woven together as an invitation to come and see what Asian American feminist Buddhists have been doing all along, and how we see ourselves and each other in relationship to Buddhism. As a contemporary sutra, this anthology hopes to nurture, grow, and suture together a community for Asian American Buddhists who have often been ignored and overlooked despite their profound practice and contributions. We hope that readers may find glimpses of themselves in these stories of ambivalence, joy, heartache, and liberation to re-imagine themselves not as overly devotional and less authentic practitioners than their white convert counterparts, but rather as potent sources of Dharma.

Readers will find, perhaps surprisingly, that many of us consider ourselves "bad" Buddhists, for our ways of being Buddhist are misaligned with received categories and expectations of us as Asian American Buddhist women. We simply do not fit the peaceful meditator mold and are often out of joint with the prevailing narrative of what makes for a "good Buddhist." Instead of lamenting our "bad" Buddhist selves, many of us have drawn inspiration from cultural critic Roxane Gay, whose self-styled identity as a "Bad Feminist" has particular purchase for this volume. Gay explains:

> I openly embrace the label of bad feminist. I do so because I am flawed and human. I am not terribly well versed in feminist history. I am not

as well read in key feminist texts as I would like to be. I have certain . . . interests and personality traits and opinions that may not fall in line with mainstream feminism, but I am still a feminist. I cannot tell you how freeing it has been to accept this about myself.[7]

Gay openly acknowledges her messy imperfect self, a self that is committed to feminism, yet is unwilling to put herself on a pedestal. Instead, as a bad feminist, Gay embraces the contradictions of what it means to be human while continuing to advocate for justice; she is unwilling to relinquish parts of herself that enjoy the things that a feminist on a pedestal could not. As she puts it, "I am just trying—trying to support what I believe in, trying to do some good in this world, trying to make some noise with my writing while also being myself: a woman who loves pink and likes to get freaky and sometimes dances her ass off to music she knows, she *knows*, is terrible for women."[8] Gay's bad feminist resonates closely with our own experiences, for by embracing ourselves as bad Buddhists, we accept the contradictions and untidiness of our Buddhist selves; we are unwilling to suppress the parts of ourselves that Buddhism can help us accept, but we also celebrate ourselves in our yearning for liberation.

We share Gay's definition of feminism, which she intentionally keeps simple despite its complexities and blind spots. Gay explains:

> I believe in equal opportunities for women and men. I believe in women having reproductive freedom and affordable unfettered access to the health care they need. I believe women should be paid the same amount as men for doing the same work. Feminism is a choice, and if a woman does not want to be a feminist, that is her right, but it is still my responsibility to fight for her rights. I believe feminism is grounded in supporting the choices of women even if we wouldn't make certain choices for ourselves.[9]

Gay makes clear that one can be a feminist (or even a feminist Buddhist), fighting for freedom for all beings, without sacrificing oneself at the altar of feminist (or Buddhist) piety. It is for these reasons that many of the authors here have appropriated the term "bad Buddhist" as a positive personal and political designation.

In this anthology you will find an alternative understanding of some of the most effective practices and features of Buddhism, outside of meditation, that are not usually afforded noteworthy attention.

Asian American Feminist Buddhist Voices

In "My Mother Remains: An Immigrant Daughter's Buddhist Reckoning with Filial Debt," Chenxing Han explores the limits of the mother-child bond as *the* iconic model for cultivating lovingkindness in her own relationship to her mother. "What if the parent-child relationship is marked by harm and rupture rather than healing and repair?" she asks as she explores her ambivalence around mother-daughter dis/affinity and in/gratitude—all as a way to grapple with the vexing question of *What do we owe our parents?*

In "Infinite Light, Infinite Life," Funie Hsu/Chhî shares how her mother's life and death opened Hsu/Chhî up to the reality of the Buddhadharma, especially in regard to the interconnection among all beings. She shares how her mother revealed the truth of their karmic affinities with other humans, as well as with nonhuman animals and spirits. Hsu/Chhî explores how through her mother's embodied experiences and teachings, she inherited both Buddhism and a connection to the world beyond the human realm. She highlights how these inheritances are more than superstition; they illuminate the expansiveness of existence. In addition to reflecting how Asian American heritage Buddhists often learn their Buddhism through being in relation with family—and particularly in relation with the women in their family—rather than through texts or religious services, this chapter highlights how such modes of Buddhist inheritance can often regard linkages to other beings (human and nonhuman, living and nonliving) as being central and significant components of belief and practice.

Jane Naomi Iwamura's "Grave Remembrance: Sustaining Connection and Caregiving Across Generations" offers a personal reflection on her family's regular practice of visiting the cemetery to remember the deceased and maintain sustaining ties to their loved ones. Born out of a Buddhist worldview of death and sense of gratitude and interconnectedness, this ritual represents the way in which she passes down her religious and cultural heritage to her children.

These often-unmarked rituals, practiced by many Asian Americans outside of the walls of the temple, suggests the "long echo" of religious transmission and equates Buddhist memorials and memory with a specifically Buddhist ethics of care.

In "Creating Desire Paths: On Being a 'Bad Buddhist Auntie,'" Mihiri Tillakaratne asks what it means that Gen X, millennial, and Gen Z Asian American Buddhists are now aunties and therefore *ancestors*. She explores how they pass on cultural and religious traditions in unique and subversive ways and asks what this means for Buddhism, where lineage is so vital. Tillakaratne reflects on the contradictions of embracing a Bad Buddhist Auntie identity: being considered a role model while also being seen as a cautionary tale; being a great auntie while simultaneously being a bad Buddhist, bad Sri Lankan, and bad American. She explores what it means for the Bad Buddhist Auntie to shape the minds of future generations of Sri Lankan American Buddhists, and how we can embrace the Bad Buddhist Auntie inside us all.

In "Threading the Invisible Flower Garland: Stories of Asian (North) American Buddhist Women I Have Known," Mushim Patricia Ikeda shares a collage of true stories, harnessing the power of brief personal narratives and vignettes to advance the Asian American Buddhist liberation movement. Beginning with "1997: My mother, with terminal cancer, declares herself Buddhist," Ikeda moves on to talk-story about her Japanese immigrant grandmother's Buddhist practice in Hawai'i; she then interweaves her experience with the Korean Buddhist laywomen, who are the backbone of Korean Buddhism, with her monastic training in Toronto, Canada, Michigan, and in the mountains of South Korea. Warmth, connection, unsung hard work, quiet support, and luminous spiritual life in the midst of everyday activities emerge as themes, grounded in the feminist principle that the personal is the political. Through real stories this chapter reflects the on-the-ground diversity, contradictions, and open questions that emerge from interacting with Asian North American Buddhist women.

Nalika Gajaweera's "Critical Affinity—A Scholar-Practitioner's Memoir of Lived Buddhism" explores her ambivalent relationship to Buddhism as an Asian American, a scholar of Buddhism, and a Sri Lankan American, one who was born in the US and raised in Sri Lanka in a Sinhalese Buddhist household during a religiously inflected civil war. Hard-pressed to separate the tradition from the ethnoreligious community of Sinhalese Buddhism and its complicity in bloody state violence against minorities in Sri Lanka, she shares that she is admittingly often bemused, and even a little envious, of the romanticized appeal Buddhism holds for many Western converts. She notes that while Buddhism seems to represent for her interlocutors a potential salve for present and historical wounds of US empire, for herself, the tradition is entangled in statecraft, power, and violence against the other. Gajaweera draws attention to the struggles, the disavowal, and the desires of relating to Buddhism, especially in relation to violence as a transnational diaspora Asian Buddhist.

In "Art for Catharsis (or an Unborn Child): Transforming Trauma, Pain, and Loss into Healing Rituals," Naomi Kasumi shares her own healing process after having an abortion. She shares how she has cultivated a "ritual" of creating handmade objects that have evolved into many large-scale installation artworks over the past two decades. These creations serve as a testament to the power of artistic expression in navigating the tumultuous landscape of grief and loss. The act of openly sharing her experience with others, a courageous endeavor given the current taboo surrounding discussions of abortion in the US and especially in Japan, became a cathartic and vital aspect of the healing journey.

In "Talk-Story from the Trenches: Asian American Buddhist Feminists in Academia," two Asian American queer-identified, feminist scholars of Southeast Asian descent utilize pseudonyms to dialogue about how to incorporate Buddhist psychological insights into teaching and how to balance work, politics, and family responsibilities in the United States. Tâm Thâm Tịnh and Thanda Aung offer a conversation about working in Asian American studies and Women's/Gender and Sexuality studies within the California public university system. Their conversation exposes how white supremacist cishetero-patriarchal institutions protect and reproduce themselves by denying difference and displacing problems onto marginalized and already precarious usual [killjoy] suspects (e.g., the unhappy feminist, the angry or "racist" woman of color, the queer or trans* "bully"). Sino-Burmese immigrant Thanda Aung speaks from her family connections with diasporic Burmese Theravāda and (Chinese) Mahāyāna communities in Southern California. Tâm Thâm Tịnh is an immigrant from Việt Nam who has been exploring Vietnamese Zen Buddhism, as taught by master Thích Nhất Hạnh, and mindfulness as a way for members of diaspora to heal from the different forms of PTSD, violence, and oppression. Their talk-story examines how Buddhism, mindfulness, and detached compassion might offer healing at personal and collective levels within academia and for Southeast Asian Americans.

Syd Yang's "Being with the Body in a Body" explores how eating disorder recovery can be a feminist endeavor, what the Bodhisattvas may have to teach about an embodiment of liberation, and how the physical body might be the raft that will take them to the Other Shore. Yang shares how recovering from an eating disorder has been about coming back in/to the body sustained through continually remembering that they have a body and that this body is worth caring for. That this body is worth loving, regardless of its transgressiveness or gender, regardless of sexuality, regardless of age. Their recovery is an endeavor that invites them into a deeper and kinder embodiment that roots into a Dharma-based feminism that honors the liberation of all bodies, all lived/living experience, and all ways of being with oneself and (in) the world.

In "Asian American Buddhist Feminist Rage, Trauma, and Self-Love," Sharon A. Suh shares how embodied Buddhist practices have helped her recognize, feel, and allow the anger and rage she often suppressed as a means of liberating herself from an unhealthy second marriage. Learning to read the signs of her body and trust her gut were the first steps she needed to cultivate self-love in a culture that silences the rage Asian American women may feel and how that rage is a symptom of things gone awry. Suh argues that Buddhism is about liberating ourselves from systems of domination and cycles of trauma, and this requires a deliberate and thoughtful process of self-care and self-love. Self-care and self-love are not the result of self-conceit or excessive self-centeredness but of an ethics of care that requires abandoning the propensity to self-silence for the sake of individual and collective liberation.

A Feminist Killjoy Infusion

Another guiding spirit of *Emergent Dharma* comes from the feminist killjoy par excellence, Sara Ahmed. In *The Feminist Killjoy Handbook*, Ahmed encourages us to engage in the difficult yet necessary task of acknowledging how whiteness, white privilege, and white supremacy have constructed, shaped, and maintained power structures that delimit access to non-whites. When we do so, we must be willing to risk upsetting or killing the complacent and often blind joy that comes from an uncritical view of one's own privilege in order to become feminist killjoys. In describing how feminists kill joy, Ahmed explains, "Feminists are judged as threatening (of happiness) because we threaten what is deemed by some to be necessary (for happiness): a belief, a practice, a way of life, a social arrangement."[10] The tightfisted investments in power structures and institutions often rest upon a dividing line between who is allowed in and centered and who is left on the margins. Ahmed makes clear that the feminist killjoy is not against joy, but rather against such joy accumulating in the hands of those in power at the expense of others. When the feminist killjoy points out this discrepancy, she is often rendered unhappy, unfulfilled, angry (rightfully so), and ultimately silenced. Ahmed further notes, "My aim is not to rescue us from the feminist killjoy but to give her a voice. . . . To reclaim this figure is to recognize a truth in her."[11]

Ahmed observes that when we point out a problem, as many a feminist killjoy does, we are often rendered the very problem that we wish to fix; that is, "If you expose a problem, you pose a problem; if you pose a problem, you become the problem. The management of a problem becomes the management of a person."[12] Managing the problem usually results in shrouding the problem in secrecy and silence in an attempt to make the problem itself go away. Ahmed is keen to show that with whiteness comes not only power, but a desire to perpetuate the accumulation of its riches (social, economic, political) in the hands of those who benefit most from white supremacist capitalist patriarchy.

It would be foolhardy to assume that Buddhist institutions are somehow free from power-hungry concerns. No matter how often Buddhist terms such as *emptiness* and *interconnectedness* are wielded to argue that predominantly white Euro-American convert sanghas transcend racial, class, gendered, and sexual stratification, our experience says otherwise. The narratives featured here show that such claims function as spiritual bypasses that do little to challenge such power structures and, instead, reinforce privilege through a quick

Buddhist sleight of hand. Claiming a deep resonance with Buddhist teachings of no self, many Buddhist converts accused of racism simply shut down or silence the real complaints of racial violence (physical and epistemic) by substituting the person of color making the complaint for the legitimate complaint itself.

When faced with accusations of racism and sexism in an institution (including the Buddhist sangha), it is far easier for those in power to maintain the status quo by personalizing the complaint and giving it a face—usually that of a woman-of-color whistleblower who undoubtedly causes eyes to roll, often before she even officially lodges the complaint. It is easy to blame the person leveling the complaint for killing the joy in the room when they challenge discrepancies in power and access. In fact, such complaints are usually blocked quickly and fail to make it up the chain of command. The feminist killjoy perseveres, nonetheless.

Such eyerolling, the kind that suggests the "oh, here she goes" response, is a retaliatory gesture aimed at debunking and taking the air out of the complaint, but Ahmed skillfully reappropriates the eyeroll as the perfect feminist killjoy method and effect. In *Living a Feminist Life*, Ahmed writes, "Whenever we speak, eyes seem to roll, as if to say, well, you would say that. From these experiences we can condense a formula: **Rolling eyes = feminist pedagogy**."[13] Much like the sensation of alienation from the bounties of white supremacist capitalist patriarchy awakens a feminist killjoy consciousness, the myriad experiences of Asian American alienation in predominantly white Buddhist institutions can turn us into affect aliens—where we sense that something is not quite right, or that we are not quite right. That is, "We are alienated by not being affected in the same way as those around us."[14] While others in the meditation hall may bask in the celebration of our presumed emptiness and interconnectedness, the feminist Buddhist killjoys in the room remain unwilling to accept what is neither wholesome nor unskillful.

When the feminist killjoy names the white elephant(s) in the room, they often receive blowback because they have named something that should not have been named yet has been there all along. Asian American Buddhists have had to contend with the whiteness of Buddhism in the room since white meditation convert centers developed and spread in major cities across the United

States. While the authors in this book may not publicly proclaim themselves to be feminist killjoys, the spirit of the feminist killjoy is palpable in each contribution. The feminist killjoy spirit inspires us to critique the hyperinvisibility of Asian Americans in American sanghas and to decry the grafting of the Asian American model minority myth onto our very bodies to render us silent. The prevailing assumption is that Asian American women are passive, silent, stoic, and more concerned with economic and social success in the United States, and therefore they will keep quiet no matter the cost. What the reader will find in this volume is that the feminist killjoy spirit is alive, well, and kicking. We engage in a critical intervention by dismantling the categories that have failed to define us or even envision us as Buddhists worthy of attention and worthy of being seen as major contributors to the phenomenon of American Buddhism.

The feminist killjoy icon thus serves as a guiding force that brings these voices together in a shared and collective space to name, to redress, to intervene, to celebrate, and to support each other. While this book was coming together, each author met with the editor to discuss their piece and each conversation led to the realization that "we are the ones we have been looking for—we are the Buddhist sangha that we have yearned to find." That is, we all share a similar desire to create the sangha that could articulate the ways that the Buddhadharma has appeared for us through our individual and collective struggles, through our anguish, through our joy, through the ways that we create rituals to restore ourselves to fullness and to integrate the parts of us that are hidden, suppressed, marginalized, attacked.

The icon of the feminist killjoy thus aligns beautifully with an Asian American feminist Buddhist method through the act of noticing. We observe phenomena as they arise and pass away and when there is opposition to that passing away, we note the three poisons of greed, hatred, and delusion as they persist, and we awaken to the habits of race and racism—these are the Buddhist methods that promise liberation, and the Buddhist killjoy utilizes these methods of observation for social liberation. What could be more Buddhist than noticing, naming, and then changing the sources of suffering to turn toward liberation?

Noticing and observing is a central Buddhist practice; it is also what makes the feminist killjoy's act of discernment so powerful and valuable. It is observation followed by action and, at times, an unpopular and often uncalled-for action. For Ahmed, noticing is an act of political labor. She remarks:

> You might notice how you are noticeable. And in noticing how you become noticeable, how you stand out, you come to see what you otherwise would not see if you participated in something, or what you could not see from the vantage point you previously enjoyed. This is why I think of noticing as political labour. In noticing the world, we hammer away at it.[15]

Part of the relief and joy of being a killjoy comes from being able to name and note what has been happening and actively work to transform it.

Herein lies the deep connection between the feminist killjoy and the Asian American Buddhists—we see, feel, note, and observe both what is happening outside of ourselves and the impact of the observables on our own bodies. We trust that our bodies are not lying to us as they register the impact of imperialist white supremacist capitalist patriarchy. The feminist killjoy also senses when things are awry, and this too is the Buddhist way—noting, sensing, and experiencing sensations and observing and labeling them. We offer this anthology as an opportunity for Asian American feminist Buddhists to come together and to share the wounds, the celebrations, and the joy-making that shape our Buddhist subjectivities. Ehi Passika!

I

MY MOTHER REMAINS

An Immigrant Daughter's Buddhist Reckoning with Filial Debt

CHENXING HAN

没有母女缘 *méiyǒu mǔnǚ yuán*: What does it mean to say this of a woman and the girl she gave birth to? To insist that they do not have mother-daughter affinity is betrayed by the pair's once-umbilical and always-biological connection. The two are karmically bound. For Buddhists, this mother-child bond serves as *the* iconic model for cultivating lovingkindness. From the seventh stanza of the Karaṇīyametta-sutta:

> As a mother would so cherish
> her child, with her life, her only child
> Now cultivate, in equal force,
> a boundless mind for all beings[1]

I am an only child. When I first chanted this Pali verse in my early twenties, the comparison fell flat. This self-sacrificing mother, who would give up not just a minute's attention but her very *life* to shelter her kid from harm—this was not my mother. Growing up, yes, I wished for such a mom. But as I pass, childless, through the latter half of my thirties, I don't know if I want a mother who would cede her own time and desires so readily. Mine did not, does not—a refusal that has molded suffering and strength into my life.

On the rare occasions when my mother talks about being pregnant with me in 1980s Shanghai, she recalls playing a rigorous game of badminton with the express aim of driving me out. There I am, too comfortable to leave, as my watermelon-bellied mother whacks the shuttlecock across the net, fantasizing that my expulsion—the end of her discomfort—will be as swift.

Her discomfort does not cease with my birth. Though not born into a pig zodiac or famine year like my father, I am voracious. To ease the pain of breastfeeding, my mother supplements my diet with sugar water.

I always wondered if this detail was apocryphal. Wasn't getting sugar water before receiving a name (my father chose 辰星 a few days after I was born) too precise a portend for the need to find nourishment elsewhere? Three decades later, I stumble across proof, in a 3×5 album no thicker than a billfold, plastic-sleeved diary entries where photos should be. Unsentimental as a hog farmer's feed log, tidy Chinese script attests to the sugar water dates and quantities.

If my mother has mastered laconic bullet journaling, I am the most purple of profligates when it comes to the written word (case in point). But we are both economical when it comes to speaking with each other, often to the level of miserliness. During one period in the latter half of my twenties, when daughter-mother communication was at an all-time low, I read Grace M. Cho's *Haunting the Korean Diaspora*.

"I want to tell you a story," Cho writes, "not of anything in particular that happened in my family, but of how silence came to define my daily fabric."[2] It had been a decade since the unhappy silences (anxious, seething, apathetic: To run with Tolstoy, each unhappy moment is unhappy in its own way) of my high school days, when my mother and I shared a roof and little else (seldom meals, never hugs) in the suburbs of Seattle, while my father lived and worked eight hundred miles away in Silicon Valley.

A decade had passed, but Cho's words summoned that unhappiness afresh: the tension, the anger, the despair, the rancor. Some of it had dissipated, but some of it remained stubbornly lodged. I was like a cucumber intent on becoming a bitter melon. That Thanksgiving—for what now, another decade onward, seems like no discernable reason—I drove forty-five minutes not to my parents' house but to my best friend's boyfriend's family home. Nobody asked, nobody commented, so the silences only grew. I thought of the narrator in Maxine Hong Kingston's *The Woman Warrior* as she recalls her mother's reaction—echoed by the other villagers—to the incriminating melon belly of the aunt whose husband had set sail to America years ago: *No one said anything. We did not discuss it.*[3]

"I imagine that one of the reasons people cling to their hates so stubbornly is because they sense, once hate is gone, that they will be forced to deal with pain," James Baldwin writes in *Notes of a Native Son*'s titular essay.[4] My pain, so desperate to be mirrored, read resemblance into Cho's book where crucial differences prevailed:

I too had lived in Washington, but in a less rural part of the state, thirty years later.

The Chinese character for the country (my last name 韓) may be tattooed on my body, but I am not Korean.

My mother has no diagnosis of mental illness, though she peppered my upbringing with many an exasperated "神经病!" (My third time watching *Everything Everywhere All at Once*, I realized this is also Evelyn Wang's signature mutterance, with daughter Joy and husband Waymond as its primary targets.) I never knew how best to translate *shénjīnbìng*. Fool? Nutcase? Crazypants? Psycho? *Why are you crying?* Her sneering question only made me cry harder. *You're never going to survive in this world if you're so sensitive.* 神经病![5]

The epithets that might be aimed at Cho's mother (war bride; *yanggongju*) would miss their mark in mine. My mother professed a hatred of politics—I took politics to mean no choice in the songs you sang, no chance of retrieving your half-brother's disappeared body—but expressed no resentment about six years of factory work during the Cultural Revolution. If anything, she sounded satisfied by her own competence. In America, she would see the price tags on clothing and stuffed animals and proclaim, *I can make this.* (She could, and did.) Mom's prowess in math matched her skill at sewing: talents cultivated in spite (not because) of six years among textile machinery. She married a fellow engineering student five years her junior, a pairing made possible by the decade of university closures. They left Shanghai for graduate programs in Ohio, Dad and I trailing Mom by eight months, by which point she'd found her way to Pennsylvania. It was the beginning of fourteen years of family separation in a successful bid for upward mobility. Monetary gains, other kinds of losses.

"It would take time to flesh out the fullness of my mother's seeming absence from our silent family dinners," writes Cho in *Haunting the Korean Diaspora.*[6] Thirteen years later, her memoir, *Tastes like War,* fleshes out how schizophrenia was part of that fullness.

I had been wrong to project hostility into Cho's family dinners. What she felt for her mother—what motivated her writing—was the opposite of hatred. Of the one-room studio in New Jersey where her mother spent her final years: "The apartment had been a labor of love and filial duty." On choosing a professorship over her baking business: "I continued down that path because I was driven by the need to repay the debt owed to her." Cho elaborates:

> There was my personal debt of knowing that her singular motivation had always been to give her children a life of opportunity, but there were also societal debts—American society's debt to the immigrants who make their food, clean their toilets, raise their children; Korean society's debt to the droves of young women who put their bodies and sexual labor on the front lines of national security, to whom no one would ever speak the words "thank you for your service." In neither case were the debtees treated with gratitude. Instead, the debtors would make them into the cause of society's ills, the very things that needed to be eradicated.[7]

I hold my mother against this frame of debt as if squinting at a photo negative before a sunlit window. Seeking contours, I find inversions.

It is not my mother's singular motivation to give her children (child, technically; there's just me) a life of opportunity. I can't imagine her choosing to come to this country if it wouldn't have expanded, first and foremost, the opportunities in her own life.

My mother has never worked in food or janitorial or childcare services, besides a brief gig selling hot dogs at the baseball stadium (preferable to answering calls at the university bookstore, since her mental math was impeccable, unlike her comprehension of what a "Bic" or "mailer" was). She has never cleaned toilets that were not her own. I can't imagine her raising other people's children. It's not the PhD in electrical and computer engineering so much as the wary distance she keeps around kids, as if faced with a burgeoning case of mildew: better not get too close, careful it doesn't get out of hand.

Debt and her handmaiden Gratitude, their kissing cousin Sacrifice—none of these characters make an appearance in my mother's stories of China and America. Matter-of-Factness prevails. The University of Cincinnati didn't pay a living stipend, so she applied to a PhD program at Carnegie Mellon and covered her costs as a bookstore clerk and hot dog hawker before the move from Ohio to Pennsylvania. The first year in the textile machine factory, she was paid sixteen yuan a month; in the second year, eighteen. Upon achieving the rank of 师父 *shīfù* and taking on 徒弟 *túdì*, her salary reached its peak: the permanent plateau of thirty-two yuan a month. (I notice that the factory gave my mother and her apprentices titles that would be at home in a Buddhist monastery: Master, Disciples.) Shifts on endless weekly rotation: 6:30 in the morning to 2:30 in the afternoon, 2:30 in the afternoon to 10:30 in the evening, and worst of all, overnight from 10:30 to 6:30. The underlings, currying favor, would occasionally buy her meals: 拍马屁 *pāi mǎpì*, my mom chuckles, sounding pleased. (Coincidentally, she was born in the right zodiac year to be on the receiving end of "patting the horse's rump.") Who can blame her for being pleased? Those meals tasted far better than the potatoes served up for lunch during the famine years of the Great Leap Forward, tubers my preschool-age mom—obstinate, ungrateful—roundly refused.

My mother was among the droves of schoolchildren made to dig trenches to straighten out rivers, yet evinces none of my father's vituperation for the forced labor ("Brain-dead!" my dad scowls). She doesn't say she is owed anything—or owes anyone. She isn't looking for gratitude—and isn't doling it out either, in fawning doses or frugal ones. If anyone tarred her as the cause of society's ills, my mother would not give a rat's ass. In the summer after my junior year of college, a group of science campers (I was the science writer intern) surprised me by predicting that, faced with a *Lord of the Flies/Hunger Games* situation, I would surely be the last person standing. (How we arrived at this macabre conversation evades memory.) I thought: You have not met my mother.

In the bittermeloness of my twenties, I read resemblance into Cho's story where crucial differences prevailed. I even managed to neglect the biggest difference of all: My mother is still alive.[8]

Before a sunlit window, I scrutinize still shots and find no Dragon Lady, no Lotus Blossom, no China Doll, no Tiger Mom either. Just my inimitable, ineradicable mother.

On the subreddit r/AsianParentStories, NC stands for "no contact" rather than the state above South Carolina; AP refers not to standardized exams but the Asian Parent who would demand that you ace them.[9]

No Contact is usually a pained choice made by the suffering child, though busy schedules and habitual silences could conspire to bring it about. If not for WhatsApp, I too might have lapsed into the estranged fate of NC with my APs. During the pandemic, my mom used the initials of our first names (Chinese nickname, in my case) to form our group thread. A recent exchange on AXX:

今天去摘草莓 🍓 很贵, 但是又香又甜 I text

👍 my mom replies, adding:

今天做了一只白斩鸡, 很好吃

(to which I add a heart emoji even though I'm vegetarian)

We can text about u-pick strawberries and Cantonese poached chicken, but I cannot imagine typing—much less saying—to my mother, "My debt to you is immense," as found in the lines of the Cambodian Dharma song "Asking for

Mother's Forgiveness," which details the debt incurred by all of us who began life in utero.

> When I was inside your womb
> I put you through constant pain
> whether you walked, stood, or sat
> and made you eat simple food.
>
> Salty, spicy, hot, or cold:
> these you eschewed for my sake.
> You suppressed your desires
> to protect me in the womb.
>
> For nearly ten months you toiled,
> the pain spreading through your body,
> without a moment's relief
> to bring you joy, ease, or peace.[10]

Another Dharma song from the Khmer Buddhist tradition, "Filial Debts," extends the tally postpartum.

> While you ate, I cried and screamed.
> You rushed over and held me,
> Gently singing lullabies
> With affection till I slept.
>
> Spit and piss and even shit
> Any nasty thing I'd ooze,
> you'd pick up with your own hands
> and wipe me clean without disgust.[11]

To chant this poem is to beg forgiveness from the "noble mother and father" who have "toiled so hard to rear me"—though, given the strictures of gender, one suspects that the lion's share of dealing with all those secretions fell on the purportedly uncomplaining mother.

Without memories of infancy, who can measure their upbringing against the ideal presented in "Filial Debts"? I can only speculate that with both parents working full time, my childhood nanny, Auntie Xu, would have done a good portion of the soothing and wiping. While I don't know if my mother complained of disgust, she did bemoan the tedium of childrearing with enough frequency and vehemence that I assumed *baby = excruciating boredom* was an equation worthy of Pythagoras.

I mumbled sheepish *sorry*s for causing her mind-numbing monotony. If you see childcare as a chosen outcome of elective parenthood, my erstwhile apologies are unwarranted, absurd even. But within the world of Cambodian Dharma songs—which entered my life through my partner, who has been learning and translating ស្មូត *smot* for longer than the seventeen years I've known him—my remorse is entirely apropos ("Noble mother and father . . . forgive my faults and failings!"). The very fact of being alive is proof of an incalculable debt to our parents ("words can't record all you've done").

Along with the badminton and sugar water, another story survives from our Shanghai *lòngtáng*: I once howled for an hour. There was no rushing over, no holding, no affectionate lullabies. *We left you alone on purpose*, my parents recount with pride. *After that, you never cried so wildly again.*

Whether they had hastened to my side or not—whether this was the ultimate victory in self-soothing or the basis for a lifetime of insecure attachment—many a Buddhist text will insist that it is well-nigh impossible to repay our filial debts. The Buddha says so himself in "Recollection of the Virtues of Parents," through an ever-escalating set of similes.

> Bhikkhus, there are two persons that cannot easily be repaid. What two? One's mother and father.
>
> Even if one should carry about one's mother on one shoulder and one's father on the other, and [while doing so] should have a life span of a hundred years, live for a hundred years; and if one should attend to them by anointing them with balms, by massaging, bathing, and rubbing their limbs, and they even void their urine and excrement there, one still would not have done enough for one's parents, nor would one have repaid them. Even if one were to establish one's parents as the supreme lords and rulers over this great earth abounding in the seven treasures, one still would not have done enough for one's parents, nor would one have repaid them. For what reason? Parents are of great help to their children; they bring them up, feed them, and show them the world.[12]

So, even if you serve as Atlas to the globe of your parents, literally shouldering their combined weight for not just a minute but an entire *century*; if you attend to them as you might a pair of well-oiled WWE wrestlers, who, it should be noted, are suffering from incontinence; if, after this herculean feat of acrobats and custodianship, you grant them reign over all the gold, silver, beryl, seashell, agate, pearl, and carnelian in the world—even after all this, it won't be enough.

Or, more concisely,

you can never repay your mother,

to quote from "The Lanyard," Billy Collins' quintessential poem on filial debt[13]—the same six words that Putsata Reang uses as an epigraph for her memoir, *Ma and Me*.[14]

If neither acts of care nor material riches resolve filial debt, what will? The Buddha grappled with this very conundrum upon recognizing the need to pay back the "price of rice and milk" to his mother, Queen Māyā, who died seven days after his birth.[15] In the bilingual Pali-Khmer sermon "Discourse on Maternal Debts," he realizes:

avasiṭṭhā me mātā/"My mother remains."

The Khmer portion expands on this realization.

"Now there's only my exalted mother, to whom I, the Tathāgata, owe a great debt, who remains to be repaid at last. So now I, the Tathāgata, should go repay my mother. As for the Buddhas of the past, they all repaid their mothers. How should I repay my holy mother?" The Lord thought deeply, using his omniscient wisdom, then said, "When all of the Buddhas of old had been enlightened to the wisdom of omniscience for seven full years, they performed the Twin Miracle and vanquished all of the heathens there, before finally going off to reside in Tavatimsa Heaven, [under] a coral tree and upon a raised seat of jewels, where they repaid their mothers by preaching the Abhidhamma."[16]

In other words, he followed a tried-and-true formula.

1. Obtain enlightenment. Teach the Dharma for seven years. (Preliminaries.)

2. Create a jeweled walkway in the air. Emit fire from the top half of your body and water from the lower half. Alternate. Use this flame and fluid to illuminate the cosmos while preaching the Dharma.

3. Make several duplicates of yourself walking, lying down, and sitting (all while still in the air).

4. Host a Q&A forum for the educational benefit of the audience: Make another duplicate of yourself to ask questions and answer them as your nonduplicate self.

5. Repeat steps 2 through 4 in your hometown and the city where rival leaders are looking for a showdown.

6. Ascend to the Heaven of the Thirty-Three to preach on the most abstruse and exacting aspects of Buddhist doctrine for three months to your deceased mother.

I don't know about you, but this recipe for paying off filial debt feels . . . not so replicable. Yet the broad principle—we owe our parents an enormous debt; the most efficacious means of repayment is spiritual—resounds across the Buddhist world.

But what if the parent-child relationship is marked by harm rather than healing, rupture instead of repair? How, then, do we reckon with the vexed and vexing question of *What do we owe our parents?*

"Struggling with the Teaching of Karmic Debt Toward One's Parents," on the subreddit r/Buddhism, opens with a post from a mental health professional who accepts the reality of karma but disagrees with transactional notions of filial debt.

I frequently work with people who have narcissistic, neglectful, or abusive parents and the idea that they "owe" their parents back for

taking care of them is a great source of suffering and regression for
them in my experience. . . . I really don't see an act of unconditional
love as something to be somehow repaid by the recipient.[17]

A muscular debate ensues. One person suggests shifting the framing from
debt to gratitude: Of course parents have faults, they're wandering through
samsara too, so why not be thankful for being born a human, at a time when
the Dharma is still being preached? Another touts the benefits of spiritual
practice: "The alternative is you stay angry and the anger burns you up. It is
very hard work!"

The original querier, Untap_Phased, counters that anger helpfully moti-
vates abused children to set necessary boundaries.

More people weigh in. Despite a bevy of other proposals—including invo-
cations of Nagarjuna's two-truths distinction between relative and absolute
reality ("There are many levels of healing/forgiveness . . . awakening trumps
all of them")—Untap_Phased is unsatisfied: "I remain disturbed and confused
at the amount of responses that immediately frame this as a matter of repayment or debt."

It's not just Redditors who find the topic contentious. Reiko Ohnuma argues
that "the tradition itself is grappling with the 'debt to the mother' theme,"[18] as
evidenced by the range of Buddhist texts—many featuring the Buddha, his aunt
and foster mother Mahāpajāpatī, and his cousin Ānanda—that can be mapped
onto "a continuum of increasing discomfort with the son's debt toward his
mother" from grudging acceptance to outright disavowal.[19] In these ambiguous
emotions around Mahāpajāpatī—who did not "conveniently die, as Māyā did"[20]
but stuck around in classic feminist killjoy fashion to plead for women's ordination into the sangha—we begin to appreciate the Buddha's relationship to his
mother(s) as "a tie both nurturing and devouring, sometimes furthering and
sometimes hindering his Dharma."[21] When it comes to a relationship as intense
as the one between mother and child, "the flip side to such love and attachment
might very well be ambivalence, guilt, submerged hostility."[22]

It's not easy to be mired in such a mess of feelings. Another Redditor
attempts a triumphant resolution to the whole quandary: If your motivation
is liberation of all sentient beings, why not be indebted to your parents? Given
how close they are, you could actually help liberate them from suffering!

Not so fast, says Untap_Phased.

This is an inappropriate and impossible task to lay at the feet of the victim of abuse, a child that has for their whole lives been conditioned to live as a reflection of their parent and hold on to the hope that they can "change" their parent into the one they deserved even to the point of dying to do so.[23]

And this, as erin Khuê Ninh asserts (in "Ask a Model Minority Suicide";[24] *Ingratitude*;[25] and *Passing for Perfect*[26]), is precisely the problem. When "clothes worn, meals eaten, air breathed" are "filial obligations to be repaid, in denominations of selfhood" regardless of how cruel the creditors and how dutiful the debtors, some of us will gamble with our very lives to try to beat the house.

The odds are particularly bad for second-generation Asian American daughters—or really any of us who answer to Filial Duty and the Model Minority success frame.[27] The Model Minority, like Duty, decrees allegiance to the pursuit of its asymptotic perfection. Yet both are siren calls hard to resist, even when we know them to be unwinnable propositions.

After all, as Ninh points out, the Model Minority is less myth or stereotype than identity, genre, aspiration, expectation, compulsion, racialized performance, operating system, prison, purgatory. If you, too, are a daughter of Asian immigrants who struggles to repudiate the Model Minority's orbit only to feel like further proof of its gravitational tow, you will know in your bones why the unnamed narrator of *The Woman Warrior* (let's call her Maxine) weaves an elaborate fantasy as Fa Mu Lan ("the villagers would make a legend about my perfect filiality"), only to fail spectacularly in Docility and Duty as a second-generation daughter (*Stop that crying!* my mother would yell. *I'm going to hit you if you don't stop. Bad girl! Stop!*).

Even well into adulthood, Maxine cannot shake free from her haunted childhood. She confesses: "When I visit the family now, I wrap my American successes around me like a private shawl; I *am* worthy of eating the food." She can't bring herself to visit often: "I had to get out of hating range."[28]

Who is doing the hating, child or parent? Kingston's obfuscation here acts as another shawl. A cloak of protection by (and for) a daughter who "would not speak words to give [her mother] pain."

Hearing in my mind's ear the perspective of an Asian American daughter litanized—into debt, unto death—I initially thought Kingston had written: "I had to get out of hurting range."

The chorus of Redditors on "Struggling with the Teaching of Karmic Debt Toward One's Parents" tenders no consensus, though one post uniquely unsettles me.

> Something else to keep in mind, being born is not a passive process. The person being born is making choices as well. It is not enough for a man and woman to have sex, the being to be born needs to be present as well. We choose our parents at some level, so we do play a role in our births. This doesn't excuse any poor treatment by parents, but any poor treatment doesn't justify having unskillful qualities of mind in relation to one's parents.[29]

I first heard this notion dramatized in Cambodian Buddhist texts that ascribe agency to the consciousness that hungers for human form. This pre-self/proto-I plays a pivotal role in the act of conception that will lead to gestation and (re)birth. Worthwhile critiques of heterosexism and gender binarism aside (perhaps we can't fault these texts for not taking queer families and IVF into account), I remember how this novel idea hit me like a gut-punch.

We choose who we are born to.

What? I'd squawked, and not just because of the ick factor of turning conception into an incestuous ménage à trois. (I prefer not to envision my parents copulating, and I especially do not want to imagine electing to participate in some way.) More disturbing: the implication that birth is no accident of genetics or act of God, but, to some degree, a self-begotten choice.

The teenage me who screamed, in a fit of misery, "I wish I was never born"—the enraged mother who agreed (*I wish you were never born*)—the tension and anger and despair and rancor before and during and after—one Buddhist response would be: *Actually, you did wish to be born, and to this particular family. Go figure.* A test worthy of Fa Mu Lan, who had to learn "to make [her] mind large, as the universe is large, so that there is room for paradoxes."[30]

In *The Woman Warrior*, a mother-daughter relationship takes on mythic proportions. An Asian American work of more recent vintage, *Everything Everywhere All At Once* (*EEAAO*), similarly renders the emotional truth of familial tensions by depicting them as epic, multiversal battles.

Alpha Joy as the ostensibly matricidal overlord Jobu Tupaki—mind-shattered by overbearing mother Alpha Evelyn, who pushed her to contain multitudes—yearns for an escape from samsara, flirts with nihilism in the form of an Everything Bagel, fantasizes about a karma-free omniverse where nothing we do matters. I've only ever watched the film with other Buddhists, which may explain why I can't help but wonder if *EEAAO* is less science fiction than Dharmic reality.

If it is not just individual consciousnesses that are reborn but relationships too, as Erik Davis contends[31]—look to contemporary Cambodian Buddhist understandings, or to the countless lifetimes in which the Buddha-to-be journeyed with his (or her) parents, spouse, children, cousin, aunt—then Joy and Evelyn are bound by volition, in mutual tenacity. As if there is some karmic entanglement that wants to be worked out, even as they maim each other across infinite universes, or manifest as desert rocks only to hurtle off a cliff's edge into the abyss.

A friend once told me about the teaching, particularly common in Tibetan Buddhism, that everybody you meet has been your mother in a past life.

Everyone has been your mother is the basis for *mettā*.

Mettā, my friend added, is not for wimps.

(EEAAO's Waymond, in Alpha or regular form: not a wimp.)

Only one Buddhist teaching on family relations has made me cringe harder than the whole playing-a-role-at-your-own-conception thing. "Every child must have a mother and it is totally natural to love her," writes Thích Nhất Hạnh in "A Rose for Your Pocket: An Appreciation of Motherhood."

> The mother loves her child, and the child loves his mother. The child needs his mother, and the mother needs her child. If the mother doesn't need her child, nor the child his mother, then this is not a mother, and this is not a child. It is a misuse of the words "mother" and "child."[32]

Every time I read this ode to mothers, I think of my white Christian classmates in Cranberry Township, school-issued flowers and hand-crafted cards passing from small hands to open palms. Teachers looking upon me with pity, less for racial incongruity than maternal abandonment. (Surely my parents were lying to me about being "separated by their jobs"?) My carnation—symbol of mother's love, blooming where the Virgin's tears fell—withered, long before I saw my mother next, on the apartment balcony by the potted plant with its paper clip–sized cucumbers. We'd have to check the old photo albums to remember how often we visited Florida (at least once, maybe twice; she worked while Dad and I went to Disney World) and how often she came to Cranberry (no recollection whatsoever) over those two years.

The Thích Nhất Hạnh Foundation website offers a caveat in its introduction to "A Rose for Your Pocket":

> For those of us who have a challenging relationship with our mother, we may instead use this reflection to develop a deeper appreciation for our father, a teacher, or another loved one who has been a positive figure in our life.

Perhaps this is meant as consolation, but it feels like a sidestep. As the Buddha said, "My mother remains." Even if my response to "Mother is a gentle and sweet spirit who makes unhappiness and worries disappear" is an emphatic *Nope*, my poetic sensibilities resist substituting *mother* with the relative who gave me bear hugs and a feeling of safety such as I have never experienced (and probably never will experience) from my mom. ("An uncle is like a spring of pure water, like the very finest sugar cane or honey, the best quality sweet rice"?)

What makes me want to squirm right out of my skin is Nhất Hạnh's prescription to sit your mother down (tonight, or the next time you visit if you live far away), make her stop whatever she's doing, look her in the eye, and then,

> keep looking into her eyes, smiling serenely, and say, "Do you know that I love you?" Ask this question without waiting for an answer. Even if you are thirty or forty years old, or older, ask her as the child of your mother. Your mother and you will be happy, conscious of living in eternal love.

Playing this scenario out in my head, all I can conjure is a baffled mother, blurting out: "Are you dying?"

But Nhất Hạnh's next sentence parries my deflection.

> Then tomorrow, when she leaves you, you will have no regrets.

"Let your elders eat while their throat is still upright," Putsata Reang's mother enjoins, and so Put (as Ma calls her) shows up with a cornucopia of fruit and pastries on every social call with her older siblings or parents or grandparents.[33] (No doubt she does this for elders beyond the sphere of her Cambodian American family as well.)

Before publishing *Ma and Me*, Reang penned a piece for *The New York Times*' Modern Love column. "At Sea, and Seeking a Safe Harbor" documents the pain of (having) a mother who is unable to accept that her daughter is gay, and the burden of living with an albatross of a story that sinks a dutiful daughter with unrepayable debt.[34]

Reang's compulsion to "live an immaculate existence" originates with her mother's refusal, on a Thailand-bound navy vessel full of Cambodian refugees, to obey captain's orders. She will not throw her listless baby overboard. That half-dead infant grows up, of course, to be Putsata.

The ending of *Ma and Me*, which I won't spoil here, evokes for me "A Tree Rooted at the River's Edge." Composed by an anonymous author in the late twentieth century, the poem owes its popularity to a monk from Northeast Thailand who chants the Thai words in a meandrous Lao melody.

The reminders of impermanence are standard enough—

We, your parents, have now grown old,
and must depart from you before long.
The times we still will meet face to face
are but a sliver of all the days to come.

but later stanzas startle for their inversion of filiality's usual logic:

We're sorry if we've hurt you.
Please remember that at all times,
in our deepest hearts, we only have wanted
to follow your progress and give our blessings.

A tree rooted at the river's edge
has little hope to stand there long.

One day it will surely collapse,
leaving the bank behind, all alone,
leaving the bank behind, all alone.[35]

At one of my language lessons during the two years I lived in Bangkok, my Thai teacher asked: "What food from America do you miss the most?"

Though I usually labored over every syllable that left my mouth, fretting over consonants and tones and vowel length and grammar, my answer flowed fluently.

อาหารที่พ่อแม่ทำ *ahan thi pho mae tham*

The food my father and mother make.

For the first time in our months of meeting together, I saw tears glaze Mod's eyes, felt them spring to my own. I had spoken an absolutely true sentence whose correctness had nothing to do with phonological or grammatical precision.

Until that moment, I hadn't known I wanted to be fed by my parents while my throat was still upright.

Now that a decade has passed, I don't regret that missed Thanksgiving per se. The three of us have never really done celebrations. Not Christmas or Valentine's, Fourth of July or Halloween, not Mother's Day or Father's Day or birthdays. (Gifts in our household: A water flosser will join my pile of mail in the guest room on a random Tuesday; I'll pick them up the next time I stop by, months later.)

Maybe I'm not so hard on myself for that one night of pretending to belong to another family because I've now steeped for two decades in the Buddhist teaching of *anicca*. Here at the tail end of my thirties, it's easier to accept that nothing lasts forever. Family dinners are numbered. They are numbered now that I'm twenty-four-hundred miles away from California. They were numbered the four years I spent in Cambodia and Thailand—and the fifteen years I lived close enough to my parents for frequent visits but refused. They've been numbered ever since my mother played a fierce game of badminton to expel me into this world.

没有母女缘: When my aunt (my mother's only full sibling; the others are from her father's first marriage) suggested this as a possibility, I felt a sweeping sense of relief even as the paradox of these five words began to dawn. It was an oddly comforting encapsulation of my strained relationship with my mother. For the first time, I considered two ever-changing selfhoods, the futility of blaming either, and the karmic field between them.

We may not have mother-daughter affinity in this lifetime. By Thích Nhất Hạnh's definition, we definitely do not. But I wonder if we might yet develop the karmic affinity of a pair of acrobats, as featured in the Sedaka-sutta.

After she clambers carefully onto the bamboo pole and perches safely to rest on his shoulders, the disciple receives instruction from the master acrobat: "You look after me, dear Medakathālikā, and I'll look after you."

She protests: "That's not how it is, tutor! You should look after yourself, and I'll look after myself."

Upon relating this story, the Buddha praises the apprentice who knows the danger of neglecting her own balance. "Looking after yourself, you look after others; and looking after others, you look after yourself."[36]

The Sedaka-sutta is about the cultivation of mindfulness, patience, non-harming, lovingkindness, and care, but it is, above all, an exhortation not to forsake one's own worth as the primary beneficiary of these virtuous practices. Daughters of the Asian diaspora, perhaps the question is not *What do we owe our mothers?* but an even harder one to answer:

What do we owe ourselves?

If we won't fit the Model Minority frame or the Filial Daughter mold, what shapes do we want to take on?

When I text my parents about the u-pick strawberries on Father's Day, I leave out some details because my dad will worry if I tell him about the fifteen-mile ride on my ill-fitting bike along the high-speed roads that I imprudently took to get to the farm, not to mention my resulting heatstroke symptoms. Nor do I say how much I want to share with them the two pounds of painstakingly picked fruit: flavor and fragrance worth the sunburn.

In *Coming Home to Tibet: A Memoir of Love, Loss, and Belonging*, Tsering Wangmo Dhompa writes: "In my mother's world my life was a success if I was literate in Tibetan, if I studied Buddhism, and if I grew to be a good and kind person."[37]

Again, not my mom.

"Home, to me, was any place by my mother's side," Dhompa writes—no surprise in a book dedicated "To Tsering Choden Dhompa, Beloved Mother."[38]

For most of my life, that sentence would only ring true if I replaced "by" with "as far away as possible from."

But when Dhompa relates that her mother regularly brought home a semi-circle of cookie or a half-eaten piece of chicken tucked inside her handbag—they were too delicious not to share—I suddenly recall the strawberry plants that grew wild outside a house in the suburbs of Seattle, a house inhabited by two warring women.

There was no AI in the early aughts, as there is now, to inform me that

> wild strawberries, also known as Fragaria virginiana, spread by sending out runners (stolons) and rhizomes that grow along the ground and take root to form new plants. These new plants are called "daughter plants."

All I knew was the miserly yield at the termini of those errant stolons—thumbnail-sized fruits in quantities so small you could count them on one hand, as if in inverse proportion to their fragrance and flavor. I never monopolized them, and neither did she. On random summer days, a tiny, perishable gem might just appear at the dining table where mother and daughter ate their meals, apart and alone. Mouthwatering, rare, blood-red truce.

These days, it is still the case that my mom's willingness to hug me rivals her enthusiasm for embracing a glowing poker fresh out of a bonfire. When I tell her I've won a grant, she clucks that all I've done is brought more work upon myself. (What was I expecting, "congratulations"?) Our relationship is no longer always hard, but it is often still uneasy. Contemplating our (lack of?) 母女缘, it comforts and discomfits me in equal measure to think: Nothing is forever, not rancor or debt, cruelties or carnations, riverbanks or strawberries, Mother or Me.

I wrote the bulk of this essay at Tavatimsa. This is my name for the steeply discounted chinoiserie I purchased from a local consignment store after I discovered that the drop-front secretary desk, cosplaying as a much older Gregorian, had exactly thirty-three cubbies and drawers. The woman who bought the meticulously hand-painted desk new, half a century ago, had passed away; it was her daughter who furnished my secondhand adoption.

Gold-embossed peonies, lotuses in pavilions, mountains and farmers and birds and willows. To my dismay, none of them could tell me what kind of stadium my mom sold hot dogs at. Was it football? (It is a mark of my sports illiteracy that I didn't guess the obvious, correct answer.) Since the phoenixes were keeping their beaks shut, I had no choice but to get the answer straight from the horse's mouth.

Open the call history in my cell phone and you'll be hard pressed to find more than a few entries a year from Mom or Dad. I originally guessed that these clocked in around 82 seconds. I overestimated. (Some sample durations: 31 seconds, 1 minute, 26 seconds, 8 seconds, 49 seconds.) My mom has a disconcerting habit of hanging up without saying goodbye, usually while I am speaking mid-sentence. (In my twenties, "Are you still alive?" was a total conversation between us. Absence and silence are habit-forming.)

Maybe it was all those years of rationed dialing to China, racking up the minutes while counting down the dollars (or was it the other way around?), the international calling card liable to run out on Waipo or Nainai before anything much at all could be said. We could've medaled for shortest sprint to the finish.

But because "Carnegie Mellon hot dog stadium" Google searches weren't getting me any closer to figuring out my mother's food service employment history, I called. Whereupon I learned that I had gotten the state wrong.

She sold the franks in Ohio, not Pennsylvania. Wait, *when* did you arrive? You stopped in San Francisco for a week before Cincinnati? I didn't know you lived in another apartment before Dad and I came! Oh yeah, good point Dad, of course you never had a car in China. Who taught you to drive that $300 Honda Accord? Dad lived in Ohio *and* Maryland at the same time? If Pittsburgh was 300 miles from Cincinnati and 380 miles from Maryland, Dad couldn't see us much, right? Is that why Mom and I had to take the bus? Hold up, let's list all the apartments, and can we figure out the right order this time?

We reached for the past in Shanghainese and Mandarin and English. In the end, we talked for a record-breaking 1 hour and 44 minutes.

Before moving to Michigan, my partner and I stumbled upon a rustic hundred-year-old *butsudan* at the antique store in Point Richmond named for its octogenarian owner. (Born in the Philippines, Guillermina and her husband had lived in Bangkok more than half a century before we did.) It was our first-ever vintage furniture purchase. (I thought it would be our last, but Tavatimsa proved me wrong.) The butsudan just fit into our new (used) car, my mom's old hybrid (she'd upgraded to a full electric).

I actually bought two Japanese art pieces that day. The other one nested easily in the palm of my hand. Brightly painted papier-mâché. Severely angled brows above frowning eyes. Focused or wrathful? Hard to say. The zodiac doll's indeterminate expression made me chuckle.

When I gave it to her, I spoke the truth. *Saw this and thought of you.* The horse's bobble head nodded in silent agreement. Meeting her scowling, determined likeness, my mother's eyes flashed in recognition. I thought of *The Woman Warrior*'s last three words. *It translated well.*

From my mother's upright throat, the song of laughter.

2
—
INFINITE LIGHT, INFINITE LIFE

FUNIE HSU/CHHÎ

Your mom told me that you asked about A+ Po.[1] "But where is *your* mom?" you wondered out of the blue. The sudden realization that you've never met your maternal grandma caused a moment of reflective pause during bathtime. "*Where* is she?"

I laughed when your mom said that she replied, "Uh . . . A+ Po's at Rainbow Bridge." That was how she explained what happened to your German Shepherd sister, Aiko. Caught off guard in the midst of suds and bath toys, it was an easier answer for a preschooler than describing cancer, the Western Pure Land, and rebirth. Plus, you were in your rainbow stage, so it was a potentially comforting response. Why not have you picture A+ Po happily frolicking with Aiko and other dogs (including Harry and Kheh-khì) like a pup-filled version of Gabby's Dollhouse?

A+ Po would have liked that, too. She grew up with all kinds of animals in the countryside and rice fields of Eastern Taiwan—from dogs and cats to water buffalo and poisonous cobras. She's the one who first taught your mom and me how to respect nonhuman beings, how to care for them as kin. A+ Po is the reason why I'm always walking around covered in fur, despite my best Chom Chom rolling. I imagine that each strand of stray cat and dog hair is a sprinkling of her presence wrapped up in the traces of their form.

A+ Po showed us that the world is not as it seems. We can lose life in an instant—and awaken to a connectedness beyond what our eyes can perceive. The Vietnamese Zen teacher Thích Nhất Hạnh famously wrote, "If you are a poet, you will see clearly that there is a cloud floating in this sheet of paper. Without a cloud, there will be no rain; without rain, the trees cannot grow: and without trees, we cannot make paper." Similarly, A+ Po floats on the rainbow clouds in the pages of this story. She is calling out to you,

> Halo! My grandchild! A+ Po is here!
> I am here in these letters!
> I am here in this!
> I am . . . .

She is excited to *khai káng* and share her stories with you.

When I was little, on the special occasions when we had guests over, the adults would gather around the second-hand patio table that served as the center of our mismatched dining set. After mealtime, they would sip oolong tea, spear cut fruit with toothpicks, and crack licorice watermelon seeds between their teeth, all the while sharing the latest updates and family stories from Taiwan. I would find my way to A+ Po's seat and wedge myself into the narrow gap between her back and her chair. I found it an ingenious way to hide (if I can't see them, they can't see me!) and still hear all the news. Turning my head to the side, I would wrap my arms around her waist and press my ear into her back, listening to the vibrations of A+ Po's muffled voice as she took in and exchanged stories about relations and places I didn't recognize.

So and so in Báng-kah had a stroke and is no longer the same.

But he was so young!

Kim-Pô is in her eighties but she still hikes in the mountains in the mornings and soaks in the hot springs!

She's always been strong and healthy!

Ear squished tightly against her back, I received these stories through A+ Po's body. They were transmitted into me through the gentle rumbling tremors of her voice, just as they were when I was a baby in her womb. Even though I can no longer hear or see her, A+ Po's vibrations still course through me.

In illuminating the reality of no death, Master Thích Nhất Hạnh used the analogy of TV and radio signals to describe how, though we may not see them, these electromagnetic waves fill the space around us, only made apparent with the right conditions—the turning on of a TV or radio. Likewise, A+ Po is still present around, and in, us. In fact, a lot of people say your mom and I sound like echoes of her. They hear her when we speak. Perhaps we are the conditions to make evident her stories and her life, how they show us that beyond death is the reality of infinite life.

This, then, is part of your inheritance.

The Practice of Compassion Is the Cat's Meow

Though we can no longer hear her words, we can still learn from A+ Po by paying attention to how she lived her life as an evolving practice of compassion for all beings. Before I continue, I'll share that A+ Po was not perfect. Nobody is. Like all people, she had moments when her temper flared. During these times, we knew to keep a distance since A+ Po was raised with corporal punishment as the norm and she freely carried on the tradition. Your mom and I learned just how quick a wooden spoon could transform from a magical culinary wand to an arm-extending slapping weapon. Just like the spoon, your grandma could instill both happiness and dread. Though she was no exemplar of human perfection (this ideal is the falsehood of a different kind of Enlightenment), she was perfectly human, making her compassionate acts of lovingkindness all the more achievable, all the more worthy of emulation. Although A+ Po may not have studied any sutras (she once shared that her education in rural Taiwan only extended through middle school), she was deeply moved by Guan Yin Púsà and was profoundly touched by the many stories of the Bodhisattva's compassionate power that she encountered in her life. The practice of compassion, then, became the expression of A+ Po's religious devotion, and the basis of the Buddhist teachings she transmitted to your mother and me.

An enduring memory I have of A+ Po is of the time we watched a TV series together that depicted one of the Bodhisattva of Compassion's many incarnations. At the time, your mom and I were still young and living at home. In the evenings, after eating the freshly prepared dinners A+ Po cooked for us after a long day at the garment production warehouse, we would often huddle together on the couch (A-Kong worked late into the night at his restaurant job). Babie, the tabby point Siamese, would curl up on one of the armrests and Harry, the Pekingese, would nestle in one of our laps. Together we would watch the evening dramas on the local Mandarin-language TV station. This time, it was the story of Princess Miao Shan and how she became Guan Yin. Your mom and I were familiar with the merciful Guan Yin, *bàibài*-ing to her at Hsi Lai temple during our visits. But watching this show gave us a whole new understanding of both Guan Yin Púsà and A+ Po's relationship to her.

Growing up in Taiwan, your grandma was raised in a diverse religious context that included reverence to local gods, Daoist healers, and tales of Guan Yin's merciful interventions. She saw firsthand how women, in particular, were emboldened by the Bodhisattva's example to create compassionate care for each other (more on this later). Due to various causes and conditions, immigrating to America led A+ Po and A-Kong to walk more intentionally down their Buddhist path. While the legend of Princess Miao Shan was not new to A+ Po, viewing the tale in the United States had a powerful effect on her. She was so moved by the dramatized scenes of Princess Miao Shan's resilient compassionate action that she was brought to a stream of tears. Repeatedly taking off her Costco glasses to wipe her eyes, she impressed upon us, while loudly blowing her nose, the incomparable compassionate wisdom of Guan Yin. More than Princess Miao Shan/Guan Yin's story, I was transfixed by A+ Po's reaction. I knew that, as is the case for so many Taiwanese women, Guan Shi Yin Púsà was a central figure of refuge in A+ Po's life. Just as A+ Po was impacted by this story of Guan Yin, so too was I stirred by observing her response. This tale transmitted through the TV was a means of familial Buddhist transmission from A+ Po to your mom and me. Like the TV of Master Thích Nhất Hạnh's description, the transmission continues beyond death. You need only to tune in.

Looking back, I wonder if for A+ Po, Guan Yin represented a liberating possibility of existing beyond the material limitations of her life—and death. Perhaps the Bodhisattva was a pathway for her to realize that even though we were a struggling, working-class, immigrant family, she could still live her life in the abundance provided by her Buddhist values. In the legend of Miao Shan, the princess defied her father's order to marry in order to devote herself to religious practice, a decision that resulted in familial scorn and a loss of material security. Her insistence on living a life of the Buddhadharma, however, meant she was supported by the Three Treasures. In committing herself to this refuge, she became a source of limitless compassion, ultimately transforming beyond her worldly form into the thousand-armed, thousand-eyed Guan Yin. While A+ Po had little choice in determining our family's economic condition, guided by the many stories of Guan Yin shared with her by other women, she practiced living beyond her earthly conditions by connecting to other beings through compassionate action.

I witnessed this unfold at a young age when a tiny kitten unexpectedly showed up at our apartment.

I remember the sun shining softly, casting a warm glow through the window as your grandma gently cradled the little orange tabby in her palms. To my preschooler self, it was as if A+ Po had reached toward the sky and grabbed a handful of the sun's rays, which transformed into a ball of breathing fluff as it entered the earthly atmosphere. I was completely entranced by this babiest of kittens, with her teeny triangle ears, tiny pink paw pads, and squeaky insistent meows. It was the first time I saw a kitten that young up close. I was mesmerized by her adorable form, astounded by her delicateness and vulnerability—this little being writhing and crying in A+ Po's cupped hands, her life, like ours, so fundamentally dependent on others. The kitten's baby blue eyes were open, but she still walked with a wobble, a sign that she was only a few weeks old, and thus in dire need of a mother's care.

All beings need lovingkindness.

All beings have once been our mothers.

I don't remember where she came from, but given her size and her sudden appearance, A+ Po must have found her near our apartment. She must have heard her tiny meows as she was sewing piecework in the living room and watching over your mom and me. I imagine that she searched for the kitten knowing that a precious life was calling out for tender care. Returning to the house, she showed me the fuzzy *tàiyáng* curiously peeking out from above her hands, like a little sunrise appearing on the horizon.

"Mew! Mew! MEW!" the little sun exclaimed.

Zhǎo bù dào māma, shì bùshì? A+ Po answered. *Kělián de xiǎo baby. OK, OK, ngài di, ngài di. Nǐ hěn è. Wǒ lái zhàogù nǐ.* "Have you lost your mom? Poor little baby. OK, OK, I know, I know. You're very hungry. I'll take care of you."

This interplay of life between different beings was engraved into my heart-mind. I was old enough to know that cats and humans don't share the same language, but A+ Po's conversation with the little tabby was so natural and instinctive, it established a new fundamental reality for me, one of interspecies regard, communication, and care.

A+ Po brought the kitty to the kitchen sink to bathe her, and I watched with rapt attention. Standing on my tiptoes, my fingers grasped the edge of the sink so I could pull myself up and peek at the kitten, I saw that with wet fur she was even smaller than she first appeared. A+ Po continued speaking to the kitten as she gently poured warm water over her head and body, one handful at a time. *Xiǎo baby, bié dānxīn. Xǐle yǐhòu jiù huì hěn shūfú.* "Little baby, don't worry. You'll feel much better after your bath," she reassured the little tabby while she lathered soap through her orange striped fur.

A+ Po showed me that a world beyond what I knew was an actuality. She taught me that by paying compassion-filled attention, we can see and hear the truth of our relations to other beings; that we can live our lives intimately connected with them; and that together, we can ease each other's suffering.

While A+ Po was bathing the kitty, the tiny feline was providing respite for A+ Po's body and spirit. As I mentioned, during these early years in the US, your grandma spent most of her days rapidly producing piecework. She sewed together small garment parts—sometimes pockets, sometimes shoulder pads, or shoulder seams—at pennies a piece. Sitting hunched over an industrial sewing machine positioned by the front door, she filled heavy-duty plastic bags with pockets full of hope while simultaneously keeping an eye on her two young daughters. Under these conditions, she soon became accustomed to breaking her hours and days into pieces—anxiously, desperately stitching together a livelihood for her young family.

Once, A+ Po was so intent on sewing as many pieces as quickly as possible that in her rush, the sewing needle punctured right through her nail, and right into the flesh of her middle finger—a painful reminder that she was not merely an extension of the sewing machine, but a sentient being. Despite her throbbing injury, A+ Po, after cleaning her wound, and wrapping an OK-bàng around it, continued sewing. This was not a bootstrapping act of immigrant industry, but the reality of being poor and uninsured in America. This was the alienated life she felt she had to endure to provide for us. It was in this context that the little kitty made her guest appearance.

The tabby's presence reconnected A+ Po to a world beyond a life compelled to work, her meows a *dhāraṇī* reminding A+ Po of her greater dharmic path. Caring for the kitten allowed A+ Po to find herself among the mountainous bags of piecework and express her Buddhist devotion through compassionate action. It also required her to reorient her laboring body toward providing physical and spiritual care for herself through connection to other sentient beings. The kitten was a little orange jewel in Indra's net, whose washing helped to reflect A+ Po's own place in the intertwined web. Thus, the tabby ushered in a moment of Buddhist practice that rejuvenated A+ Po's life.

It also left a lasting impression on me. Watching A+ Po rinse and delicately towel dry the newly clean ball of fluff reminded me of the way she would dry off my own hair after she bathed me. Observing this act of care taught me to viscerally empathize with other beings, to understand that in many ways they, too, have physical and emotional needs just like me. Just like you. When you asked your mom about A+ Po, you, too, were being bathed and taken care of like that little tabby, the two of you both showered in a transmission of A+ Po's compassion.

We Are Held By One Thousand Hands . . .

Your mom's two hands have cleaned and cared for you countless times; in each of these moments, they were guided by the many invisible but ever-present arms that have cared for her. If you look deeply at her hands, you will see a thousand hands: A+ Po's hands, her mom's hands, A-Chó's hands, her mom's hands, and so on and so forth. You will also see hundreds of hands belonging to nameless figures who offered compassionate care to our family and ancestors. Even though we may not know who they are, or they us, we have been shaped by these karmic connections. A+ Po's brief life showed me that all of these hands continue to leave an imprint on us.

Growing up at A+ Po's side, I experienced the reality of this truth slowly unfurl. I first became aware of this connection during a quick trip to 99 Ranch (of all places) with A+ Po when I was in middle school. It was a routine stop to get groceries. As we walked through the parking lot toward the entrance, I was focused on how I would persuade her to buy me snacks (I-Mei Milk Puffs. If had to, I would settle for Pocky sticks.) when A+ Po suddenly stopped a few feet from the doors and fished out her wallet. An older Asian woman was standing in front of the entryway next to a sign and a collection box. She was a volunteer from Tzu Chi, a Taiwanese Buddhist organization that was focused on providing social aid, A+ Po explained. *Tāmen hěn yǒu àixīn. Měi cì fāshēngle zāinàn, tāmen dōuhuì bāngzhù shòuhài zhě.* "They're very caring. Whenever there's a disaster, they are always quick to help the victims," she added. *Wǒmen lái juān yīdiǎn qián.* "Let's donate some money."

A+ Po explained that there had been a recent earthquake in Taiwan and that the volunteer was raising money on behalf of Tzu Chi to help provide assistance. I was familiar with the Salvation Army's Red Kettles and learned to view the sight of their volunteers ringing bells in front of the Stater Bros. as a staple of the Christmas season in the US. Seeing this Tzu Chi volunteer, however, struck a deep chord. Outside of a temple, it was the first time I had witnessed Buddhism so prominently displayed in the midst of American public life. Notably, it was also the first time I saw Buddhism in social action in the United States.

That the volunteer was a woman was no surprise. Growing up, it seemed to me that the temple was a female space. Whether it was the many *bhikkhunīs* organizing the services and activities, the lay volunteers, or the attendees, the dominant presence of women was a significant element of my experience of Buddhism. Thus, though it was quite ordinary that the Tzu Chi volunteer was a woman, it was also meaningful, nonetheless. I thought it was valiant of her to spend her day standing in front of a grocery store, being mostly ignored by passersby, to raise disaster relief funds for people she didn't know. Watching her stand there, I began to see our connection with other beings we may never know. The volunteer's hands, folded in front of her lower waist, were at the same time spiritually outstretched, reaching out to provide compassionate relief for others. I later learned that Master Cheng Yen, the founder of Tzu Chi, often described the organization's many volunteers as the thousand arms and eyes of Guan Yin. It made sense that A+ Po was inspired and impacted by their work. Through her modest *dāna*, she felt compelled to be part of the many hands coming together to provide refuge for others.

I would think back to this memory years later when A+ Po and I visited her rural hometown in Taitung County. Little did I know how much the women of Tzu Chi had impacted A+ Po's life until we took her mom, your A+ Tai, to the hospital when her health declined. For those living in the eastern countryside, fully resourced medical facilities were limited. For those contending with poverty, what medical care was available was cost-prohibitive. Responding to this context, Master Cheng Yen organized local housewives to raise funds and establish a free clinic in Hualien County. By 1986, Hualien Tzu Chi General Hospital was established. According to the organization, it remains the only medical center in Eastern Taiwan. This was the hospital that treated your A+ Tai, and later, eased her into her transition.

As we entered through the hospital doors, I remember A+ Po showed the same reverence for Tzu Chi as she had when she first told me about the organization in front of 99 Ranch years earlier. Understanding this context, and physically standing in the hospital that served as the realization of Tzu Chi's impact in Eastern Taiwan, I felt that I was piecing together a more complete picture of both A+ Po and our fundamental interdependence with others. A+ Po was deeply grateful for the compassionate care the hospital and its medical staff provided. I recall standing in the lobby and looking around to take in the details of the hospital for the first time while A+ Po explained how it was no ordinary hospital, but one driven by Buddhist values. She shared this with a sense of relief, not just for the fact that A+ Tai would receive medical attention, but that she would be in spiritually caring hands. The hands of the attendants that pushed A+ Tai's wheelchair, fed, bathed, and nursed her are part of the hundreds of helping hands folded within your mama's own two hands. She cares for you with the loving force of a thousand hands.

Recently, Tzu Chi representatives in the Bay Area kindly attended a Buddhist memorial for Asian American ancestors I helped to organize. When I met them in person at the ceremony, they gifted me *Jing Si Aphorisms* by Ven. Cheng Yen. *To jiéyuán*, they tenderly explained as they handed me the book. To form connecting ties. Later, they generously contributed dāna in support of our memorial event. I thought about A+ Po standing in front of 99 Ranch and her modest donation to the Tzu Chi volunteer. A thousand hands joined together make a full circle—a meditative *ensō*.

> *When our spirit and actions are in harmony; when our heart and thoughts are in accord, that is deep meditation.*

> —SHIH CHENG YEN, *JING SI APHORISMS*

. . . And Paws

The blackbirds told her, she said.

A+ Po and A-Kong were away camping in a remote national park when your mom received the news that A+ Tai had passed away in Taiwan. Your mom frantically called A+ Po but couldn't reach her for quite some time. When she was finally able to speak to her and relay the sad update, A+ Po was bereft. But she was not surprised. Earlier, she said, blackbirds were circling and cawing loudly above her. They must have been there to tell her about A+ Tai, to let her know that her beloved mother had transitioned from the earthly realm and gone beyond.

To others, this might sound like magical thinking. In our family, our experience and our religious belief confirm that we are connected to all sentient beings—and that these ties extend beyond the physical realm. When A+ Tai died, she visited your Uncle Andrew while he was sleeping. He awoke to the feeling of a presence in his room and saw her sitting at the foot of his bed. A+ Tai helped to raise your uncle and held him dear to her heart, so she came to say a final goodbye. He was understandably shaken! It wasn't until he was at work the next day that he received a call from family in Taiwan notifying him of A+ Tai's death. Even before we heard about Uncle Andrew's story, when A+ Po mentioned the blackbirds we believed it to be true.

As A+ Po taught us through the little orange tabby kitten, sentient beings of different species are our kin. We join hands, paws, wings, and hooves to take care of each other through our suffering. This, too, is a circle.

Before A+ Po mentioned the blackbirds at her camping site, your mom told her she found a little injured bird in our backyard. It was a baby blackbird. She carefully picked it up and put it in a box but wasn't sure what to do next. A+ Po told your mama that she must take good care of the little one and do her best to help it. That's when A+ Po told her about the blackbirds that flew over her and how they must all have shared a connection with A+ Tai. As A+ Po's daughter, your mom could sense these ties. She made several phone calls to local vets and shelters looking for medical attention for the little bird. Finally, she found a wildlife rehabilitator and drove the little bird an hour away to Riverside so that it could be cared for.

Years later, when we didn't realize A+ Po was sick, your mom and I witnessed another experience of deep interspecies kinship. One night when I was in grad school and living in Oakland, I received a call from your mom in the early hours of the morning. "Something's wrong with Babie," she shared, urgently getting to the point. "I don't know what it is. Ma's sleeping in your room because Dad's snoring and Babie keeps meowing in front of your door and pawing at it. He won't stop. He's been doing it for a few nights now." Babie was notoriously stubborn and insistent, but this behavior was uncharacteristic of him. We were both concerned, and at a loss for what to do. Your mom decided she would keep him in her room through the night and monitor him.

A short time later, A+ Po was diagnosed with stage 4 lung cancer. She passed away a week after her diagnosis. Though she had seen several doctors about her chest pain and difficulty breathing, they dismissed her, telling her it was only a cold, or asthma. Having been convinced that her symptoms were mostly in her mind, A+ Po sought little comforts. She stacked her walk-in closet with boxes of Salonpas, jars of Tiger Balm, and tins of Little Nurse Mentholatum. Sitting in the middle of the closet floor, she adorned her chest and back with the medicated patches and rubbed the ointments into her skin, hoping to finally catch a deep breath. It wasn't until she saw Dr. Chang, the

Chinese medicine doctor by the temple, that she was told something was seriously wrong. Babie, your mom and I believe, must have sensed it that night, meowing and pawing to be by A+ Po's side.

I know this can sound like wishful anthropomorphizing—trying to create a tender story to soothe our human-centric selves during times of suffering. However, the ethologist Frans de Waal cautions us not to engage in anthropodenial and dismiss the shared commonalities between species. Babie, too, cared for A+ Po. This I am certain of. Though I secretly brought him into our home as a tiny kitten and named him (baby, but with an "ie" so we could be twins), A+ Po was the one who advocated for him when A-Kong found out. She was the one who consistently looked after him when I faltered on my enthusiastic teenage promise to take care of all his needs. She would naturally talk to him, just as she did with the little orange tabby, addressing him as Mr. Babie and carrying on conversations about his day and mood. He would chat with her, meowing to answer her questions. I imagine that his little paws tapping on the bedroom door, desperately trying to get to A+ Po, must have been his attempt to tell her that things were not right, but that he was there to accompany her through her suffering.

The day we came home from the hospital after A+ Po died, the three of us—A-Kong, your mom, and I—collapsed into unimaginable despair. We each found different nooks of the house to fill with our inconsolable bawling. Our worlds were turned upside down. For the first time, I began to understand the Buddhist idea that our perceptions are not reality. Suddenly, in the midst of our sorrow, we heard a series of deep, guttural wails. Snapped out of our own sadness, we all went in search of the sound. Looking into his bedroom, A-Kong stopped. "Babie," he said, surprised and moved. There in the middle of her rented hospital bed was Babie. He was turning circles and letting out loud, pained calls. It was as if he knew A+ Po would never return to the house in human form and he was speaking to her in a different realm. I had never heard such a sound before—and have not heard it since. I did hear, though, clear as day, the sound of A+ Po's voice in response. "Good boy, Mr. Babie. Good boy."

In her death, as in her life, A+ Po showed us that the world is more than we think it to be. It is more expansive, more interconnected than we know.

Almost a decade later, after Babie, too, had passed, I was back in the family house the night A-Kong died. As I finally fell asleep crying in my childhood bed (in the same room A+ Po slept in when your mom called that night years ago), Uncle Hondo saw Babie laying peacefully on my back. "Good boy, Babie," he whispered.

In the End, There Is Infinite Life

The day A+ Po died, everything happened so fast. At the hospital it seemed chaotic, especially so since we were coming to terms with the fact that we had no control. No amount of treatment, or medicines, or pleading would change the fact that A+ Po's body was spiraling, that it would soon stop supporting life. The only thing we could do was seek comfort. The doctors administered high dosages of various drugs to keep her as pain-free as possible, but this put her in a panicked and confused mental state.

At one point, I couldn't understand the words coming out of her mouth, but I could tell she was trying to tell me something important. I made out that she wanted my pen and my notebook, the one where your mom and I took hurried notes, frantically trying to capture everything the doctors said about her evolving status and her medications. I flipped the notebook to a fresh page and handed it to her. A+ Po struggled with the pen but determinedly wrote a few characters in Chinese. In her drugged state, they came out as scribbles. No matter how I tried, I couldn't make sense of what it said. Each wrong guess led A+ Po to repeat her incoherent words with more forceful urgency. Finally, she pointed at my wrist, at the *Fózhū* I got at Hsi Lai temple. I took it off and placed it on her wrist and asked her if she wanted to recite Guan Shi Yin Púsà and the Buddha's name. This brought her a sudden relief. I held her hand as we recited and she calmed down to a peaceful rest.

During a brief care-taking break, I called Auntie Anh to share the heart-breaking update and to seek comfort of my own. She had known A+ Po since we first became friends in middle school and shared in the pain of the anticipatory grief. Auntie Anh, having also been raised Buddhist, reached out to Hsi Lai and contacted bereavement volunteers so that they could be by A+ Po's (and our) side. I could not know how important this would be in creating a space of refuge that would hold us during this time of unimaginable loss.

When the volunteers arrived, they brought a compassionate kindness that served as a light to guide us through the thick uncertainty of our anguish. They plugged in a little device that chanted the Buddha's name in a loop so that A+ Po's mind could focus on her transition. They taught us what to do after her last breath, how to provide a sense of calm encouragement for her, how to recite for her body for eight hours following her final exhalation in her hospital bed, and how to continue to recite for her at home for the next forty-nine days. In thanking them for the generosity of their time and care, I shared with them how confused and lost we felt. How I couldn't even understand what my mom was saying or writing, and thus, couldn't help her in the way that I wanted. One volunteer asked to see what she wrote. "This is very clear," he said upon seeing the notebook page. He passed the notebook to the other volunteers, who confirmed it among themselves.

Held in the compassionate hands of strangers, A+ Po's final message to me unfolded like a lotus: *Amítuófó. Amitābha.* Infinite light, infinite life. We had been reciting it together all along.

A+ Po's Final Written Message

I mentioned earlier that A+ Po loved to *khai káng*. Sometimes the stories she told were not that interesting (even pretty boring and pointless!), but she would always end by asking, insisting, *Nǐ shuō, hǎobù hǎoxiào a?* "Don't you think that's amusing?" In the spirit of her stories, I'll close by sharing one that I think she would have liked.

A month after A-Kong died, a dear spiritual friend passed away. I found out about Aaron's death while I was getting ready for my work commute. At school, in my office, I shut the door and let myself cry for a few minutes before I had to collect myself and go teach. It was rough getting through the day. On the bus ride back to the train station, I let myself get lost in thoughts of Aaron. When the bus was about to pull up into the station, I saw a modest burgundy sedan drive into the drop-off zone and park. The car's back windshield prominently displayed a decal that spelled out in large letters "AMITABHA," as if yelling it to the world. Interesting, I thought. Knowing that Amitabha is not an uncommon Indian name, I reasoned that the stickers must simply be a reflection of the driver's confidence in himself. As the bus got closer to the car, though, I saw the dashboard was decorated with Amitabha Buddha figures, and that the front windshield was similarly adorned with the "AMI-TABHA" decal. This driver really loved Amitabha Buddha! I couldn't help but smile and think that it must have been Aaron. He must have sent this driver to deliver this message loud and clear from beyond. "It's real! It's all real!" I imagined him squealing to me, delighting in his infinite life.

Nǐ shuō, little one, *hǎobù hǎoxiào a?*

3

—

GRAVE REMEMBRANCE

Sustaining Connection and Caregiving Across Generations

JANE NAOMI IWAMURA

"It's time to visit the cemetery. How about this Sunday?" I say. My teenage children and husband agree, and we set the date. Sunday, we hop into the car. We pick up flowers on the way and make the hour-long journey to Pacific View Memorial Park. My daughter reads and my son and husband nap in the car.

Twice each year, my family and I visit the cemetery where my parents are buried. This is not unique or unusual; visiting the grave is a common practice among many Buddhists. Thích Nhất Hạnh notes that "the most precious gift we can offer anyone is our attention. When mindfulness embraces those we love, they will bloom like flowers." Such attention takes many forms and is built into the rituals we enact for the living and the dead. Visiting the graves of the deceased is common among Buddhists, and here I reflect and reframe the practice from the standpoint of an Asian American Buddhist mother and daughter—attending to those I love—living and dead. Beyond simply honoring my deceased parents, these visits have become occasions for a radical caregiving that forges bonds between my parents, myself, my children, and the larger chain of being—between the human realm (Sahā, world of suffering) and the Western Pure Land. The ritual has become a way to share and pass on to my biracial children a legacy that is life-enhancing and part of their spiritual inheritance.

Death

We arrive at the cemetery. Pacific View Memorial Park is a lovely, well-kept site with a view of the ocean in the distance. My parents are buried in the Veterans' Cemetery section—a plot my father secured as a US military veteran. We glimpse my parents' grave from a distance.

Selecting a burial site was important to my parents. They had briefly considered returning to the cemetery where my grandparents and many aunts and uncles are buried: Floral Memorial Park in the San Joaquin Valley, about three hours away. But they knew that my visits would probably be infrequent given the cemetery's distance from Southern California, where I live. Burial sites in Southern California, however, are both expensive and difficult to procure. My entrepreneurial father realized that he had the option of sites in cemeteries dedicated to military veterans, and my parents identified two options for their final resting place: the Los Angeles National Cemetery (near UCLA in Westwood) and Pacific View Memorial Park (in Newport Beach). Among their considerations was the likelihood that I would come and visit them at either site. My mother argued for the Los Angeles National Cemetery ("Jane will visit us more often since the cemetery is close to her home."). My father preferred Pacific View Memorial Park ("Westwood is so noisy with the traffic from UCLA and freeway, and from the gravesite in Newport Beach, one has a view of the ocean. It's not too far for Jane to travel."). My father's preference won out. While I was a part of these conversations, I would often say very little since I felt the decision should be my parents'. I did reassure them that I would visit them no matter where they chose to be buried.

I note that my parents never explicitly or directly demanded that I visit them after they passed, but this expectation was implicitly built into our discussion of burial sites and something that I always assumed. As I look back on this conversation, I am struck by my parents' need and desire for an ongoing connection with me, my husband, and their grandchildren and the continued acknowledgment of their existence *as if* they were alive. They, themselves, recognized their parents and loved ones as so—taking part in memorial services and regularly visiting the cemetery themselves. While I now recognize this as a duty and obligation, I had always seen it as something that I would simply do. This assumption was forged through practice and wrought from a view of death, not as non-existence, but as passage.

My mother died in 2001. She suffered an extended illness for over a year and was in the hospital and hospice care for the final two months of her life. We never found out the cause of her death. As she reached the end, she would say, "I have so much still that I want to do." My mother's death was especially difficult for me, as well as for my father. Because she was only seventy-two when she died, my mother's death felt premature; we always felt and expected that she would live a long life. Like so many other *Nisei* (second-generation) mothers, she was the caregiver of the family—generous, caring, and attending to our needs—especially to my father who rarely had to cook his own dinner or do his own laundry. She was a master at the iron and would assiduously press my father's shirts, pants, and handkerchiefs. Upon her death, my father and I realized that these everyday expressions of love and care, and her friendship and indeed *being*, were something that we took for granted. We just expected that she would always be there. For my mother, who had dedicated her life to her family, aging brought the anticipation of both more time to pursue pastimes and projects and, potentially, grandchildren. Although she never pressured me to have children, I know that she would have gained immense joy as a grandmother and would have loved her grandchildren deeply. When she died, perhaps greater than mourning my own loss, I mourned the sacrifices she had made and the life that she had still hoped to lead.

Mourning my mother's death became the occasion for my father, my husband, and me to visit the cemetery. As I was growing up, my mother and grandmothers would take me to the cemetery with homegrown flowers to pay respects to deceased relatives—some of whom I did not know. We would *gassho*—put our hands together and silently recite the *nembutsu* ("Namuamidabutsu") before the graves of our relatives. Visiting the cemetery also became a time to recount memories and honor those who had died. It there-fore seemed most natural to visit my mother—to care for our memories of her and let her know that we still cared for her.

In 2004, my son was born; and my daughter in 2008. We would continue these visits with my children in tow—once around Mother's Day (around the time my mother passed away) and once between Christmas and the New Year.

In 2013, my father passed away. He was ninety-one years old. I took com-fort in the fact that his death was swift, at home, and doing something he loved—watching Monday Night Football on the television. I also found solace in the fact that he got to know his grandchildren (aged eight and four at the time of his passing). We had many happy memories together through our weekly visits and travels to family reunions, and I was appreciative that my children were able to gather an early sense of connectedness with their grand-father and our extended family. My father's passing was especially difficult for my son, who shared an especially close relationship with my father; we would find him crying and bereft when he was trying to go to sleep. My husband and I would comfort him, letting our son know that we understood his grief; we felt it, too. And I would reassure my son that his grandfather loved him and that my father was still was still here—even though he physically was not. Our visits to the cemetery would come to reinforce these words, offering ritual assurance of my father's (and mother's) continuing presence and love and providing a foundation for him to understand our "Buddha nature."

When each of my parents died, I made arrangements for their funeral and burial with ministers at the Orange County Buddhist Church (OCBC) that is part of the Buddhist Churches of America (BCA), a Jodo Shinshu denomination. Practitioners of Shin Buddhism, which emerged from the Jap-anese Pure Land School and is unlike other Buddhist traditions, believe that the faithful, upon death, pass on to Amida's Pure Land (Sukhavati), where they enter a world of non-suffering and eventually attain Buddhahood. The deceased person is given a new name (*homyō*) recognizing their spiritual transformation and enlightenment and is referred to more generally as *hotoke* (literally, "Buddha"). In their new existence, the dead are released from the cycle of birth and death (*samsara*) and no longer suffer. Death rituals within the Jodo Shin tradition can entail a number of services: the funeral, burial, and memorial services (*hoji*) on the seventh day, the forty-ninth day, the first year, and years 3, 7, 13, 17, 25, 33, and 50. My grandmothers (*Issei* or first-generation) would keep track of these death anniversaries and arrange for these services. However, with the demands of everyday American life and living in an environment with no comparable rituals, Japanese American Jodo Shin Buddhists observed the set of services less and less. My parents were no exception; my Nisei mother did not arrange for hoji beyond the forty-ninth day. She did however regularly visit the cemetery—remembering her parents, our extended family, and even the woman who had introduced my parents to one another. This woman was not a relative of ours, and I have since forgotten her name. I do remember that my mother was insistent on visiting her matchmaker's grave. Not only did this woman change the life course of my parents and indeed make possible my own existence, but she apparently had no children to remember her. Visiting this woman's grave brought her back into a circle of connection and care through memory.

There are many reasons for the decreased observance of these death rituals among Japanese Americans (Nikkei)—including the decline of Buddhism that some attribute to a focus on such rituals. Scholars note that Japanese Buddhism is often disparagingly called "funeral Buddhism" due to its attention to the dead.[1] This is no less the situation among Japanese American Buddhists who contend with Western conceptions of death. The BCA makes an effort to guide practitioners from "perpetuating the image of Buddhism as a religion for the dead and the afterlife" by reorienting their attention away from the deceased.[2] Instead, they emphasize that one's focus should be on Amida Buddha and living one's lives with wisdom and compassion.

In response to this image of Japanese Buddhism and the ambivalent perceptions toward these observances, scholars highlight how Buddhist death rituals provide solace to the bereaved, and enact reflection, healing, connection, and spiritual growth.[3] (The BCA itself acknowledges this significance.) Although the cycle of formal rituals has become abbreviated in the American context, death care remains a vital part of Shin Buddhism and the larger Buddhist tradition. We still remember and deeply care for the dead. Such care through remembrance remains a touchstone and a part of our heritage.

Connection

My parents' grave is a short distance from where we park. As we walk up the hill,
we pass from the mundane to the sacred—a time and space full of special meaning
and connection. We take a look at the grave marker, which has weathered since
our last visit. It is right that we are here at this moment.

When my father was alive, we would visit my mother. And when he
passed, we would visit him. My mother and father enjoy seeing their grandchildren. Over the years and through our visits, they have seen my children
grow and flourish. I know they are pleased and look forward to our visits.

Our family's story is a typical Japanese American one. As a *Sansei*
(third-generation Japanese American), I was raised as a Buddhist. I attended
a small rural temple that was part of the BCA from an early age and fell in love
with the sutra chanting performed each Sunday. Growing up in the "church," I
also took part in Dharma school, danced at Obon festivals, frequented dances
that were part of the Jr. Young Buddhist Association (Jr. YBA), and played
the piano for memorial services. While attending a Mennonite high school, I
moved away from temple and came to adopt a Christian identity. In college I
briefly joined an evangelical Christian church and later studied Christian theology in graduate school. During my studies, my deep affinity with a Buddhist
perspective became apparent, and I came to embrace my Japanese American
Buddhist roots in my late twenties.

My grandparents, Jodo Shin Buddhists, migrated from the southern
Kyūshū region of Japan. They were part of a large wave of Japanese who immigrated in the late nineteenth/early twentieth century—the majority of whom
were Buddhists. As they settled, these Issei (first-generation) established
temples and sponsored ministers from Japan. My parents, Nisei (second-
generation), were raised in the temple and within a thriving Japanese American Buddhist community. As they grew into adulthood, Buddhism for my parents was simply a given. Beyond sending their only child to Dharma school,
their connection with the temple centered around weddings and funerals.

My grandmothers were a different story. Although they did not go to
temple, they maintained home altars (butsudan) and chanted the nembutsu at
home. Their Buddhist faith was key to their survival. The Buddhist worldview

that my grandmothers embraced provided an anchor in a sea of suffering that they experienced as Japanese immigrants in a new and often hostile world, and the Japanese American Buddhist community served as a means of sustenance and support. Buddhism also allowed immigrant Japanese Americans such as my grandparents to maintain their connection with their spiritual and cultural heritage and shore up a positive sense of self—deep and meaningful—that resisted the tides of oppression. My father's mother, Natsuye, was especially devout and her devotion was built into the care she took with her family, and especially my grandfather. When my grandfather was alive, my grandmother would shred carrots, bundle these shreds into a cheesecloth, and painstakingly squeeze a cup of carrot juice to nourish her ailing husband. When he died, she took care in arranging his memorial service and maintaining his memory at her butsudan.

In addition to these practices, her day included setting a place at the table for my deceased grandfather and having conversations with him. This seemed odd to me at first. But as I grew accustomed to this ritual, I would come to appreciate my grandfather's continuing presence and my grandmother's love for him through this gesture. The daily place settings and conversations were my grandmother's way of taking care of my grandfather even as he had passed on to the Pure Land. Through my grandmother's actions, I learned that death does not mean the end of our relationships with one another. I also came to realize that she was modeling an ethics of care that extended beyond the loss of my grandfather's human existence and physical presence and served as an expression of deep compassion and enduring obligation to the Buddha realm. It is this model of care that I carry forward in our visits to the cemetery.

In her study of Zen Buddhist women practitioners in Japan, Paula Arai recognizes how the dead are transformed into "personal Buddhas," who play an important role in the process of healing and spiritual cultivation of the living. She notes:

> Recognizing the deceased as personal Buddhas means the living and dead are not separated. The concept of personal Buddha takes the teaching of interrelatedness and stretches it across the illusory boundaries of life and death. Intimate relations people have with their personal Buddhas function to dissolve the delusion of separate entities.[4]

Setting a place at the table, reciting the nembutsu at the butsudan, and visiting the cemetery are ways of interacting with our personal Buddhas. As Arai notes, this relationship is intimate and ongoing and connects the living and dead across time and space. Beyond the significant function it plays for the living, these acts of remembrance and lovingkindness pay homage to the dead and lets them know that they dwell among us.

Caregiving

My son fetches water to clean the grave and for the flowers. My daughter cuts and arranges the flowers. I wash the grave and cut away the grass. We stand to look at the grave—fresh and beflowered. It's time for pictures. My children stand next to my parents. Click. We stand in various configurations and take pictures. Click, click, click.

When my children were young, they would roam the cemetery while I prepared the flowers. They would often gather fallen pinecones and fir branches during their exploration and arrange these treasures around the grave. Their beautiful display was my children's way of interacting with and caring for their grandpa and grandma.

Our cemetery visits can be viewed as a practice grounded in an *ethics of care*. Feminist theorist, Carol Gilligan, articulates such an ethic as one

> grounded in voice and relationships, in the importance of everyone having a voice, being listened to carefully (in their own right and on their own terms) and heard with respect. An ethics of care directs our attention to the need for responsiveness in relationships (paying attention, listening, responding) and to the costs of losing connection with oneself or with others. Its logic is inductive, contextual, psychological, rather than deductive or mathematical.[5]

In contrast to theories of moral action solely guided by universal principles and rational thought, an ethics of care places emphasis on emotion and relationality. Gilligan further notes that, "the ethics of care starts from the premise that as humans we are inherently relational, responsive beings and the human condition is one of connectedness or interdependence."[6]

Here I find strong parallels between Gilligan's conception and Buddhist thought. Jodo Shin Buddhists, who recognize a radical interdependence, view being inherently interrelational and intercausal on a most personal level. It is not only I, as a human being, that is coming into relation with Amida Buddha, a transcendent figure; I exist within buddha-field(s) that are constituted by all living beings and the myriad of Buddhas. Recognition of this radical interdependence compels one to act ethically. It is also an acknowledgment of the causes and conditions and beings to whom we are indebted for our existence. Beyond these connections, we are nothing. In terms of our visits, framing the ritual within this web of ongoing connection highlights the emotional dimension of the practice and the role that empathy and compassion play in our lives. Understanding Buddhist death practices within an ethics of care and a Buddhist sense of interrelatedness highlights the significance of an enduring connection and ongoing moral obligation to the living and the dead.

Framed in this way, our visits constitute a type of caregiving. *Caregiving* is conventionally seen as an activity of regularly looking after someone who is unable to fully care for themselves, such as a child, the elderly, or a disabled person. A caregiver also provides emotional and personal support. Caregiving stands in contrast to the function played by *caretakers*, who primarily attend to physical, material needs—usually in a professional or formal capacity. When we go to the cemetery, we certainly perform caretaking duties: clearing the weeds and washing the marker. I increasingly served as a caregiver as my parents aged: overseeing my mother's care when she was ill and attending to my father's everyday needs. After they both had passed, I looked after my parents in a different, but no less significant way. I assure them that they are loved and not forgotten and that they are still very much a part of our lives. I bring their grandchildren to come visit. *We are not simply caretakers of the grave, but caregivers of the spirit.*

According to the Shin Buddhist tradition, the dead who believe in Amida Buddha's Compassionate Vow attain rebirth in the Pure Land. Shinran, the founder of the Jodo Shinshu sect of Buddhism, of which my family and other Japanese American Buddhists belong, radically rejected previous conceptions of death rituals by presenting salvation as instantaneous and assured at the time of one's death. In Shinran's words: "Individuals in whom faith has arisen dwell at the stage of those whose birth in the Pure Land is certain; thus they are in effect 'equal to buddhas.'"[7] Unlike other Theravāda and Mahāyāna Buddhists, Shin Buddhists hold that the deceased do not dwell in an intermediate state but are reborn in the Pure Land. Intercessions by the living on behalf of the dead (deathbed and death rituals, merit-making) are not necessary. Upon their passing, they become a non-differentiated part of the Buddha realm—a state through which we, the living, come to realize our commitment to the Buddhadharma and to all sentient beings.

Put another way, death rituals become ways for the living to "understand dharma, great truth, and to encourage us to appreciate this life and our connection to everything and everyone around us."[8] According to Shin Buddhism, our ritual acts are built around this concept and viewed as ones whose focus and benefit are turned back onto the living. Hence, care for the dead essentially represents care for the living. While philosophically, and perhaps even ontologically, this may be the case, this articulation glosses over an important step that a feminist ethics of care helps to highlight: that our ritual visits to the cemetery play a key role in our own healing and rededication to the Dharma. However, this focus on the living does not preclude caring for my parents *as such*; my attention and love, my duty and obligation, are to my mother and father, even though they have passed on to the Pure Land where they seemingly are no longer in need of my care.

Remembrance serves as the lynchpin of this dynamic of care. Congruent with a Buddhist view, our existence is lived out over many lifetimes and across many realms. Passage to the Pure Land represents the ultimate stage of this existence. However, I not only honor my parents in their perfected state but also remember them as they were and continue to be for us. For me and my children, they remain the parents and grandparents who love us and whom we love. My parents' wish that I visit them after their death and remember their human existence remains present and real and I carefully and joyously heed it. I hear and attend to their voices.

Death does not sever our connections with the deceased. The living and the dead are interconnected and forever bound within a continuous chain of being. While caring for my mother and father does not entail any direct interventions, such as the transfer of merit or the offering of food and other items to sustain them in the afterlife, we continue to sustain and nurture the bonds that connect us. Within a web of care and devotion, we acknowledge the continued existence of the deceased, give thanks for what they have given and who they continue to be for us, and communicate our enduring love. Honoring the deceased is not simply for the sake of the living, but for the dead as well.

Western psychology frames religious and spiritual rituals around the dead in terms of processes of mourning and healing. However, by focusing on how these rituals operate for the living, they do not (directly) speak of the needs of the dead. Such needs are only recognized through a practitioner's viewpoint and practice. As is made manifest in death rituals, many Buddhist adherents acknowledge a person's existence beyond death. The meaning of death is not final but a passage into another form of being. The dead and the living are linked to one another in a web of being, highlighting their interconnectedness. To ontologically realize such radical interconnectedness between all sentient beings, beings along the path, and the myriad of Buddhas is a hallmark of Buddhism. *Interbeing* makes possible the interpersonal relationships across this web. Death rituals therefore do not negate the existence of the deceased but affirm their being and significance—albeit on another plane. The care of the dead therefore becomes an affirmation of their continued existence throughout the web.

John Traphagan sums this up well. In his examination of death rituals in Japan, he writes:

> the living and the ancestors depend upon each other for continued well-being and, ultimately, for their existence—the living would not exist without the ancestors, and the ancestors depend upon the living to keep them involved, as memories, in the world of the living and to provide the basic love and attention that all humans require. In other words, living and dead are mutually involved in enacting and maintaining each other's well-being.[9]

As we continue to care for my parents, we do so for the mutual well-being of the living and the dead. Through remembrance as care and attending the grave, we give thanks for my parents' lives and recognize how they still care for us.

Legacy

After we have cleaned and put flowers on the grave, we move to the memorial bench shaded by a beautiful tree a few steps away. My husband, children, and I all squeeze onto the bench and do our best to take a selfie of the four of us.

Ever since we began our visits, we take pictures at the cemetery. It was one of the few opportunities in which we were all together—my son and daughter, my husband, myself, and my father when he was alive. As I scroll through these photographs, I witness the passing of time: the weathered marker, the grave sites that have emerged next to my parents', and the maturing tree next to the site. I see my father from the time he accompanied us on our visits to his final resting place. I witness myself and my husband as we age. Bittersweet, I view my children as they have grown from infants and toddlers to young adults. While time brings change, our love remains constant.

My parents are always included in the photos we take. They are not only our "personal Buddhas," but part of our family. Taking these photos acknowledges their living presence. Through our visits, we secure my parents' well-being through acknowledgment and remembrance. Rituals that recognize and care for the dead reverberate throughout the web of existence. They touch not only those who have passed on to Amida's Pure Land, but also those beings who have yet to enter this world. As sentient beings, we are but one link along a great chain of being. We are an important link, however. As I tend to my parents, I not only connect my parents with their grandchildren, but I also connect with the sense of responsibility for caring for the dead and for each other. The Vow of Great Compassion, in which we seek enlightenment not only for ourselves, but also for others, envelops us all—across time and space—and compels us to act wisely and compassionately. I pass on to my children an expansive view of the world based on Buddhist faith. By looking after the dead, we are able to recognize and embrace impermanence, suffering, interconnectedness, and gratitude and continue to forge bonds of compassion. And our acts of care serve as the emotional force that animates and helps realize an otherwise abstract worldview.

My children's sense of the world has been shaped by our cemetery visits. When my son and daughter were born, I had every intention of raising them in the Buddhist tradition. We had several temples with active Dharma schools in the area. But somehow our Sundays were always too busy—with kid activities and visiting my father when he was alive. My encounter with evangelical Christianity and my choice to pursue the academic study of religion had also made me wary of religious institutions, despite my own positive memories of being raised in the temple. I also felt strongly that my children's spiritual path was their own.

While some might view my children (and myself) as proof of an increasingly secularized society, this does not mean that religious and cultural connections are lost.[10] My daughter and son have come to understand my connection with Buddhism and its centrality to their Japanese American identity through the funeral services they attended and my grandmother's home altars, which I inherited. They also have come to understand Buddhism on their own—through Osamu Tezuka's eight-part graphic novel series, *Buddha*—which they have read many times, and unlike previous generations, they have been exposed to Buddhism in their high school history courses. But I believe that it is through our visits to the cemetery that they have most intimately come to share a Buddhist worldview. A worldview in which death brings the realization of suffering and grief, but also, one in which death is naturalized and viewed as part of a larger cycle; in which the bonds are personal and deep; and in which such human connection is not lost, but at the same time must be actively maintained through care and compassion. And as Traphagan notes: "ultimate concern is expressed in terms of immediate concern" for friends and family, both dead and alive.[11]

Being Buddhist and visiting the cemetery is also part of the legacy of being Japanese American. This ritual embodies the history of our family and community. My mother and our extended family were incarcerated at Gila River during the Second World War. My father served in the 442nd Battalion during the Second World War and was honored with a Purple Heart and Bronze Medal. His marker includes his rank and service, as well as the

Buddhist Dharma wheel. (The Buddhist symbol was only available after my father died.) Our cemetery visits have served as prompts to share this story of courage, struggle, and injustice with my children. As my children visit the grave and roam the cemetery during our visits, they are reminded of my father's service and my mother's incarceration—all part of their Japanese American heritage and identity. Our personal Buddhas encapsulate our family's history and the history of the community. Suffering is a condition that we humanly endure and make good through our choice to remember, acknowledge, and care.

We take one final look at my parents' grave and head back down the hill to the car. I say a few quiet words to my parents—wishing them well and saying how good it is to see them; I end in gassho. We discard the clippings, tumble into the car, wave goodbye to my parents—and make our way home.

In the present day, we continue our ritual of visiting the cemetery. Now that my children have grown, our visits are brief and more somber. We do not speak much but attend to our ritual. My children recognize that our visits are important to me, and they do not question, fuss, or complain. Like holidays, our visits are built into the year and something that we simply do. While the meaning of our visits will continue to evolve, I feel I have instilled in them a Buddhist sense of connection, caring, and hope.

I hope that one day, after I have passed, my children will continue to visit me—with their families and those close to them. I hope my children remember that they are not alone but are part of a great chain of being. That they have responsibilities to the living and the dead and an obligation to care. After I pass, I look forward to seeing them and hope these times will give them comfort, joy, and connection that such visits have given me. *Namuamidabutsu.*

4

CREATING DESIRE PATHS

On Being a "Bad Buddhist Auntie"

MIHIRI TILLAKARATNE

I have a T-shirt that says, "Auntie's Worst Nightmare." The words are emblazoned across the chest in horror movie font. It's accurate. I'll never be an "appropriate" Sri Lankan American Buddhist: I'm unmarried and childfree by choice; I'm loud, I curse, I take up space (metaphorically, physically, and conversationally), and I'm fat. Worst of all, I'm totally content with it! As I have grown older, I've moved from "Auntie's Worst Nightmare" to "Bad Buddhist Auntie."

I grew up in a Sri Lankan Sinhalese Theravāda Buddhist environment, yet I consider myself a bad Buddhist, a bad Sri Lankan American, and a good auntie. I don't fit the typical Sri Lankan vision of auntiehood, especially as someone born and raised in the United States. When I've encountered others uncomfortable with their children calling me "Auntie," they've always been adult immigrants born in Sri Lanka. They simply can't conceive of someone with my Valley Girl accent being "Auntie."

In this chapter, I reflect on the contradictions of embracing a Bad Buddhist Auntie identity: being considered a role model while also being seen as a cautionary tale; being a great auntie while simultaneously being a bad Buddhist and a bad Sri Lankan American. As I grow older, like other Asian American Buddhists, my relationship with both younger generations and my temple has changed reflecting the uncertainties I've heard from leaders at Asian American Buddhist institutions handling generational shifts. Part of my role as associate editor for *Lion's Roar* involved meeting with different Asian American Buddhist communities. One issue that almost always came up is the question of generational continuity: How do we keep our sangha members who were born and/or raised in the US?

I see these shifts happening in real time as my former Sunday School students grow into young adulthood. I've written about how my temple—Dharma Vijaya Buddhist Vihara in Los Angeles, California—has successfully kept multiple generations of Sri Lankan American Buddhists engaged with our community. In 2011, I shot a documentary featuring Dharma Vijaya, *I Take Refuge*. The children in the film are now teens and young adults who are still active members of the temple. While the adults no longer attend Sunday School weekly, they stay involved financially by being monthly donors, attending religious events and festivals, and taking leadership roles. For example, the October 2022 Kathina celebrations were entirely organized and funded by former Dharma Vijaya Sunday School students, now adults in their twenties, thirties, and forties.

What does it mean that Gen X, Millennial, and Gen Z Asian American Buddhists are now aunties and therefore *ancestors*? How are we passing on our cultural and religious traditions in unique ways? What does this mean for Buddhism, where lineage is so vital, if the "Bad Buddhist Auntie" shapes the experience of future Asian American Buddhist generations? How can we embrace the Bad Buddhist Auntie inside us all? In this chapter, I explore what it means to take on the mantle of the Bad Buddhist Auntie as a practice/praxis in response to the contradictory and disjointed nature of diaspora. Taking on the responsibility of "ancestor" is a vital reframing of temporality for embodied diasporic subjects. Actively disengaging with the role of "descendent" or "inheritor" of homeland beliefs and practices changes how Asian American Buddhists born and/or raised in diaspora relate with time.

First, I examine how the experience of diaspora is fragmentary, multivocal, disjointed, contradictory, and temporally misaligned. Second, I describe how the "doing" of diaspora lies in attempting to make sense of these fractures and inconsistencies. Auntiehood is one strategy/tactic of doing diaspora and an active process of creation that is practical and focused on the present moment. Doing auntiehood involves creating, committing to, and reinforcing alternative desire paths that deviate from the normative institutional practices and beliefs in service of practical and relevant strategies that relate to a community's specific context. Finally, I describe practical strategies for creating desire paths in your own Buddhist community.

The Fragmentary Experience of Diaspora

The diasporic body participates in a particular construction of reality and perceived authenticity in diaspora. This is the so-called *Good* that reflects narrow definitions—of *Asian American*, *Buddhist*, and so on—existing in opposition to the *Bad* of "Bad Buddhist Auntie" that reflects lived experiences. This capital-G Good involves narratives of power that reflect systemic institutional hierarchal perspectives; Good reflects what is defined, perceived, and continually upheld as "normal." In this, Good is both judgmental—for example, "That's a Good Buddhist"—and prescriptive—"That's how it should be." In it is the normalization of a prescriptive *should*, and an instructive attitude in how to do the should—how the "should do's" should be done, *must* be done, in order to uphold normalcy. In reinforcing the normative, *should* has a close relationship to *is*. Good is singular, not plural—making claim to a singular/eternal/unchanging state of being that doesn't reflect plurality of experience—and reinforces hierarchies, inequities, and inequalities. Good is a monolith, reflecting singular, acceptable views on society, culture, gender, sexuality, religion, and so on.

While Good is a noun describing what supposedly is, thus making a claim to a static and stable identity, Bad reflects a verb—the doing, the process, the active nature of diaspora. The *Bad* in "Bad Buddhist Auntie" acknowledges that the experience of diaspora is fragmentary, multivocal, disjointed, and contradictory. Bad emphasizes doing, action, agency, active processes. In this, Bad reflects the constantly changing and impermanent (*anicca*) experience of diaspora in which there is no eternal identity (*anatta*) of soul, nation, or diaspora. The Bad is the messiness of diaspora: the multivocal, the fragmentary, the unsteady.

Since Good is a statement while Bad describes experience, Good and Bad are constantly conversing with each other. In fact, Good needs Bad in order to define itself; it defines itself in relation to what it is not. There is discomfort in the Bad, in standing on wobbly ground, which is why sometimes Good can be so rigidly defined that anything with nuance is automatically Bad. Since Good is a claim to authenticity, "normal/normative" and "authentic" must be defined in relation to what is "abnormal" or "inauthentic."[1] There is discursive power to the Good. However, discursive power also adheres to the Bad, in an acknowledgment that our identities, experiences, and institutions are not fixed.

I've experienced the messiness and fragmentary nature of diaspora firsthand. Over the past few years, whenever I go to a different country, I make sure to visit the Sri Lankan diasporic community there; so far, I've visited communities in Paris, Zurich, and Toronto. In 2022, I spent a few hours speaking with the owner of a Sri Lankan restaurant in Zurich called "Don't Worry Eat Curry." He came to Switzerland as a refugee from Sri Lanka, a Tamil teenager with only the clothes on his back, and built a very successful life as a restauranteur and educator. This path was vastly different from my family's departure from the homeland; my mother came to begin a PhD program at the University of California, Los Angeles. Your experience as a member of the Sri Lankan diaspora—and even defining yourself as "Sri Lankan"—depends on your ethnicity, religion, the location in which you settle, and your circumstances of departure.

Similarly, the experiences of Asian American Buddhists in diaspora depend on many factors. Situations are different depending on the community to which they belong. Members of refugee communities affected by American imperialism/war, like Cambodian and Vietnamese Americans, have different experiences from Chinese Americans. Differences are found even within the same ethnic group, like the experience of Japanese Americans in Hawai'i compared to those on the mainland. In addition, legacy Asian American Buddhists have different experiences with Buddhism than convert Asian American Buddhists.[2] These histories and experiences are layered and fragmentary. They are disconnects, hypocrisies, at odds with each other. Diaspora offers contested, messy, and sometimes volatile spaces and subjects of analysis.

The Temporal Misalignment of Diasporic Subjects

This experience of diaspora, which rejects binaries between here/there or leaving/settling, also involves a fragmented relationship to time. The work of creating home in diaspora—homing, making home, or home work—is a continuous process rooted in affect, where "being at home and the work of home-building is intimately bound up with the idea of home: the idea of a place (or places) in the past, and of this place in the future. Making home is about *creating* both pasts and futures through inhabiting the grounds of the present."[3] That is, the work of a diaspora is entwined with the temporality of home through constructing a past, present, and future.

This generates another heteroreproductive binary between parent/child and ancestor/descendant in diaspora, a time of inheritance that "connects the family to the historical past of the nation, and glances ahead to connect the family to the future of both familial and national stability."[4]

Recently, a Sunday School student interviewing me for a school project asked how I would preserve Sri Lankan culture. I responded, "I don't like the word *preservation*: There's nothing to preserve. What you *think* is 'Sri Lankan culture' is just a snapshot of a specific moment in time." My answer sprang from my work on embodied memory and the Sri Lankan American experience in which I contend that diasporic subjects, especially Asian Americans born and/or raised in the US, are temporally misaligned.[5] The temporal and spatial distances of diaspora can "freeze" time at the moment of departure, complicating temporal understandings of homeland and place. The everyday practices of diaspora—the clothes we wear, the music we listen to, the food we eat and smell—are also caught in time, affecting diasporic subjects' perceptions of the homeland politics and cultural practices. For example, when immigrants tell stories about the homeland to their children who were born and/or are being raised in the US, they do so about a past homeland that no longer exists in the present time. The cultural markers that shaped my understanding of Sri Lanka—stories, songs, cultural and religious traditions—come from before 1981, the year my parents immigrated. This temporal rigidity in diaspora is offset by a fluid temporality. Homeland culture, politics, and norms have changed from what my immigrant parents knew because the homeland has continued to change in their absence. In the Sri Lankan context, this becomes fraught, considering that the civil war began in 1983. War changes a culture and how it understands cultural, socioeconomic, and religious dynamics.

Temporal misalignment is further accentuated when this past homeland becomes the present reality for those later Asian American generations who attempt to embody that past through family traditions, cultural events, and religious practices, reenacting homeland cultural practices and norms in diaspora that no longer exist or have changed. As new waves of immigrants come to the US, they bring with them new epistemologies, new cultural and religious practices. Further, those born and/or raised in the US face a temporal misalignment as not only children of immigrants (or as immigrants themselves), but also as current parents, aunties, uncles, and mentors to younger generations. As a result, the tensions between time, memory, and diaspora take on contradictory meanings that affect the experiences and identities of Asian Americans born and/or raised in the US. My comment "There's nothing to preserve" describes the competing ideas of what Sri Lanka is and what it means to be Sri Lankan. The Good—the monolithic idea of "Sri Lankan culture"—does not exist. Temporality, nostalgia, and affect complicate and work to both make and unmake ideas of the nation, so memory becomes contradictory, ambivalent, even haunted.[6]

"Doing" Diaspora: Making Sense of the Mess

Temporal misalignment creates discomfort and confusion with the messy, fragmentary, unsteady, and disconnected nature of diaspora. In Buddhism, no singular eternal state of being exists due to impermanence; likewise, diaspora is mutable. Therefore, instead of engaging with a false sense of the eternal, embodying Buddhist teachings requires acting intentionally and making strategic choices, since kamma/karma literally means "action" or "deed." Similarly, the "doing" of diaspora lies in the active attempts to make sense of these multivocal, fragmentary, and messy fractures and inconsistencies. One strategy of comprehending our experiences is in reflecting on our own histories. We are embodied archives, made up of lived experience, memories, and traumas, trying to hold the fragmented pieces of ourselves together. Being in diaspora forces us to question our inheritances, metaphorically and literally, and makes entrenched ideologies visible.

I understood nationalist extremism early on: I was in high school during 9/11, so I came of age during the War on Terror. Though I was born and raised in the US, I feared that I, my family, and my community, would be targeted. Later, as an undergraduate at Harvard learning about Sinhalese Buddhist nationalism, I saw similarities between the rhetoric of the War on Terror and that used during the Sri Lankan civil war. As a result, I began rethinking my relationship to Sri Lanka and Buddhism itself, culminating in a horrifically necropolitical ending to my college experience. In May 2009, during my senior year finals, the Sri Lankan government's last push against the Liberation Tigers of Tamil Eelam (LTTE)—which ended the Sri Lankan civil war and lead to the death of tens of thousands of civilians used as human shields—coincided with a fatal shooting on campus. As I was processing news reports of horrific state violence in Sri Lanka, I was simultaneously experiencing the terror of American policing, as officers wandered in and out of my dorm room while detectives interviewed me about the shooter, my dorm neighbor's boyfriend.

Learning about Sri Lankan history altered my relationship to my homeland, religion, and language. This experience is common for many Sri Lankan American Sinhalese people born and/or raised in the US. Some don't learn about Sinhalese Buddhist nationalism at all, so they grow up with superficial understandings of the Sri Lankan civil war. When they realize that this erasure is itself rooted in Sinhalese Buddhist nationalist epistemic violence, it reframes their perspective on their culture and religion. When they discover the influence of Sinhalese Buddhist nationalism, these individuals begin to reevaluate and resynthesize their views on their identity. In doing so, they begin to develop an awareness of multiple racial and ethnic hierarchies in multiple locations and nation-states, which I call a *transnational social justice orientation*.[7] Developing this orientation involves recognizing the inequities and marginalization they experience as racialized diasporic bodies in the US, while simultaneously becoming aware of their privileges as Sinhalese people in Sri Lanka and in diaspora.

I felt this transnational social justice orientation deeply during my first visit to Jaffna, in northern Sri Lanka, a place that was inaccessible during the Sri Lankan civil war. The Jaffna Public Library's atrium had pictures from after the building burned due to arson in 1981, a moment that remains a powerful symbol for the Sri Lankan Tamil diaspora. Seeing the destruction of Tamil historical artifacts, literature, and documents, I suddenly wept.[8] The physical and psychic violence involved in destroying a place that held such cultural value reminded me of the burning of churches, mosques, and synagogues in the US. I thought of Balbir Singh Sodhi, murdered in the aftermath of 9/11. I thought of the mass shootings in religious spaces: the 2012 Oak Creek, Wisconsin, Sikh gurdwara; the 2015 Charleston church; and the 2018 Pittsburgh synagogue. I am a bad Sri Lankan American and a bad Buddhist because through my transnational social justice orientation, I am critical of nationalism and the use of nationalism to justify violence, whether as a racialized diasporic subject in the US affected by wartime nationalism or as part of an ethnic majority that benefits from wartime nationalism in Sri Lanka and its diaspora.

Auntiehood as Praxis: A Strategy for Doing Diaspora

Developing a transnational social justice orientation is one way to attempt to make sense of the unsteady nature of diaspora. Auntiehood is another strategy/tactic of "doing" diaspora, wherein Bad Buddhist Aunties lean in to nuance and proudly stand on wobbly ground, creating desire paths in their cultural and religious communities that offer alternative approaches. An *auntie* can be a biological relation (a parent's sister or cousin) or a generational one (between a young person and an older mentor, guardian, or relative), but aunties can just as well be strangers. As an important figure of fictive kinship, considering the roles and resonances of auntiehood provides us with "forms, structures, and aesthetics to make sense of lived conditions and to create alternative sociopolitical ecologies."[9] Aunties are flexible in the different roles they play in family networks, as members of cultural institutions, in their changing relationships to other aunties, and in their maintenance of diasporic spaces:

> Despite male figureheads, aunties ensure the day-to-day operations of diasporic religious and cultural institutions. Aunties are the machinery that keeps the project of diaspora moving, making certain that the mission of being [Asian] in America is constantly negotiated through these spaces.[10]

Their flexibility in affiliation and allegiance, however, can also be transgressive, which makes the auntie a dangerous figure. Aunties reside outside of the nuclear family unit but also within extended family networks, and they facilitate connections, moving across and between biological and nonbiological networks, blurring heteronormative definitions of "family."[11] In moving within the in-between spaces, at once belonging to both and neither, Aunties "potentially destabilize and disaggregate the social units we think we know so well."[12] As meditators between children and their parents, and in supporting younger generations in navigating parental conflicts, aunties can complicate and even threaten nuclear family dynamics.

Like *Bad*, I consider *Auntiehood* a verb, an approach to one's relationship with biological and nonbiological family, communities, and younger generations. Instead of a state of being, it is set of actions, strategies, and tactics. Since Auntiehood is something that you *do*, anyone, regardless of gender, can be an Auntie. *Doing* Auntiehood—or *Auntying*—means accepting, moving forward, and acting with the knowledge that you are now, in this moment, an *ancestor*. This involves remembering our pasts and the support we did or did not get from family and other community elders, visualizing alternative futures, and then altering our behaviors and ideologies in the present to tangibly produce those possibilities, an active process rooted in a commitment to what Layla F. Saad calls "become[ing] a good ancestor."[13] The *descendent* in diaspora inherits homeland traditions, so the practices of diaspora attempt to instill cultural and religious norms in diasporic children, since "the child, as concept and figure, is an embodiment of the temporal misalignment of memory. The child is an investment who exists in the present, who represents a future that has not yet come to pass, and who we teach about the past."[14] Envisioning ourselves as ancestors, however, allows us to reckon with temporal misalignment by discarding heteroreproductive notions of diasporic subjects as passive vehicles/vessels receiving cultural practices, instead reconsidering ourselves as active forces of a now-focused, needs-focused, and desire-focused approach to diasporic life.

Auntiehood as praxis is doing diaspora intentionally by having a temporally focused mindset, one that is rooted in present conditions and current context. Auntying makes sense of temporal misalignment and the fragmentary nature of diaspora using practical, appropriate strategies for the here and now. In this present-focused view of diaspora, instead of working for a hypothetical future child that is the symbol of nation or culture, auntiehood as praxis asks, "What are things we can do in this moment?"[15] This considers communities' particular context in space (transnational and specific diasporic location of city, state, country) and time (historical moment, age, and generation of laity), and creating alternative possibilities. In considering what actions are relevant and sustainable for *this* specific context of diaspora and location, auntiehood as praxis reflects interdependence and dependent origination (*paticca samuppada*). The understanding of how *kamma-vipāka*, or the ripening of our actions, affects us and others helps us envision ourselves as part of an interdependent web of existence. Auntying is intentionally working toward a specific effect by actively attempting particular causes. In this, capital-"A" Auntying is not only an active process of creation, but it is also care work, community work, and activist work simultaneously.[16]

While a Good Buddhist Auntie embodies a prescriptive "should do" mentality, a Bad Buddhist Auntie embodies a supportive "can do" perspective. Auntying as a politics of care involves helping, nourishing, and having empathy for younger generations navigating the complexity of being temporally misaligned and racialized diasporic subjects and being willing to show vulnerability through sharing our own struggles. Instead of a rigid, top-down relationship between ancestor and descendent, in meeting younger generations on their level and encouraging communication between generations, the Bad Buddhist Auntie horizontalizes the bond between auntie and younger generations. Auntying also encourages healthy skepticism of authority—even of us as aunties!—because what we aunties create now may not be applicable in thirty years, allowing for change and improvisation.

What Kind of Ancestor Do I Want to Be? Auntying Through Desire Paths

To accept the mantle of Auntiehood is to be given a certain cultural and societal legitimacy. Gen X, millennials, and Gen Z have been in the US for decades, so these generations have the legitimacy of time that recent immigrants do not, a legitimacy that can facilitate these generations' ability to be heard as stakeholders in their communities. In Asian American Buddhist communities, the Auntie's flexible and undefined role—not a parent, not a monastic—combined with their cultural and social cachet/legitimacy as elder allows the freedom and authority to criticize institutions and authority figures, offer alternative possibilities, and redefine what it means to be an Asian American Buddhist. An important strategy of Auntiehood is creating *desire paths*, a term originating in landscape architecture and referring to informal trails worn down by many feet. Desire paths are inherently social, as they are "lines on the ground left behind by users who have not followed official paths" and "remind us where we have been . . . [and] tell us where to go to find each other."[17] *Social desire paths* are acts made by individuals, rooted in these individuals' values, in response to "limitations in existing structures."[18] As a result, social desire paths challenge or conflict with existing spaces, and eventually affect or change these spaces. The Eightfold Path is a desire path: The Buddha broke away from the institutions of his time to find a path to enlightenment accessible to all, and following that path requires intentional actions.

Asian Americans who grew up in the US can forget that temples are *our* spaces. We've been part of these institutions for years and *decades* longer than those recent, first-generation immigrants bringing their young 1.5- and second-generation children to these spaces. We know the experience of being diasporic Buddhists and have more knowledge and understanding of being

Buddhist in America. The Buddhism my friends and I grew up practicing is different from the Buddhism in Sri Lanka, but we call it "our heritage" regardless. Part of being in diaspora is getting to decide what *heritage* and *tradition* mean. Desire paths begin with small numbers of "pioneers," who, unsatisfied with an existing path, create an alternative path that is "sufficiently obvious" for others to follow.[19] Instead of seeing desire paths as "the result of individual, independent actions" that arise "without explicit contemplation . . . to create social change," I contend that creating desire paths as a Bad Buddhist Auntie requires intentionality.[20] What we say *being Asian American Buddhist in diaspora* is becomes the defining narrative of what *Asian American* is. Just as we have followed the footsteps of the supportive Bad Buddhist Aunties before us, we can name the cultural priorities, the organizing principles, and the motivating interests of the community, illustrating how "authenticity can also be employed to build alternative cultures."[21] We have the power to remake and reframe our institutions, creating alternative paths.

Making desire paths in our Asian American Buddhist institutions requires us to create new epistemologies and claim those new ways of being as "our culture." This involves recognizing what ideologies and practices work and do not work in the social, cultural, political, and historical context of the US. Once we do this, we can then redo the practices, rhetoric, and beliefs that are divisive, harmful, or dysfunctional. Ultimately, making desire paths necessitates reworking the normative, creating new ways of being, and sustaining those alternative nonnormative epistemologies.

Desire paths are, by necessity, worn down, so they take time and effort to create. Such paths require work: contributing to your community in practical ways and getting involved, consistently. A Bad Buddhist Auntie creates desire paths by addressing the practical needs of their community, using their abilities and expertise to improve their community, and developing a relationship with clergy.[22] Contributing to your temple's monthly bills to help keep the lights on or buying supplies like disposable flatware are tangible ways to support your institution.[23] Further, see your time and energy as a dāna to your community, and use what you're already good at to get involved. If you're computer-savvy, help with your temple's website and social media. Or offer workshops or lessons in your area of expertise. For example, if you're a doctor, lead a workshop on an illness that disproportionately affects your community. If you're skilled at a sport, start a team for the kids in your temple. If you are a great writer, musician, or artist, teach what you've learned to young people. For almost fifteen years, I've used my experience in higher education to help Sunday School teens with college applications for free. Even if you can't do so weekly or monthly, in contributing to the temple community, you can make a difference. This will allow you to become a mentor and positive role model for younger generations so they can see what is possible for Asian American Buddhists.

Building, Not Burning: Working Within Institutions

Desire paths remake what is already there, so often we can create alternative paths within the existing structures of institutions. There is no need to "burn it all down" or disengage with our communities, though if the institution has irrevocably harmed you, leaving the community can be the only beneficial option. Working within our existing institutions however, is far more sustainable since desire paths have already been created in your community by previous Bad Buddhist Aunties, "not as the result of formal rule-breaking, but often by using existing structures in unintended ways."[24] The Bad Buddhist Aunties creates desire paths using "little tactics," cutting across the metaphorical grass intentionally to explore alternatives.[25] In doing so, "a line is drawn, yet this line is not a mapped coordinate from point A to point B; it is a register of movement."[26]

This register of movement is more effective in pragmatically working with clergy and other institutional leaders. Age and auntiehood bring with them a certain level of power, so this is the time to flex it! While I respect monks, I'm not overly deferential. I speak plainly and—if necessary—bluntly, especially when monks have unrealistic expectations for kids growing up in the US. Attempting to create desire paths in your community can reveal "the institution's willingness to tolerate, accept and sometimes absorb alternative routes" and how the institution responds to the "small rebellions" and "persistent disruptions that desire lines represent."[27] You can guide monks on their approach to younger generations. If you have kids, offer advice from your own experiences as a parent. Since I'm childfree, I offer my understanding of being born and raised in the US. You can encourage them to make adaptations to ceremonies and traditions so that Buddhist practices are applicable and relevant to our lives in the United States. Don't be afraid to disagree with monks! I realize this may not work for everyone; in other Asian Buddhist traditions, access to monastics can be restricted if you're a woman. However, I've found that Sri Lankan clergy in the US generally appreciate that I want to be involved and are willing to listen to my ideas, even if we disagree.

I have a complicated relationship with the abbot of my temple, Venerable Walpola Piyananda. He gives young people leadership roles in the temple, purposefully abandons rigid standards, and has deliberately horizontalized/equalized the relationship between laity and monastics, instituting what he calls Dharma Vijaya's "Children First" policy, which reframes the priorities of the temple toward the younger generation. Dharma Vijaya is a well-known training ground for Sri Lankan monks hoping to start their own temples in the US, so this approach to the younger generations has far-reaching effects on other temples across the country. We've had many conversations about temple dynamics and younger generations, where he's discussed how young people must "feel like they are not only included, but their presence is truly wanted. That their input and participation is important."[28] To do so, he says:

> I always assign [the children] key roles in temple celebrations and ceremonies. This lets them know that they are important not only to me and the other monks, but to the temple community. This training enables them to assume leadership roles—not only at the temple, but in the schools and organizations in which they participate.[29]

Over the years, I've judged many speeches, essays, and debates that allow our Sunday School kids to demonstrate their knowledge of Buddhism. Every time, I'm proud that Dharma Vijaya is developing young people who clearly understand and embody what it means to live guided by Buddhist principles.

When I go to other Sri Lankan Theravāda spaces in the US, I'm shocked at how fiercely hierarchies, certain traditions, and strict standards of behavior are enforced by immigrant aunties and uncles. They approach their kids' relationship with the temple as if they were Sri Lankan kids attending a temple in Sri Lanka. As a result, these kids see their temples as a rigid and restrictive places where they're scolded for breaking rules they don't understand. When these kids become adults, they simply stop coming to the temple. This "should do" that encourages "Good Buddhist" behavior illustrates how ideological rigidness interferes with the practical realities of the present context. Instead of seeing opportunities to educate young people about Buddhist thought and practice, this ideological purity actively prevents kids from positively engaging with their Sri Lankan Buddhist heritage.

Part of my work as a Bad Buddhist Auntie is pointing out to these parents that their kids are Sri Lankan *American* and their temple is in the *United States*. Something like requiring kids to memorize Pali chants without teaching their meaning is nonsensical for kids who are growing up in the US. Instead, Dharma Vijaya incorporates English translations of Pali chants into our temple practices. This allows young people to know and appreciate their traditions, instead of repeating words by rote that have no meaning to them. Moreover, in diaspora, temples are not solely religious spaces like they are in Sri Lanka but vital community spaces. Children don't see other Sri Lankan kids in school every day, so the temple becomes an important space of connection for young people sharing an ethnicity. Dharma Vijaya offers space for kids to be kids. Our Sri Lankan New Year celebrations are full of screaming kids running around the supposedly serene temple space playing traditional games. I ended my 2011 documentary *I Take Refuge* with kids playing tag because that captures the joys of our temple space—where kids can be themselves and make friends, even as they learn about Buddhist traditions and practices—a place where people of all generations enjoy being.

However, Ven. Piyananda and I have vehement ideological differences about the place of Buddhism in Sri Lankan politics. For example, I don't think monks should be involved in politics at all and firmly believe in the separation of church and state, while he believes Buddhist values should influence Sri Lankan governance and that Sri Lanka is at its core, a Buddhist nation. We are close, so I've talked to him at length about how strange it is for him to be dismantling "traditional" Sinhalese Buddhist conventions in the US while supporting Sinhalese Buddhist nationalist dogma. Even though we have these ideological differences about Sri Lanka itself, when it comes to thinking about what it means to be a Sri Lankan temple in the US, we are aligned where it matters: We believe in rethinking cultural and religious values and remaking them to work within the American context because we both understand the complex dynamics of being Sri Lankan American.

In this way, being a Bad Buddhist Auntie is about more than saying no to institutional norms—it's about building something. Working with clergy allows us to learn from our institutional leaders about how and why things are done in certain ways, which helps us to view our institutions with nuance. A Bad Buddhist Auntie rejects a purity culture mindset, where anything imperfect about an institution is automatically wrong. Instead, creating a desire path involves finding and nurturing the places where you and the institution align. In this way, we can view the "desire" aspect of the desire path as "a multidirectional, affective assemblage."[30] A desire path as an assemblage "[unites] a multidirectional set of relations that intersect in unanticipated ways."[31] In this way, a desire path "is not a space that serves as a container, where things happen; instead, it is a space that is the result of an action, and it produces bodies, spaces, and events in a web of relations."[32]

I feel more aligned with my temple than to any Sri Lankan American community organization because it understands that its younger generation lives in a complicated US racialized context. For example, in May 2020, Dharma Vijaya released a statement on the death of George Floyd signed by Ven. Piyananda, which read:

> I have been a Buddhist monk for sixty-seven years. I am also an American citizen. I am so saddened by the disregard of life that occurred in Minneapolis by four police officers that led to the death of George Floyd. In Buddhism, we learn that each one of use is accountable for our actions; that a human being is responsible for their actions or inactions. . . . Those people in positions of power should not abuse their power, but use it to promote understanding through communication to generate mutual respect.

This was the only Sri Lankan Buddhist temple in the United States that released such a statement. Later, some monks at the temple called my family asking how to support protestors since Dharma Vijaya is located on a main street in a primarily and historically Black neighborhood. After our conversation, the monks began moving the temple's stockpile of water and snacks to the driveway to give if protestors came by. I was incredibly proud of Ven. Piyananda's public statement and the monks' willingness to support their protesting neighbors.

Conclusion

Auntying requires a commitment to sitting with the tangles and messiness of diasporic life, acknowledging its complexities, and not flattening the experiences of Asian American Buddhists. As a Bad Buddhist Auntie, I am undisciplined, skeptical of religious authority, and critical of Sinhalese Buddhist nationalism in Sri Lanka and the US. However, I recognize that just like merely reading Buddhist philosophy is not sufficient to living a Buddhist life, shaping my community is not merely an ideal to theorize about: It involves being grounded in the realities of diaspora and prioritizing what is important within my community's specific context. A Bad Buddhist Auntie thinks critically about their cultural, societal, and religious heritages and intentionally creates alternative paths, reinforcing them until new ones are created. They understand that desire paths result from collective action—we can't do it alone. A Bad Buddhist Auntie strategically taps into already established networks to build, finding places where they align with religious authorities and lay members. In undertaking this duty to be a good ancestor, a Bad Buddhist Auntie takes ownership of their institutions, changing the normative from within. Just as grass is slowly trod underfoot until it eventually creates a trail, a Bad Buddhist Auntie makes a lifelong commitment to creating new paths for others who will follow.

5

—

THREADING THE INVISIBLE FLOWER GARLAND

Stories of Asian (North) American Buddhist Women I Have Known

MUSHIM PATRICIA IKEDA

Just as from a heap of flowers

many garland strands can be made,

even so

one born & mortal

should do

—with what's born & is mortal—

many a skillful thing.

CHAPTER 4, VERSE 53, THE DHAMMAPADA,
TRANS. THANISSARO BHIKKHU

1. 1997: My Mother, with Terminal Cancer, Declares Herself Buddhist

"Religion?" the two hospice volunteers, who are polite white Army wives, ask. We are in the house my parents had built on a large, rural, man-made lake in Virginia, and they are filling out the intake form for my mother to be a hospice patient. My mother is pleased, since they tell her this means she can receive free cartons of Ensure, which she drinks daily to try to keep some weight on her bones.

I open my lips slightly, about to butt in and say, "None," when my mother, probably sixty-five at the time, says confidently, "I'm Buddhist."

Since when? I think, shocked.

My mother, who has grown to look like an old tortoise as cancer has stripped weight off her body and her formerly carefully permed hair has fallen out, flashes me a triumphant glance.

You may be my oldest daughter and my firstborn, but you don't know everything about me, she beams at me, straight into my brain.

I wonder, for a second, if I know her at all.

I think I know that she grew up on Oahu in a Buddhist family and her parents had immigrated there from Japan as young people, my grandfather as a young man seeking adventure, we were told, and, separately, my then-fourteen-year-old grandmother, with her sister, for reasons unknown. The two sisters got a job cleaning officers' quarters at Pearl Harbor. Grandpa, whom we called Ojiichan, was Soto Zen Buddhist and grandma, Obaachan, was a Shin Buddhist. However, all the Buddhist temples in the Hawai'ian islands were shut down during World War II and, in many cases, the priests were arrested, some in their robes, and sent to the internment camps. My mother was maybe around seven at the time, and unlike her older sister, didn't return to being a practicing Buddhist after the war ended.

She and her siblings were Nisei, the so-called second generation of Japanese Americans. *Ni* means two. I am Sansei. *San* means three. I don't speak Japanese, but my mother did teach my brother and me to count from one to ten. We grew up in Ohio during the sixties, where even Catholics were an exotic minority, where school field trips occasionally took us to what may have been one of the first megachurches in the US, the Akron Baptist Temple. It had a gigantic plexiglass cross suspended from the ceiling, filled with colored light bulbs, that could be switched on and off by hand, most likely to create a light show.

During my childhood in Ohio, my mother had never mentioned Buddhism or, for that matter, any religion. Our family never went to church, although I, always a spiritual aspirant, had begged and was allowed to go to a Baptist Sunday school class with our neighbors. It was a friendly class in a sunny basement, as I recall, and no one ever pressured me to believe in Jesus or God.

I still don't know, exactly, what my dying mother means when she says, "I'm Buddhist."

The hospice volunteers simply nod and write it down on the form they are filling out, and we proceed with their get-to-know-you visit. They exclaim in delight over the big bowl of scattered sushi I had made for lunch, since one of them had been stationed in Japan with her husband and had loved being there.

After they leave, I am exhausted, but relieved that my mother will now receive occasional visits from trained hospice volunteers. I long for some time to myself, in which I'm not thinking about the large-cell lymphoma that is silently multiplying inside my mother's bones and blood. I'm restless within the role of dutiful first daughter.

"That sushi was good," my mother says. "Make it again."

2. "You Were Enough": Obaachan, Hawai'i Grandma

My brother, sister, and I had two grandmothers. We called our mother's mother Obaachan, or "Hawai'i grandma." We called our father's mother "Indiana grandma." Both were immigrants from Japan and spoke almost no English.

I visited my mother's childhood home on Oahu twice, once when I was five, and the second time when I was around fourteen, and I think I remember comparing notes with my brother after the second visit.

"Did you hear what Grandma was muttering when she lit incense in the corner of the house and bowed?" I said.

"Beats me. It sounded like *namdabs, namdabs, namdabs,*" my brother said.

We agreed we had no idea what she was doing or why. It wasn't until I was in my thirties, most likely, that I heard the word *Nembutsu* and realized that was my grandmother's practice. Since we didn't know Japanese and had grown up in semi-rural Ohio, the mumbling and bowing was just another mysterious thing among many things that were strange and interesting to us, like eating soapy-tasting avocado halves sprinkled with white sugar for breakfast, and bathing in the *ofuro,* the wood-fired hot tub in the garage.

This conversation with my brother must have been in the late 1960s, after we'd returned to Ohio. My parents called themselves Oriental. The term *Asian American* hadn't yet been invented, I think, and if anything, my parents thought of themselves as Japanese or Japanese Americans, not Asian Americans. Although they raised their three children to "be American," they also clearly communicated that we were different—smarter, cleaner, more hard-working—than our white, mostly working-class, friends and neighbors. Using the term from Hawai'i, they called white people *haoles.*

Obaachan was my stealth model of an Asian Buddhist woman living in the US. And when she was very old, she surprised us all by becoming a naturalized American citizen. My mother speculated that Obaachan may have found a way to hack the test, since to our knowledge she did not speak or read English. My maternal grandmother was Japanese, she was American, she was quietly Shin Buddhist, and she lived most of her long life in Hawai'i, raising five children who spoke English and Japanese and pidgin. She died peacefully on December 22, 1988, and I wrote this elegy for her in 2015:

Obaachan: Haruko Sawada

(for my grandmother)

1.
Haruko Sawada, born in springtime
in Japan, came to Hawai'i at age 14,
died there in late December at age 89,

still speaking only Japanese. Through an aunt
I asked her, Tell me about yourself.
"Nothing to say!" she says, laughing,
an old woman surrounded by her daughters
in a Ramada Inn. They're all sitting on beds
eating soft yellow Portuguese sweetbread.
Then she remembers
how she worked as a maid in Pearl Harbor,
married, had her first daughter. "Yes, yes,"
she says, "and in that first house
we used to net rice birds. You press
a spot on their breasts and they die."
Before her death she remembers,
and forgets.

2.
Sunlight lights the yellow oilcloth
on the long table, the greasy black avocados
halved, sprinkled with white sugar for breakfast,
the dented pots and chopsticks.
Like magic, from colored rice flour
you make us pink and green mochi,
us, your mainland grandchildren who can't
speak Japanese, can't even correctly say
Ikeda, our own last name!
Later I find you
lighting incense on the little shelf,

bowing, fingering dark beads,
muttering namdabs, namdabs, namdabs.
It took me years to know
you were really chanting
Namu Amida Butsu!—Hail to the Buddha
of infinite light and space,

the golden one from the Western Paradise.
But it was nothing I needed to know then.
You were enough.

3.
From the Hawai'i funeral my cousin brings me
a bundle wrapped in purple cloth.
An old green kimono, a flannel nightie, a fan,
a few stained aprons, crocheted baby clothes.
Odd-smelling odds and ends. Junk.
My inheritance. I'll tell you a story,
Obaachan says, making writing motions.
Write it down.

3. 1987 or 1988: You Had Everything (but You Lost the War)

I am sitting in a small kitchen across the table from a middle-aged Vietnamese immigrant couple, a husband and wife who are members of this temple in Phoenix, Arizona. Asian Buddhists often will purchase a modest tract home in the suburbs of an urban area with a concentration of Asians and Asian Americans of their ethnicity and quietly conduct services, offer residence to monks and people in need of a temporary room, and make friends with their neighbors in the hope that they won't be reported for a housing code violation.

The kitchen is very clean, the fixtures and countertop are older and bare. In these temples, the living room is usually emptied of furniture, an altar is assembled, and people sit on the carpeted floor. Sometimes there are a few house plants, or a temple cat or dog.

The Vietnamese wife and husband look polite, but determined to tell me their story. It's clear that they don't see me as an Asian Buddhist, they see me as an American citizen who happens to look Asian.

"I was arrested," the man says in English. "It was during the war in Vietnam and I was arrested and taken to another city and put into prison. I was so worried because I had to leave my wife and our little child."

The woman sitting next to him nods. "I worked and saved money and sent him packages of food and clothing, but nothing ever got to him," she says. "The prison guards, they took everything."

They hold themselves with dignity, as though in telling me their story there is some justice to be had. It is the husband who tells the story, but the wife looks neither silenced nor tense—and, in this memory, I can't remember who spoke next. It doesn't matter, and the story is both of theirs, but I was looking at her face as they spoke and said, "Our daughter was only six, and one day she went to school and got a vaccination. The shot was contaminated, and she died."

I am dressed in gray Korean Buddhist clothing, and my head is shaved. And none of that matters, really. In that moment there is only their huge sorrow, which makes the walls of the small house bulge outward, the refrigerator go silent, the world, their world, stop completely.

The husband leans forward slightly and looks me in the eye.

"You Americans," he says slowly. "You had soldiers. You had guns. You had bombs. You had *everything*. And you still lost the war. You lost the war."

The mother of the dead child nods and they both look expectantly at me, as though I have the power to offer reparations for the irreparable. It is clear they have no living children, only each other, and the temple.

There is nothing to be said, and so I say nothing. I think of the woman, trying to hold her family together, cleaning and cooking and packing her daughter's lunch and carefully packaging food and socks and trousers and clean white T-shirts to send to her husband. I imagine the mother and child slept together, bathed in each other's warmth and smell, since that is what we do, as Asians.

The kitchen feels very tiny now, like a time capsule, a bubble in which the three of us might sit forever at the small empty table, now slightly avoiding eye contact because that is what we do to show respect, to communicate that we will not suddenly begin to scream and flail about, to express that we understand that the past is the past and the present is unbearable.

Years later, I recount their story in a poem, a poem about prayer. Being Buddhist, I don't pray to a God or gods, but when I run out of options in holding suffering, I do pray. I remember reading somewhere the phrase describing the posture of some depictions of Kwan Yin, Bodhisattva of Compassion, who has many names and who is said to be a form of Avalokiteśvara, the One Who Hears the Cries of the World. Kwan Yin, often thought of as the Great Mother, beautiful, gracious, inclines slightly toward us, sometimes carrying a child on her lap. The words that describe her posture are: "kindly bent to ease us."

But what if ease is not possible? And sometimes loss is loss is loss is loss, unending as a drenching heavy rain that never stops.

4. He Was My Baby and I Loved Him

In this writing I am remembering, and I am surprised that what I am remembering is so often about loss and grief. There are, no doubt, reasons for this. People seem to like to talk to me about their lives, often, and among the hundreds of stories, certain ones persist for me. I really don't know why and it may not matter, since this is not meant to be an attempt to describe all Asian American Buddhist women. The direct realization of death and the impermanence of existence is, after all, central to the Buddhist teachings.

In 1990 and 1991, I lived for a year in a mostly white, rural Zen Buddhist community in the US. I was fortunate to be there, since I was a single mother at the time, with almost no money, and as a resident working a lower-level administrative position, I received childcare in the mornings so that I could work my job and receive a small stipend that covered toiletries, diaper services, a subsidized landline phone, and insurance and gasoline for the second-hand car that my parents had purchased for me. I was exhausted, and I had a persistent anxiety that if I collapsed, my child would be taken from me by Social Services, so I pushed myself to keep going.

There was a young woman of Asian descent in residence among the other Zen students at that time, and one day she asked if I could please take a short walk with her. I was able to arrange for a babysitter, and she and I met up and walked slowly among brown meadow grasses, the glittering ocean in the distance. It was a beautiful place to practice Zen meditation and community life, although I was so tired that one day I remember gazing up at the sunlit hills and thinking to myself, "If I were in better shape I know I would think 'This sunlight, these hills, the ocean in the distance . . . I know this is what would be called a lovely day, but in reality, I can barely feel anything. I have to keep going and I'm scared and I have to take care of my baby.' That is all I have room to feel and think. If it isn't enough, then too bad."

The young Zen student and I met at the appointed time and slowly walked together. She told me about her life, where she'd grown up and how she had become a spiritual seeker. She got a job, worked, and used the money she earned to travel in India. She met a young European spiritual seeker, fell in love with him, and they journeyed together, until one day she discovered she was pregnant.

"We didn't really know each other very well, we didn't have money, we didn't want to get married, so it was hopeless," the young woman says to me, as tears streak her face and she continues to walk, automatically, by my side. We have to keep moving, even if we're not hiking to a goal. Life in a Zen Buddhist community tends to be simple and repetitive by design. Before dawn the bell rings, we get up, get dressed, go to the meditation hall, sit in silence, do some chanting, the bell rings, we go to breakfast, then the work day begins. The next day begins the same way. If we keep going in circles instead of running away, it's possible we'll find a way to get closer to what it is that scares us the most.

"So I had an abortion," the young woman says. "And he and I, we went in separate directions. I don't know where he is right now."

I nodded sympathetically. I could relate to what she was saying, in more ways than one.

"But you know," she says, "My baby was still my child, and I still love him."

5. The Invisible

I'm not sure what year it was, maybe around 2015, and I was sitting in a crowded dining room of a conference center that was hosting several large groups, with nothing connecting us except for the fact that it was dinnertime. The tables were long, institutional tables with benches attached alongside so that the greatest number of people could eat together, and children and teenagers might have been in the room because it was primarily an educational nature center. What I do remember is that it was very loud and echoey and hard to hear anything at all. Sitting at my long row of tables were people who had gathered for a four-day conference to talk about diversity work in the United States; some of us had come for the first time to the group, and others, like myself, had made it a yearly ritual.

"I'm here for the first time," a middle-aged white woman with brown hair said to me. "What do you do?"

"I'm Buddhist," I said, "and most of my work has been antiracism work in American Buddhist circles."

"I'm Buddhist too!" she exclaimed.

We felt a certain sense of camaraderie, and for a moment I thought, "Perhaps we can be friends."

"So you're doing antiracism work in Buddhist communities?" the woman continued. "But there aren't many Buddhists who are people of color."

There was shouting and clapping from the tables around us. It was extremely difficult to hear anything in a private conversation and I had to remind myself to be respectful and to make an effort because these were the values of the conference that had brought us together.

"I disagree with you," I said as evenly as I could. "Buddhism comes from Asia, and the majority of Buddhists worldwide are people of color."

She looked confused.

"Maybe I mean Black people," she said.

"There are Black Buddhists," I said.

Whether it's Asian Americans in general, or Asian American women, or Asian American Buddhist women, or Asian American artists, or Asian American Buddhist poets, we tend to be invisible to the white mainstream US culture, unless we're seen as a threat. Most recently, since 2020, the start of the Covid-19 global pandemic, anyone with an Asian-looking face can be seen by anyone who doesn't look Asian as being responsible for the so-called China flu. Invisible or a visible threat seem to be the two boxes given to us: Check one.

And maybe that's why Buddhist women of Asian descent might need more places to gather for cross-lineage conversations, around kitchen tables, on walking paths, in conference centers, in cafes and classrooms and whatever spaces we can find so that we can tell our stories and be heard, and so that we can write our stories down and publish them and be seen and heard.

6. Posalnim [보살님]

I don't remember any of their names and mostly they didn't speak English or share their stories with me. *Posalnim* are women who are devoted lay practitioners of Korean Buddhism. Often, although not exclusively, they are older, having raised children and devoted many years to being householders, and they may or may not live in a Buddhist temple or monastery. They may or may not be married and may or may not be widows. However, something has happened so that, as an American Buddhist teacher I know says, they feel "touched by the Dharma." They coexist with both male and female monastics, often working in the temple kitchen, and the ones I've known seem to be rock solid in being quite content with being who they are and doing what they do. They don't need fancy expensive robes or ordination certificates.

I first met Posalnim in the Zen Buddhist Temple in Toronto, Canada, around 1984. I was a renunciant member of their first affiliate temple in Ann Arbor, Michigan, but, being a good typist, I had the opportunity to serve for brief periods of residency in Toronto, engaging in very steep learning curves on various machines to process articles and essays for the mother temple's Buddhist journal, *Spring Wind*. During this time I was mildly mocked and ridiculed for being an American—I think one of the Canadian monks even called me John Wayne—and, just as was the case in the Vietnamese temple in Phoenix some years later, no one seemed to hesitate about accepting and even pigeonholing me as an American woman. My experiences of being Othered in offensive ways have almost exclusively been in encounters with white Americans who ask me the classic questions, "Sure, sure, you say you were born in Ohio . . . but what country are you *really* from?" and "What language do you *really* speak?"

The language I "really" speak is standard American English with a flat Midwestern accent, and so I like being accepted for who I feel I am when I'm with Canadian Buddhists and immigrant Asian Buddhists in the United States. And it was always very interesting to me how the Posalnim, Korean Buddhist immigrant women who had lived in Canada for many years without having learned either English or French, seemed to establish themselves so easily in a kind of parallel universe, often living with the convert monastics who were Canadian and American and Mexican, working around our meal and meditation schedules in order to make kimchi, and occasionally inviting us to the Sunday lunches they prepared on the one day of the week when the larger Korean Canadian Buddhist sangha gathered for a traditional service in the main shrine room/meditation hall in the basement.

We didn't speak Korean, and the Posalnim didn't speak English. I remember two women, possibly in their fifties, who came regularly to the Toronto temple; they would stay several days, cook, share a room, and they could sometimes be heard laughing raucously at night.

Their affection and support for everyone in the temple was expressed wordlessly, through washing and kimchi making and cooking and being joyful and loud at times, silent and invisible at others. They're either dead or almost a hundred years old, most likely, at the time of this writing. *Kwan Seum Posal. Kwan Seum Posal. Kwan Seum Posal.*

7. She of Many Names

Avalokiteśvara, Bodhisattva of Great Compassion
the one who hears the cries of the world

also known as Guanyin or Kwan Yin
also known as Kwan Seum Posal
also known as Kannon and Kanzeon
also known as Quan Thế Âm
also known by the many Names
Khmer, Indonesian, Nepali, Thai, Hmong, Burmese, Sinhalese . . .

Hear us now
hear us now

8. Becoming Mushim 무 심

No ignorance and also no extinction of it, and so forth until no old age and death and also no extinction of them . . .

THE GREAT WISDOM HEART SUTRA

I was born and named Patricia Yoshiko Ikeda by my mother, Alice Hisako Sawada Ikeda and my father, Robert Yoshizo Ikeda. By the Japanese American count, they were *Nisei,* or second-generation Americans, born and raised in the US. This makes me *Sansei* or third-generation and my adult son *Yonsei* or fourth-generation.

I became Mushim in May 1983 in the Zen Buddhist Temple–Toronto, where I received the Bodhisattva Vows and Precepts and a Dharma name, along with a cohort of my American and Canadian sangha mates. I was the first person to be called forward in the private ceremony, and when my new name was announced, I recognized it as being from the Heart of Wisdom Sutra—"no eyes, no ears, no nose, no tongue, no body, NO MIND (Mu = no and Shim = heartmind)"—and I thought to myself, "Oh no, this is a very high-class name, and the teacher is going to try to work me to death!"

My Dharma name is a no name, an "Emptiness" name, a go big or go home name. There are many other Mushims and Mushins around in the Buddhist world, so it is by no means a special name or a unique name. My practice, in a very real way over the past forty years, has been to live into my Dharma name, failing repeatedly and going to sleep and waking up and trying again.

In Mushim there is no woman no Asian no American no old age and death and also no extinction of my being seventy-one years old and having limited time left in this particular social security number identity. I am attached to my middle-aged, half-Korean adult son because we have lived together through the global pandemic and he is my child and I love him. However, I regularly tell him: "Okay, here's the scenario. I've just dropped dead and now demonstrate to me that you can get into my computer and email and all my accounts so that you can pay my bills and settle my affairs. After that we can cook dinner together. Is tofu and rice and greens okay with you?"

6

CRITICAL AFFINITY

A Scholar-Practitioner's Memoir
of Lived Buddhism

In the field of Buddhist studies, the term *scholar-practitioner* has emerged to describe scholars who not only have expertise in Buddhism but who also have a connection to the tradition rooted in personal Buddhist practice. The scholar-practitioner concept counters the traditional emphasis in religious studies on objective, critical distance, which often casts doubt on the credibility of the intellectual analysis of those who practice religion. However, scholar-practitioners such as Charles Prebish argue that their dedicated commitment to contemplative Buddhist practices can offer unique insights into Buddhism itself. They contend that the contributions of scholar-practitioners are particularly significant in North America, where, in the absence of traditional scholar-monks, such individuals often fill the role of quasi-monastics, guiding students in their understanding of the Dharma.

The scholar-practitioner is most commonly associated with Buddhologists who also have a dedicated meditation practice. They are often Western converts to Buddhism and their practice of the tradition is most often through contemplative practices such as meditation, which has become the primary icon of Buddhism in the West. However, I propose expanding the scholar-practitioner category to include Asian and Asian American scholars like myself who, in addition to our academic expertise in contemporary Buddhism, bring critical perspectives about the tradition through our lived experiences as Asian American Buddhists. I argue that our scholarly engagement with Buddhism is deeply influenced by our lay engagement with the tradition as Asians and Asian Americans, and these embodied life experiences shape the significance of our contributions to the study of Buddhism.

My relationship to Buddhism is deeply influenced by my embodied Buddhist life experiences as a Sri Lankan American woman immersed in Sinhalese Buddhist culture, history, and politics. My personal connections to the tradition as a transnational Asian diaspora lay Buddhist informs my intellectual investments in the critical analysis of Buddhist worlds. Recognizing my positionality as a Buddhist and the situated knowledge my lived experiences produce informs my commitment to critical analysis of Buddhist worlds. I call this perspective *critical affinity*.

In what follows, I use small pieces of personal memoir as a form of autoethnographic writing to reflect on how I navigate inhabiting this critical affinity in relating to Buddhism as a scholar-practitioner of lived Buddhism. I describe how, as a Sri Lankan American, being born in the US and raised in Sri Lanka—during my childhood and young adult years in a Sinhalese Buddhist household during a religiously inflected civil war—has shaped my affinity toward Buddhism. I also explore how these experiences have influenced my critical intellectual investments as an anthropologist of Buddhism. Furthermore, I examine how these lived experiences critically challenge the essentialist meanings often attributed to "heritage" Buddhist identity, including how my so-called cultural baggage reflects the influence of European colonial modernity and its enduring postcolonial legacy.

The Karma of Giving Blood, Spilling Blood

In October 2023, my husband and I arrived at the USC medical hospital at our scheduled appointment for a blood donation. It was our first time donating blood and we both were eager and certainly a little nervous. But the newsletter from the Keck Hospital of USC announcing a series of local sponsored blood donor events for university staff could not have arrived in my email inbox at a more perfect time.

Yes, donating blood responded to the critical blood shortage the nation faced; the American Red Cross had recently declared a national emergency due to a blood shortage, citing the lowest number of people in the United States donating in the last twenty years. While this urgent need was a compelling reason to donate, our motivation was more personal.

For Sri Lankan Buddhists like ourselves, donating blood can hold unique spiritual significance. That first week of October marked two significant dates for us: the fortieth anniversary of my father's death and my late mother-in-law's seventy-fifth birthday. Many Buddhists believe donating blood is a karmic act that yields merit (*pin*), which in this instance we dedicated to our departed parents, buoying them in their karmic journey toward ultimate liberation from samsara.

In Sri Lanka and many parts of Asia where Buddhism is practiced, the practice of organ and tissue donations is considered a form of dāna. At one level, it is a means through which to cultivate and perfect an ethical disposition of generosity, a cornerstone of Buddhist practice. By giving blood and enacting the practice of letting go, one seeks to break free from the illusion of a separate self. But beyond this more doctrinal interpretation of dāna, at a more mundane personal level, for many lay Buddhists, giving blood (*léh dan deema*) also serves as a means of cultivating and transferring merit to the departed (*pin anumodana*). For my husband and me, it was an extension of our reciprocal responsibilities to our late parents; a familial duty and an act of care intimately tied to our Buddhist upbringing.

Many converts to Buddhism in the West often struggle with the constellation of "supernatural" ideas around the theory of karma that are so fundamental to the way Buddhists in Sri Lanka and its diaspora navigate their moral lives. Indeed, in some Western meditation-based convert circles, it is not uncommon to hear the term *cultural baggage* to refer to the ritualized acts, cosmological ideas, and devotional practices of Asian and Asian diaspora Buddhists. In my own engagement with convert Buddhist communities through my research, I have often noted a reticence among Western convert

Buddhist communities to take these practices and ideas seriously, with many interlocutors commenting on ideas of karma and rebirth as perhaps being cultural accretions that they believe are incompatible with "true" Buddhism that is consonant with a modern rationalized worldview. As a researcher, I've often been struck not only by how such claims of cultural baggage render the spiritual lives and everyday practices of heritage Asian American Buddhists like myself invisible and illegible but also by the underlying conceit of authority to define what constitutes authentic Buddhism.

Yet, it is precisely this constellation of ideas around the theory of karma that have engendered the spiritual life of Buddhists. Although in a Western context, karma is held up as advancing an ethic of autonomous individualism, for many who were raised in Buddhist cultural contexts, these ideas of karma offer a perspective into the relational and intersubjective dimension of our lived experiences. For example, one of my earliest childhood memories is of a *pirit* ceremony held in our home upon the passing of my father. Buddhist monks were invited to chant Pali Sutta verses and tie white protective strings around our wrists. Like dāna, Buddhists believe that chanting pirit cultivates good karma or merit that can create favorable conditions for one's own and one's loved ones' samsaric journey. It is an enactment of this Buddhist worldview that posits social and personal relationships as intertwined in karmic entanglements, connecting individuals across past, present, and future cosmic distances. Now, decades later at USC, I hoped and believed that transferring merit on behalf of my father at his fortieth death anniversary through a secular blood donation event would have similar karmic efficacy.

At the clinic, the latex band bit into my arm, and I felt a tight cold pressure. As I watched the nurse expertly insert the needle and my gaze drifted to the blood bag slowly beginning to fill, my mind drifted to 1999 and a memory of my first attempt to donate blood when I was eighteen years old in Colombo, Sri Lanka.

It was the summer before I was to return to the United States for my first year in college, having spent nearly my entire childhood in Sri Lanka. Though I was born in Virginia, after my father's sudden death at forty-four, my young widowed mother decided to return to Sri Lanka to raise my two sisters and me among the safety and support of her homeland. At this time, my sisters were fourteen and twelve and I was two and a half. So when I first attempted to donate blood, it was at a Buddhist temple in Colombo against the backdrop of the civil war that had been raging since we arrived in Sri Lanka in 1983.

Throughout the 1980s and 1990s the demand for blood was high as a result of the war in the north of the country with the Liberation Tigers of Tamil Eelam (LTTE). For the Sinhalese majority government, the LTTE's demand for a separate homeland, or *Eelam*, for Tamils in the northern and eastern regions of Sri Lanka constituted a threat to its sovereignty and territorial integrity. For the majority Sinhalese, who have viewed Sri Lanka as the *dhammadipa*—the island (*dipa*) of the Buddha's teachings (*dhamma*)—a sacred Buddhist space meant to be secured by the Sinhalese as the "chosen race," the LTTE demand for an independent Eelam impinged on their nationalist sensibilities. It was against this backdrop of Sinhalese Buddhist nationalism that Buddhist clergy made their appeals to the Sinhalese for blood to help treat soldiers injured on the battlefield or civilians injured by bomb blasts, and their appeals for blood donations resonated strongly with the Sinhalese Buddhist nationalist consciousness.

Many Sinhalese, including those from affluent middle-class families like mine, volunteered in large numbers at the time. Buddhist institutions, from civic organizations to monastic establishments, were significant sources of support for the blood drive campaigns, often framing their appeals in Buddhist terms. For example, a popular narrative positioned military service as a form of dāna and rhetoricians would often describe military servicemen as committing the selfless sacrifice of *aes, his, mas, leh* (eyes, head, flesh, and blood). In Theravāda Buddhism, these bodily organs denote a special category of meritorious giving referred to as *dāna paramita* that is rooted in Buddhist folklore (of the extraordinary bodily sacrifices made by the Buddha in previous lives as recorded in Jataka tales). By connecting the military defense of national sovereignty to the righteousness of dāna paramita, rhetoricians were able to appeal to the public to donate blood to soldiers as a form of reciprocal support for the cause of protecting Sinhalese sovereignty. Ideas of blood donation as a form of national service merged in this way with more traditional appeals to the meritorious nature of giving.

Alas, my body weight as a young teenage girl was just shy of the weight requirement to donate blood and I was turned away. Nearly twenty-five years later, as I sat there at the USC hospital in Los Angeles having my blood drawn for the first time in the memory of my late father, I could not help but wince in recalling this memory—at my own participation in these everyday forms of Sinhalese Buddhist nationalist consciousness that fueled a bloody war and that have continued to uphold Sinhalese Buddhist hegemony in Sri Lanka.

Reckoning with My Heritage Buddhist Identity

Momentum is growing within the Asian American Buddhist diaspora to make known and to amplify the contributions and significance of heritage Buddhists, namely Buddhists whose Asian ancestral and cultural heritages have historically preserved Buddhism. This call to honor heritage Buddhists is particularly significant as Asian American Buddhists face the experiences of racism, erasure, and cultural appropriation that endure in a culture of white dominance.

Yet, at the same time, the violence and everyday racial oppressions that Sinhalese Buddhist have dealt in the name of preserving Buddhism in Sri Lanka gives me pause in embracing my own heritage Buddhist identity. In fact, I have had to spend a good deal of my adult life deconstructing my Buddhist identity and heritage, especially as it has been defined within the constraints of the Sinhalese Buddhist nationalist consciousness that I was immersed in as a Sinhalese girl growing up in Sri Lanka. Because I find that the dominant Sinhalese Buddhist racial consciousness leaves almost no Sri Lankan Buddhist community space, even in the diaspora, really free of its specter, I admittedly have often felt reluctant to actively engage in these cultural spaces. I've certainly witnessed how, in the name of preserving Buddhist heritage, the racist rhetoric of Sinhalese nationalism has sometimes been even more amplified and bellicose in the Sri Lankan American diaspora than in Sri Lanka itself.

Yet, my embodied experiences as a heritage Buddhist woman with transnational ties to Sri Lanka and the United States, combined with my scholarly training, have also provided me with unique insights into the diverse local meanings that animate the spiritual life of Sinhalese Buddhists that challenge static views of Asian and Asian American Buddhism.

I'm seated in the meditation hall on the second day of a five-day meditation retreat at an Insight meditation center in the Northeastern United States. This retreat is a historic moment for the local community, addressing the growing need for more accessible spaces for communities of color beyond its predominantly white demographics.

As I look around the room at my fellow retreatants, a diverse group of practitioners from various parts of the country guided by two women of color, I can't help but feel a sense of belonging. One of the teachers guides the group in the first "sit" of the day, inviting us to turn our attention to the present moment, to the embodied experience of the self, and to observe the sensation of breathing. Our collective silence and focused breathing invite a stillness of mind and body.

My reason for being here is to experience this momentous occasion first-hand as part of my ethnographic research on the institutional efforts of North American Buddhist convert communities to respond to the institutional whiteness prevalent in Insight meditation communities. While meditation isn't a regular practice for me and I rarely have a disciplined meditation practice outside of retreats I attend for participant-observation, I nonetheless have an intimate familiarity with it.

I have a vivid memory of my young mother sitting on the verandah of our Sri Lankan home, headphones on and a Walkman in her lap, meditating. She had started this practice shortly after my father's sudden death in Virginia Beach. She was engrossed in cassette tapes by Bhante Rahula, a North American Theravāda monk based at the Bhavana Society in West Virginia. A few years prior, she had received these recorded guided instructions on Vipassana during a visit to the society's founder, the Sri Lankan monk Bhante Henepola Gunaratana, whom my family knew through the tight-knit Sri Lankan diaspora in Virginia. I remember the large, white binder holding a dozen or so of these cassettes as one of her most cherished possessions.

Amid her profound grief and despair as a young mother navigating a transcontinental move, selling a home, and caring for her daughters, the guided Vipassana meditations provided her with a lifeline, grounding her in the present and nurturing joy and resilience. As a Buddhist, my mother believed that karma—my deceased father's, hers, and ours—were the conditions of his untimely demise. However, she found solace in the Buddhist principles of suffering (*dukkha*) and impermanence (*anicca*) cultivated in the practice of Vipassana that helped her accept his death and find strength to persevere through her grief.

Later, when I was around seven years old, I also learned *anāpānasati bhāvanā* (meditation) at the Buddhist girls' school I attended early on in my schooling in Sri Lanka. Poya days, lunar monthly holidays commemorating the Buddha's life, were often dedicated in school to taking *sil* (ethical precepts) and meditating. Unlike in the US, where mindfulness meditation is taught for secular purposes, Sri Lankan Buddhist schools introduce bhāvanā for spiritual formation. Despite our otherworldly aspirations, I vividly recall my white uniform dress sticking to my skin in the sweltering humidity. The pungent odor of a room full of sweaty schoolgirls filled my nostrils with each meditative breath.

Buddhist girls' schools like the one I attended were a direct legacy of the broader Buddhist revivalist movement that unfolded in the early twentieth century in the face of growing aspirations for independence from colonial rule. A significant aspect of this movement was the emphasis placed on lay people undertaking high-level spiritual pursuits once reserved for spiritually advanced monks, alongside formalized training in studying Buddhism and the Sinhalese language. Along with religious formation, including meditating and learning to recite numerous Pali gathas and the Buddhist Jatakas, the school curriculum I recall emphasized a particular framing of Buddhist mytho-historiography—one centered on the ethnoreligious exceptionalism of Sinhalese Buddhists.

Scholars of Buddhism have characterized these transformations as laicization and part of the broader process of Buddhist modernism that unfolded in South and Southeast Asia during colonial modernity, where North American and European Theosophists played a pivotal role in establishing educational institutions like the one I attended. Musaeus College, the Buddhist girls' school that I attended, bore the names of its Western Buddhist-Theosophical founders: Marie Musaeus Higgins, a German educationist who served as the founding principal along with Peter De Abrew, a Sri Lankan philanthropist. The school houses were named after prominent figures associated with the Theosophical Society's work in Sri Lanka—Henry Steel Olcott, an American co-founder of the society; Annie Besant, an English supporter of independence movements; and Higgins. Their framed portraits hung on the assembly hall walls. As a young girl, during those long Poya observances in the assembly hall, I would often find myself distractedly glancing during meditation practice at the founders' portraits. I was puzzled by this incongruity. What did these white figures have to do with a school so invested in Buddhism? My confusion deepened when a teacher revealed that one of the founders, Colonel Olcott, was like myself, an American.

The presumption of Theosophists like Colonel Henry Olcott was that the Buddhist laity of Sri Lanka were ignorant of their own tradition and felt it their white savior prerogative to provide middle-class Sinhalese youth with a knowledge of Buddhism through education. The Buddhism they introduced in school was thus a rationalized one, shorn of traditional Sinhalese Buddhist engagement with deities and spirits, and one decidedly oriented toward a Buddhism distilled down to its philosophical and ethical premises. Teaching children to meditate at an early age was part of their vision of a Buddhist religious formation.

Yet, despite the aspirations of Theosophists and their native coconspirators like the Buddhist revivalist Anagarika Dharmapala, a thriving Buddhist heterodoxy exists in Sri Lanka, defying reformist attempts to rationalize traditional Sinhalese Buddhist practices.

Indeed, one of my childhood memories involves sitting with my mother and two teenage sisters in a small, dimly lit shrine at a Buddhist temple dedicated to Kataragama Deviyo, the guardian deity of Sri Lanka. Our visits to the temple happened around the same time my mother began practicing meditation, soon after we left Virginia. I recall the air was thick with the fragrant scent of burning incense as we participated in a private *pooja* seeking blessings. Adorned with colorful flowers and flickering oil lamps, the shrine, nestled within the grounds of a prominent Buddhist temple, was a place of both reverence and mystery. A bare-chested priest solemnly recited Vedic verses while gently fanning us with peacock feathers, a symbol of the deity's divine power in the syncretic blend of Buddhist and Hindu beliefs.

While the Buddhist modernist versions of Sinhalese Buddhism emphasizes a purist interpretation of the Theravāda tradition shorn of non-Buddhist rituals and popular "superstition," to this day popular Sinhalese practice incorporates a diverse pantheon of deities and spirits—including Kataragama, Pattani, Vishnu, Ganesh, Lakshmi, Shiva, and Kali—who are revered as protectors offering worldly assistance to help devotees navigate themselves through the vicissitudes of samsara. Hence, even as the Buddha remains the central figure in this syncretic tradition, with Maitreya holding a prominent place as the future Buddha, Sinhalese Buddhists often turn to divine intervention of this pantheon of local gods to offer external support, personal empowerment, and inner strength to address life's hardships.

In my mother's case, her turn to Kataragama at this juncture in her life was to buoy us through her rebuilding of a life in Sri Lanka as a widow while raising two teenage daughters and a young child. Later as a graduate student at UC Irvine, when I called my mother, who was living at the time in Sri Lanka, to share my fears about finishing my doctoral degree, she turned to Ganesha, the god of letters and learning, offering a pooja in his honor to favor me in my educational pursuits.

When my mother remarried, my stepfather's personal shrine in his office room at home exemplified the multi-religiosity and religious syncretism of Buddhists in Sri Lanka. Alongside the statue of the Buddha at the center of the shrine, it also featured a statue of Ganesh, an image of Vishnu, a photograph of the South Indian guru Sathya Sai Baba (an image my mother brought back from her pilgrimage to the Sathya Sai Baba ashram where she witnessed his miracles), and even a statue of Saint Jude; the latter two were his own adaptation into the traditional pantheon of Hindu and Indigenous gods, but their significance was no less. On road trips outside of Colombo, my step-father would invariably stop at the Church of St. Jude and have us leave a candle at his shrine.

Over the years, the syncretic practices of Sinhalese Buddhism in my own home waxed and waned, often influenced by periodic waves of Buddhist

reform on the island. Similar to the early twentieth-century reform movement led by figures like Anagarika Dharmapala and Henry Olcott, who prof-
fered Buddhism as a "rational religion" that centered on the individual and
his or her own nirvanic salvation and viewed Christians and non-Sinhalese as
outside aliens, the turn of the twenty-first century in Sri Lanka saw the rise
of charismatic Buddhist nationalist monks who advocated for a "pure" Buddhism. These reformers frequently criticized popular religious syncretism in
the media, contrasting it with the Buddha's original "true" teachings. Their
rhetoric constructed an idealized vision of Sinhalese Buddhism, positioning
it against perceived external threats from the idolatry and superstitions of
religious others, including Hindus, Christians, and Muslims. Likewise, they
posed the popular "idolatry" of Sinhalese Buddhist (such as my own family's)
as internal threats to the tradition. Indeed, for Sinhalese to practice forms of
Buddhism beyond their essentialized rationalized version was construed as a
perversion and therefore a betrayal of one's religion itself.

These life experiences as a transnational diaspora Asian Buddhist have had
an undeniable impact on the critical affinity stance I take toward the study
of contemporary Buddhism. For instance, the irony is not lost on me when,
in my current research on race and whiteness in North American Buddhism,
Buddhist convert practitioners of color describe to me the resistance they
face from white spiritual leadership on engaging issues of identity and race
through a Buddhist framework, particularly claiming that their approach is
one of "watering down the pure dharma teachings." I am particularly struck
by such rebuttals, for I find the rhetorical resistance they encounter similar to
that of Buddhist reformers in Sri Lanka who critique popular forms of devotional Buddhism in favor of the "pure teaching of the Buddha." I am intrigued
by how both reformist formulations of contemporary Sinhalese Buddhism
and the dominant expression of meditation-based convert Buddhism share a
common historical legacy in the project of Buddhist modernism.

Thus, when we in the Western academy of Buddhist studies debate the
merits of using conceptual categories like Buddhist modernism to describe

cultural history shifts and the development of contemporary forms of Buddhism, the intellectual conversation is not one I can honestly enter with critical distance. As a transnational diaspora Buddhist, Buddhist modernism might even be considered my cultural baggage. Yet, a sketch of my own biographical itinerary as a scholar-practitioner of lived Buddhism has also demonstrated, I hope, how a paradigm like Buddhist modernism is relevant to understanding how the project of modernity has shaped the social environment of Sinhalese Buddhism, while it has also highlighted the paradigm's limitations in explaining the lived forms of Buddhism that unfold. Put another way, a concept like Buddhist modernism is dominant but does not determine the diversity of embodied perspectives that contemporary Buddhists inhabit.

In conclusion, this essay has aimed to demonstrate that while the concept of the scholar-practitioner in Buddhist studies offers a profound rethinking of the relationship between academic scholarship and personal practice, it also needs to be expanded. By embracing the lived experiences and critical perspectives of Asian and Asian American scholars, we can further expand the boundaries of what it means to engage with Buddhism both intellectually and personally. My journey as a Sri Lankan American woman, deeply rooted in Sinhalese Buddhist culture and shaped by transnational experiences, exemplifies the unique contributions that scholar-practitioners can make. Through autoethnographic reflections, I have illustrated how my critical affinity toward Buddhism is informed by both my academic pursuits and my embodied life experiences. This dual engagement challenges essentialist notions of Buddhist identity and highlights the complex interplay between heritage, colonial history, and contemporary practice. Ultimately, recognizing the value of scholar-practitioners, especially those who are Asian and Asian American, enriches our understanding of Buddhism and fosters a more inclusive and nuanced approach to its study by incorporating critical perspectives rooted in lived experiences.

7

—

ART FOR CATHARSIS (OR AN UNBORN CHILD)

Transforming Trauma, Pain, and Loss into Healing Rituals

NAOMI KASUMI

From my earliest memories, Buddhism has been a constant presence in my life. I was born in Kyoto, a city renowned as a main center of many Buddhist sects, and I grew up in a typical household with a Buddhist altar in the tatami living room. A monk from Kennin-ji Rinzai Zen temple would visit our home two or three times a year for various ancestral and seasonal events, as well as for family memorial *hōyō* ceremonies. After completing my compulsory education, I attended a private Buddhist girls' high school (京都家政学園) and then proceeded to Bukkyō (佛教大学) University, managed by Chion-in temple, the Jōdo-shu (Pure Land sect) headquarters, and one of many designated National Treasures in Kyoto. We were required to take religion classes for three years. Despite the external markers of a Buddhist background, I never really perceived a strong religious connection to my own upbringing and beliefs. I assumed that most of the people in Kyoto, except for the elderly or those involved in cults, shared a similar outlook. Even now as an adult living in the US and as an artist collaborating with Buddhist temples in Japan, my relationship with Buddhism is still not clear. Since I was a little child, I was spiritual, imaginative, and creative, but I also had little interest in Buddhism and almost no inclination toward religious practice. At the same time, much of my creative work as an artist has somewhat unconsciously taken up Buddhist themes and forms to express and heal from grief, trauma, and loss. In this chapter, I share my artistic practice and creative process and, in so doing, seek to unravel my own connection to Buddhism and spirituality, which I still struggle to clearly identify.

Douglas Eby observes that "creative expression can transform painful reactions and situations, providing strength and understanding to change how we feel and interact with the world. Works of art made by others can remodel our inner realities."[1] Any art, regardless of its medium or content, inherently carries the artist's life experiences. For me, art has always been a powerful medium for expressing the inexpressible and channeling emotions that words alone cannot capture. This chapter delves into my process and journey of art-making as a means of catharsis—transforming trauma, pain, and loss into healing rituals. Drawing from my deeply personal experience of loss, I explore how creating handmade objects and large-scale installations has become integral to my emotional reconstruction process and how Buddhist themes and forms have taken on a much more meaningful role than I had previously thought.

Over two decades ago I began a personal journey and exploration of my innermost self. On this journey, I discovered how the process of making art not only helped me come to terms with feelings of sadness and loss but also served as a catalyst for dialogue. My art explores and addresses the concepts of *presence* and *absence, memory/memorial, loss* and *trauma,* and *testimony* related to my experience of having an abortion in 1998. In this chapter, I explore these intertwined concepts and my gradual shift toward healing in which I spontaneously created hundreds or thousands of handmade objects through ritualistic, meditative, repetitive action that have since evolved into many large-scale art installations. These creations serve as a testament to the power of artistic expression in navigating the tumultuous landscape of grief and loss. The act of openly sharing my experience with others, a courageous endeavor given cultural and societal taboos surrounding discussions of abortion in the US and Japan, became a cathartic and vital aspect of the healing process.[2]

The connection between catharsis and the concept of *art as healer* engages with artistic expression on human well-being through narratives that illustrate how art can be utilized as a therapeutic tool, offering healing and solace to individuals facing physical, emotional, and psychological challenges. In *Why Art Can Offer Us Catharsis and Healing*, Vivian Manning-Schaffel observes that "when you can channel emotion into a piece of work, it draws in others, and they get what you are going through. It brings us back to a feeling of not being alone".[3] She notes that this can often be found in musical form such as in the popular songs of Adele or Taylor Swift. Expressing pain through art is a way of seeking connection and validation while externalizing complicated feelings.

Memorials play important roles for individuals and society. They serve as a means of commemoration and remembrance, ensuring that the significance of a person or event is not forgotten. They provide a space for reflection and mourning, which can offer healing and a sense of closure. Memorials encourage reflection, stimulate dialogue, and strengthen cultural and community identity, fostering a sense of shared memory and unity. Memorials, often in the form of monuments or art pieces, promote healing and catharsis for both artist and viewer. Creating memorial art helps artists process emotions and grief, while the finished pieces offer solace and reflection for others. The relationship between memorials and art is profound, with expressive art pieces emphasizing a person's absence through the presence of a physical monument.

A Personal Journey

Since my life-changing abortion in 1998, I have been making handmade objects spontaneously and obsessively, engaging in a timeless ritual that reflects my personal struggle to come to terms with intense feelings of grief, sadness, loss, anguish, confusion, and depression. These objects also represent a therapeutic and redemptive process to atone for what Japanese culture believes to be a transgression against the sacredness of life.

Over the past twenty-five years, these rituals have gradually resulted in a restorative, emotional, and creative shift in me, both as a person and as an artist. What I have found is that my artistic practice has a particular resonance with Buddhist memorial rituals for unborn children, which has deepened my indebtedness to Japanese Buddhist traditions that I grew up with, but with which I never consciously engaged. I have, since beginning to create these handmade objects, even returned to collaborate with Japanese Buddhist temples to show my work on healing. What this experience has revealed is that even though an abortion may be considered a transgression against the sacredness of life, Japanese Buddhism has also provided profound culturally relevant rituals to support my healing. Sharing the truth of my experience with others also serves as my catharsis, and it becomes a significant part of the healing process. I know I am not alone in dealing with this experience. Through interactive storytelling, my memorial pieces invite people to identify their own memories of loss and secrecy. And in a series of memorial projects entitled "MEM: memory/memorial," I attempt to articulate my story in a rich and honest public forum.

I was twenty-seven years old, living in New York as a newly-transferred international art student at State University of New York (SUNY) from Oregon when I discovered my unexpected pregnancy. I experienced an initial stage of complete shock and an emotional roller-coaster along with persistent, uncontrollable tears and a sense of numbness. High anxiety led to a loss of appetite and dramatic weight loss. I also suffered from insomnia triggered by overwhelming shame, guilt, and overthinking. I struggled with the psychological and physical changes associated with the responsibility of becoming a "mother," something I had never experienced or even considered before. Watching TV commercials involving kids made me cry out loud. I felt a constant nausea and ache deep inside my throat and in the pit of my stomach as if I were being squeezed by sharp nails every day. An unmarried student-pregnancy is a huge taboo in Japanese society, especially in my family, so I couldn't tell my parents, and I kept the pregnancy and my suffering a secret.

During the initial two months of anxiety, however, I also started hearing something I never expected. A voice. From inside me. I started communicating with the origin of the voice—the fetus. He said "Mom . . . mom, don't, I want you to live. You must live no matter what . . ." I continued to hear his voice and we conversed every day. Sometimes his voice magically echoed in my dreams. I couldn't see him. He spoke to me in the darkness, "Mom, I am okay. I accept your decision as my fate." My heart was squeezed with guilt and sorrow. I could not stop my tears.

In Japan, it is a bad omen, but I named the voice, the unborn child, Shion [SHE-on], inspirationally after a purple wildflower, a type of aster, that is called Shion (紫苑) in Japan. I still believe his spirit resides on the moon, watching over me from a higher place. Every full moon night, I have a conversation with Shion to keep him up to date on my life. I feel a profound spiritual connection with this invisible being. Many years after my abortion, I spontaneously wondered about the meaning of my unborn child's name. Shion (紫苑) holds significant symbolism in Japanese floriography (the language of flowers: 花言葉), encompassing expressions such as "I will not forget you" (君を忘れない), "thinking of someone far away" (遠くにいる人を想う), and "reminiscence" (追憶) and revives memories of "a lost loved one or a distant lover." These symbolic meanings trace their origins to narratives found within the *Konjaku Monogatarishū* (今昔物語集).

After over two months of emotional struggle and turmoil, including repeated thoughts of suicide and nearly one-sided discussions with the father, as well as considering all possible factors—social, financial, psychological, and relational (family)—I chose to have an abortion. As a dependent international student without the legal ability to work and support both myself and the baby, I felt this was the most responsible course of action. After the spring semester ended in May, I flew back to Oregon to talk to the father of the child and made an appointment to visit the clinic. A nurse spoke to me on the phone, and she gave me a name that I had to use on the procedure day. An old Irish name—"Cornie."

On that day, I stood in front of the large heavy doors of the clinic, rang the interphone, and said "Hi, I am Cornie." Inside the clinic, I was given several pages of paperwork that I had to read and sign. A nurse said, "Take your time." It wasn't enough time, but I had already taken three months of contemplation to arrive at my decision. But I was surrounded by guilt and hesitation. Ten minutes before my surgery appointment schedule I finally signed off and said to my unborn child, "*Gomen ne*, (I am sorry) . . . I am sorry, Shion."

I anticipated I would go through emotional grief and sadness; however, I didn't count on the severe trauma, persistent dark feelings, guilt, and intense pain that followed. These feelings were compounded by my best friend's affair with the father, which led to a prolonged and terrible breakup. According to counseling professor Debra Mollen, "It's important for people to know that abortion does not cause mental health problems. . . . What's harmful are the stigma surrounding abortion, the lack of knowledge about it, and the lack of access to mental and emotional support."[4] I struggled with all of these factors, but naming the aborted fetus Shion and engaging in his personification or "play" allowed me to maintain an imaginative, intimate, and silent conversation with the spirit of the unborn child that was crucial for my mental stability during the pregnancy. While I believed I was communicating with Shion, others perceived it as delusional mumbling. However, when this form of communication ceased post-procedure, my resulting depression was compounded by an intense grief that became significantly more severe. When I ended my pregnancy in Oregon, thousands of miles away from home, I couldn't find a culture willing to acknowledge my loss. Moreover, I was unable to share this experience with my friends or family in Japan. I kept my pregnancy and termination a secret from my parents for ten years.

Reflecting back, I see that I was falling into a "period of being trapped in an abyss." My mind was overwhelmed with vivid memories of the process of termination at the clinic, physical fatigue, feelings of guilt and loss, and the aftermath of continuous betrayal and emotional abuse by my boyfriend.

I went to school every day, never missing a class, even though my home-work remained unfinished. My personal diary from the time reads, "Driving to school, my body sat in the classroom, eyes fixed on the backs of my boy-friend and my best friend together, sitting a few rows ahead . . ."[5] My mind was absent, lost somewhere I couldn't identify. Smiling felt impossible; my facial muscles were frozen in a stiff mask. Sleepless nights plagued me or they were filled with haunting nightmares. Numbness consumed me, leaving me feeling nothing.

I began to engage in repetitive behaviors, such as compulsively chew-ing all my fingernails and repeatedly typing the same lines of a poem on an antique typewriter. Almost unconsciously, I would continue these actions over and over on countless pages of paper.

Poem:

he stopped writing me letters,
he stopped calling on the phone,
instead, he started lying,
he started meeting her when I was alone
he started sleeping with her,
she sent me flowers with a note:
she said "This is for your unborn child"

Over time, this behavior evolved into an obsession, a ritualistic act to main-tain my sanity. Upon regaining awareness, I would find my room buried under a mess of crumpled paper balls. I then spontaneously uncrumpled and flat-tened the paper balls, organizing them into small bundles tied with hemp rope to restore some semblance of order. Although these bundles still clut-tered my floor, they seemed somewhat more organized. I repeated this pro-cess of typing, making a mess in the room, organizing, and bundling several times until I eventually exhausted my supply of paper. This obsessive ritual continued for two years and culminated in the creation of an artwork that I entitled *hidden voice* (2001). I had arrived at a point where the act of repetitive production of handmade objects became an artistic process of cleansing and healing that has continued and transformed up to this day.

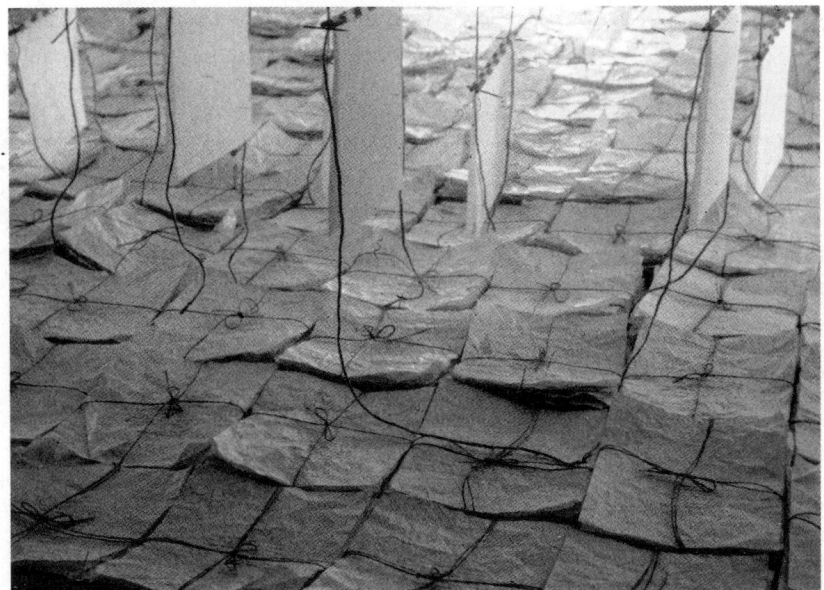

Figure 1: hidden voice, 2001, detail of the installation. Photo: courtesy of artist (Naomi Kasumi).

Art as a Healing Ritual

In *Alchemy of Art*, Eby notes that "deep hurts" can also fuel creative projects.[6] Roxanne Chinook, a tribal member of the Confederated Tribes of the Warm Springs Indian Reservation in Oregon, shares that "My art emulates a personal and cultural experience, from the spirit of the trickster to healing from the traumas of my past. The process of creating strengthens and restores my spirit, and has rendered me a relationship with the sacred."[7] My own response to finding myself in the depths of an emotional abyss was to spontaneously and obsessively make handmade objects without any specific purpose or artistic goal. This creative ritual was a timeless loop that seemed like it could continue endlessly. Eventually, I began consciously creating these multiple repetitive objects that became sources of my public artwork. These objects reflect my personal struggle to come to terms with multiple feelings of grief, anger, sadness, loss, confusion, and depression. They also embody a therapeutic and redemptive journey to atone for what Japanese culture views as a karmic transgression. Over the past twenty-five years, these rituals have gradually resulted in a restorative, emotional, and creative shift in me, both as a person and as an artist.

The Third Voice

In 1999, I created my first monumental work, entitled *The Third Voice*, as my BFA terminal project. This piece marked the inception of what I have coined *traumatic–expression art* and served as the first public exposure of my personal experience. Throughout the year after my abortion, I designed a chamber/installation space that encapsulated the day of the event. The design aimed to immerse guest audiences/viewers in my experience as they navigated through the temporary monument. Structured as an artist's book, the installation embraced a factual "story-telling" concept, guiding viewers through the space from right to left, counterclockwise, akin to reading a Japanese book, to evoke a sense of loss and pain. However, I faced challenges in openly sharing my experience in cultural contexts in the US. While my work did not directly engage in the pro-life/pro-choice debate, it unintentionally became politically charged due to the factual nature of my abortion documentation. The political reactions of American viewers to my artwork— particularly to the word *abortion*—were markedly different from those in my native culture, where the topic remains taboo but does not typically provoke such overt political responses. This whole experience surprised me.

hidden voice

I then began working on another conceptual artist's book entitled *hidden voice*, which extended the theme of *The Third Voice* but concentrated on purging the darkness of my mind. The components of the initial *hidden voice* installation were crafted over two years as I obsessively and ritualistically typed out pages on a manual typewriter. This work, on the other hand, was constructed like a small cave with floating book pages and evoked a cold, sad, and painful atmosphere (Figure 1). This installation featured a single obsessively typed poem on wrinkled, bundled paper and hundreds of intricately braided long hemp ropes that suspended the fragile floating "piano-hinge" binding pages of the "book" in the air from the ceiling. Despite the seemingly dark and chaotic context, I meticulously organized the elements of the *hidden voice* installation, which reflects how my obsessive ritual creation helped heal my fragmented mind. In creating this, I explored the tension between order and disorder to reflect past emotional abuses and feelings of emotional coldness, numbness, madness while obsessively typing the same text forever, the sadness of loss, and healing. This process allowed me to delve into the meaning of human relationships, my abusive family history, and Japanese culture and society to reveal a unique beauty in the contrast between emotional chaos and the meticulous organization of the work. Through my art, I found that I could share my concealed emotions and personal experiences in public, using book art and installation practices as catharsis, and a way to heal my own pain and loss while acknowledging the suffering of others.

Cultural Context and Comparison

Unlike the politically charged post-abortion experience many women have in the US, Japanese culture and the Japanese Buddhist practice in particular reflect concern for both the terminated spirit of the fetus and compassion for the woman/mother who, due to difficult circumstances, has had to resort to an abortion.[8] Japanese culture and a majority of Japanese people accept the existence of the aborted spirit, known as *mizuko* (fetus), as a continuing form of life, which I learned is quite a mystery for most Westerners and other religious practitioners. In the US, there is little to no public acknowledgment of miscarriage and abortion. Reflecting on her own experience of a miscarriage and the absence of mourning rituals for pregnancy loss and termination in the US, Peggy Orenstein observes, "Without form, there is no content."[9] Westerners often do not consider a fetus without a tangible form in their hands as a form of life. Hence, Western women have no ritual for cleansing the grief that clings to these silent sorrows. Even in this time of relentless confession, women seldom speak of their loss aloud. Orenstein further remarks: "I had never previously considered that there is no word in English for a miscarried or aborted fetus."[10]

In Japan, culturally it is called mizuko (水子), which translates as "water child," "child of the water (womb)," or "unseen child" (見ず子). Historically, Japanese Buddhists believed that existence flowed into a being slowly, like liquid. Children began to take shape as humans gradually over time. They were not considered to be fully in our world until they were seven years old. The mizuko is perceived to float somewhere along the continuum in a liminal space between life and death but belonging to neither.[11] Because of its belief in transmigration and rebirth, Buddhism does not view abortion or miscarriage as the end of life for the mizuko. Rather it is expected that the bodhisattva Jizo would help the mizuko eventually "return" to the world or find another pathway into being at a later time.

Jizo (地蔵, "womb of the earth") Bosatsu is revered as a guardian deity of children within Japanese villages and communities who also protects the spirits of children who have passed away. In the late 1970s, when abortion rates reached their peak in Japan, it became common to see rows of multiple Mizuko Jizo statues resembling both a child and the guardian deity at religious sites established for the ritual of apology and remembrance known as *Mizuko kuyo*.[12] Prior to my abortion, I had preconceived notions of Mizuko kuyo as a taboo stemming from 1970s Japanese TV shows and from my grandmother's cautionary tales before I immigrated to the US. However, after producing *hidden voice*, I realized that my creations, which I interpreted as a formal ritual, would be viewed as a Mizuko kuyo ritual that Japanese women have traditionally practiced.

Mizuko kuyo rituals originally began as informal rites for the mizuko spirits that were developed and carried out by women without priests. These rituals serve as a poignant and profound cultural practice aimed at reconciling grief and loss, and they embody a deeply personal expression that continues to provide a communal and personal space for healing and remembrance.

MEM: Memory/Memorial Project

My project started as a story-telling approach with *The Third Voice* and *hidden voice* as forms of traumatic–expression art, but a few years after I produced those two large installation pieces, I traveled to Japan to research the cultural and religious contexts for the Mizuko kuyo ritual and abortion in Japan. I now consciously incorporate the meaning and significance of the religious and cultural context into my annual memorial rituals and creative practice. This transition from spontaneous art-making to a deliberate series of memorial art practices has continued to shape the body of work that I have since pursued.

This lifelong project consists of annual memorials structured around my own temporary monuments that reflect the Buddhist notion of impermanence. For each memorial, I privately make numerous objects that I place in either the natural or given environment. These objects began as instances of traumatic-expression art that capture my raw feelings, confusion, and expressions of pain embodied in *The Third Voice* and *hidden voice*. After creating these emotional and dark-themed installation pieces as a form of purging, I began to address and integrate the concept of annual memorial "offerings" as a ritual for apology and remembrance, similar to Mizuko kuyo rituals. This body of work, collectively titled *MEM: memory/memorial*, comprises twenty-six individual pieces or installations that build on the project's main concept. With each successive commemorative piece, my personal need for apology and remembrance is performed as I engage in the therapeutic and redemptive process of repetitively making numerous handmade objects. The ritual seems timeless and endless. My initial actions were simply obsessive and haunted by the idea that I did not have enough pieces to reflect my apology. However, over the past twenty-five years, these rituals have led to a restorative, emotional, and creative transformation in me, both as a person and as an artist.

My Creative Philosophy

My creative journey centers on the search for a moment of stillness, a point where time and space merge. Through the creative process of ritualistic repetition, I unconsciously open a gateway to my inner self. This "point" connects me to another reality (dimension) where a dialogue between art objects and nature, or art objects and humans, becomes possible. However, this process unfolds in absolute silence. My work involves creating an artistic space where viewers feel "safe" and spiritually connected to elements of nature—air, wind, fire, earth, water—and even the universe. I collect materials from the local environments I inhabit, using indigenous or everyday organic materials to craft what I call a sacred space and an ancient home for my spirit. I aim to visualize an imaginative world by exploring materials as metaphors and vehicles for transforming spoken or written language into a spiritual language. This process involves channeling my five senses and human-centered (self-centered) emotional interpretation of small incidents in nature, producing a large quantity of handmade symbolic objects to express my inner voice.

Art-Making and Ceremonial Installation as Ritual

I achieve my own sacred space through my personal ritualistic process of art-making and creating a ceremonial installation. For example, the space might become an imaginative landscape of a riverbank with empty eggshells, an estuary adorned with pinwheels, a circular portal featuring hundreds of palms arranged like lotus petals. The space may become a cosmic river (like the Milky Way), with the 大悲心陀羅尼, the Great Compassion Dharani, applied to the flow of teaching that expresses the profound unity of life within the vast cosmos as is advocated by Zen Buddhism.

My work consistently embodies both macro and micro perspectives: large-scale installations with meticulously detailed elements that invite viewers to engage more closely with them. Furthermore, I create my repetitive objects in specific numbers; I choose each for its symbolic meaning. I often select the numbers 108 and 365 for my personal rituals. These numbers are deeply rooted in Buddhist cosmology and prayer practices. The number 108 has been considered sacred in the Indian subcontinent for a long time. For example, a traditional rosary or set of mantra beads in India consists of 108 beads. Similarly, in Japan, 108 is regarded as a sacred number representing 煩悩, worldly desires, or accumulated sins within an individual body. On New Year's Eve, Buddhist temples in Japan toll their bells to cleanse individuals of life's impurities and sins before the new year begins. This ritual starts at 11:30 p.m. and continues until the bell has been rung 108 times.

These projects start as intimate, private, manufactured artworks that initially find their form in the studio and are then installed as ephemeral artwork, sometimes within my house, or discreetly within nature in a quiet public space without the viewers' perspective in mind. After I have privately initiated the work, I can then consider it for public exhibition; at this point, I scale up the overall volume of the work to suit the specific exhibition venue. Some of these monuments, however, remain as my personal ritual and are not shown in art galleries or publicly.

The installation work, created through ceremonial processes, has a life of its own and morphs its form to suit the environment and its purpose. The act of creating a space or artwork to fit in a specific environment is often ephemeral and only on occasion is it semipermanent. It is mesmerizing to see the works take on a life of their own and invite viewers into dialogue. It is impossible to have a true experience without being actually present in the space, activating all your senses.

Samples of MEM

In this section, I share those pieces from the series that are particularly connected to Japanese Buddhism as well as the authentic characteristics of Japanese culture that seep out of my body and body of work. I introduce a very limited selection of these MEM projects accompanied by a brief description and an image to reveal the ways that Buddhism has shaped and given me a form in which to express and transform my suffering.

MEM: no. 5 limbo

My sixth memorial piece called *MEM: memory/memorial no. 5 limbo* was held on May 23, 2005. In this memorial ritual, I created a monument of 108 empty eggshells with red bibs to resemble the Jizo statues that I saw roadside or at temples in Japan.

In Japan, my MEM creation would be considered a Jizo ritual, which was originally developed and practiced by women.[13] I got the title, *limbo*, from

Figure 2: MEM: no. 5 limbo (2005), Details of Memorial ritual installation, Seattle, WA. Photo: courtesy of artist (Naomi Kasumi).

many interesting sources and ideas in Asian and Western culture as well as from Dante's descriptions of limbo in *Inferno*, which is a holding place for the spirits of dead/souls of children who are destined for neither heaven nor hell. However, the most definitive influence on my naming and space design for this project was from an old tale in Japan. I remember my grandmother telling me a sad story before bed several times. It was a tale of Sai-no-Kawara (the riverbank of Sai), which was a place existing between this world and another, a place of oblivion. At the riverbank, unborn babies are playing and creating a *stupa* with river stones, dedicating merit for their older siblings and parents, waiting for their mother and father to pick them up. But, the parents never come. . . . The fact that I remembered my grandmother's bedtime story was odd enough, but I also began to wonder if my grandmother had her own mizuko.

For this installation project, I created a space, my imaginative riverbank of Sai, with empty eggs that could have been the origins of life. The field of 5,140 white, empty, eggshells created a sense of purity, sensitivity, and the fragility of life, as well as an overwhelming visual sensation; it also suggested the quietness of the emotional aftermath of a traumatic event, and the process of making this body of work. This project became an extremely meaningful and important project to me.

It took me over eighteen months to finish blowing the contents out of the eggs—a timeless ritual in itself. This process was vital for my healing. While

Figure 3: MEM: no. 5 limbo (2005), details of solo exhibition at International Gallery of Contemporary Arts, Anchorage, Alaska. Photo: courtesy of artist (Naomi Kasumi).

using a simple tool to empty each egg, I heard painful squeaking sounds, reminiscent of the last cries of a tiny life, many times over. The process also reminded me of the mechanical actions of the doctor who performed the abortion. Among the five thousand eggs I presented, a few wore the red bibs inspired by Japanese Jizo statues, symbolizing the mizuko of other women. As a contrast to this repetitive robotic action, the red, tiny, crocheted bibs evoke a mother's dreams for her unborn child. In my case, this process came after ending my pregnancy, emphasizing both the grief of loss and my need for apology.

MEM: *no. 7 scriptorium*

This was my eighth installation—a book-art memorial piece, crafted from numerous used tea bags that I had collected, dried, dyed, and cast in wax. While creating this work, I sought to install it in a nontraditional indoor space in Japan, thus marking a departure from the art gallery context. I approached a Japanese Buddhist temple to explore their interest in hosting such an exhibition in the summer of 2007. The concept of "installation art" in a Buddhist temple was too untraditional for the Japanese head monk to immediately grasp, but after several phone conversations, I secured a space for the world premiere "experimental" exhibition of *MEM: memory/memorial no. 7 scriptorium* at a famous Buddhist temple in Nagano, Japan. With it, I intentionally created a sacred space where visitors could calm their spirits and engage in silent reflection amid the hanging tapestries I had constructed. Five tapestry-like books were installed in the main hall of Kogen-in Temple in Iiyama, Nagano. This temple, originally built in 1295 and converted to the Sōtō Zen sect over 620 years ago, is designated as a National Important Cultural Property in Japan, which marks the temple's recognition of the significance of healing from trauma, grief, and loss.

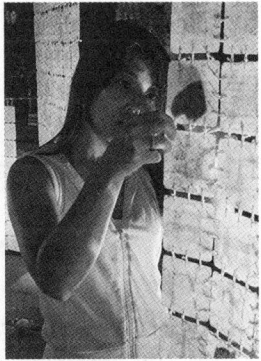

Figure 4: MEM: no. 7 scriptorium (2007), solo exhibition at Kogen-in Temple in Iiyama, Nagano, Japan. Photo: courtesy of artist (Naomi Kasumi).

As an installation artist, I found this project was both exhilarating and challenging. This marked the first time I installed my artwork in a non-gallery indoor space. I had some constraints I had not faced before: I was prohibited from using nails and had no lighting tracks or any support structures that are typically found in gallery spaces. Even though it was intended as a meditative and highly experimental project, I found the main hall space proved to be perfectly suited for the installation. It was meant to be.

In January 2008, *Scriptorium* debuted in Osaka, Japan. With this book-art installation I sought to create an immersive, sensory experience, encouraging viewers to see, read, touch, smell, feel, think, interact, and share. While conceptualizing the eighth memorial piece, I reflected on the fact that my unborn child would have been nine years old, which inspired me to create a bedtime story reminiscent of those my grandmother read to me. The installation consists of nine books, each containing 108 encaustic cards. These cards feature Japanese sutra calligraphy, digital and Xerox images, personal writings, and natural elements such as maple leaves and butterfly wings. The books are colored using natural tea dye (derived from tea bags collected over two years of my evening tea rituals) and beeswax, as well as contributions from friends, colleagues, and students. This organic dyeing process, beyond my control, symbolizes my practice of letting go and flowing with nature, making each page visually unique.

Creating Dialogue

Japan is a country where over 52 percent of people consider themselves non-religious,[14] yet religion, spirituality, and everyday life are intertwined and harmoniously embedded into cultural customs. These mixed socioreligious customs are often transmitted within families, especially by grandparents, as part of family tradition and respect. My spirituality is greatly influenced by this socioreligious cultural custom combined with my uniquely artistic imagination.

My work is deeply influenced by my native Japanese culture and history. Now, however, I navigate and blend Japanese and American cultures. I spent the first twenty-five years of my life in Japan, and my current life and art reflect my native beliefs and culture in dialogue with having lived, studied, taught, designed, and created art in the United States for almost thirty years. This experience has uniquely shaped my approach to creating art and these artistic memorial rituals have led to a restorative, emotional, and creative transformation in me, as a person and in how I live as an Asian, an Asian American woman, and as an artist.

Conclusion

The body of work I share here represents my growth as an artist from the beginning, when I began making art to process the experience of having had an abortion and dealing with the resulting trauma, grief, and depression. The work portrays my life, experiences, and memories combined with latent cultural influences and beliefs. At the same time, it reflects cathartic release and my healing process. At the beginning of my artistic career over twenty-five years ago, I avoided involving others in my creative process because my work was deeply personal and addressed my secrets and emotional issues. I was unable to discuss my work and did not want to be questioned about my experiences or ongoing projects. As an extremely private person, I felt that my creative process needed to remain confidential. I referred to this process as *nurturing*.

From another perspective, the repetitive rituals of my artwork can be likened to the Buddhist practice of 作務: *samu,* or daily tasks, which refers to the physical labor performed as part of monastic training. This includes activities such as cleaning, cooking, and other communal duties, all carried out with wholehearted dedication. Looking back on my artwork, I have come to see that although I have never considered or referred to myself as a Buddhist outright, it has become abundantly clear that the form of my work is indelibly shaped by Buddhist rituals and practice. Without the form of Buddhism, there would perhaps be no content or no context in which to share my experiences. Revealing my secrets through public installation art was uncomfortable to begin with; however, sharing my emotions and realizing I was not alone has alleviated so much of my internal pain. Furthermore, as an artist, exposing this aspect of my life publicly has fostered dialogue with so many community members; although I work alone and often in secret, the public nature of my work transcends beyond myself. In addition, I often refer to the exhibition of my work as a "funeral," where Buddhist monks perform rituals to celebrate the person's life in a public setting.

Repeating this process—which sometimes requires over a year of production, ritual ceremonies, and public installation art exhibitions—is akin to repetitively stitching and suturing a wound. I never know when the stitching will end or when the wound will be completely closed and healed. It may take forever. This creative project represents just a few pages of my never-ending story, resembling samsara, the eternal cycle of transmigration or reincarnation. I will continue my ritualistic creation until the end of my life, and I am content with this journey.

8

—

TALK-STORY FROM THE TRENCHES

Asian American Buddhist Feminists in Academia

TÂM THÂM TỊNH AND THANDA AUNG

This conversation explores our respective relationships to Buddhism and more. Both of us are immigrants from Southeast Asia. We met as undergraduates in Claremont, California, and our friendship evolved as we completed different PhDs at UCLA. In addition to our regional and family histories, our consciousnesses have been shaped by Southern California, our education, and our employment at public universities for more than three decades. For the bulk of our teaching careers, we have worked and taught in interdisciplinary departments focusing on Asian American studies and gender and sexuality studies.

Over the past year, we had multiple in-person and Zoom conversations and edited this sample to share. Together we trace our roots and routes: the ways in which we were introduced to Buddhism through our ancestors and cultures and our current relationships to religion. We discuss how Buddhism affects our praxis and orientation toward academia, suffering, inherited or intergenerational trauma, resistance, and interbeing.

Because our conversation delves into abuse and trauma, we use pseudonyms to respect the privacy and reputation of our elders and family members.

Roots: Family Backgrounds

Tâm Thâm Tịnh: *I am a 1.5-generation queer Vietnamese American sociologist, who is a follower of Thích Nhất Hạnh's teachings on Engaged Buddhism. As a practitioner of what I consider pragmatic Buddhism, and not the esoteric nor the superstitious Buddhism, I loosely identify as a Buddhist because I "loosely practice mindful interbeing." I am an uninvited guest and settler in the lands of the Tataviam, Chumash, and Tongva.*

Thanda Aung: *I am a Sino-Burmese immigrant feminist professor who is also an uninvited guest and settler, and a naturalized Asian American citizen of the United States. I currently live and work on the unceded lands of the Cahuilla, Tongva, Luiseño, and Serrano peoples. My training is in comparative cultural studies and literature. I call my family "doubly diasporic" because of our ancestral ties to China and historical ties to Myanmar, which was called Burma until 1989.[1] I appreciate your "loose" identification and the centrality of "mindful interbeing" as part of your Buddhist practice since it mirrors my own religious ambivalence and my investment in interdependence, reducing harm, and advancing social justice—which I mostly learned from Women of Color teachers and feminist theorists/visionaries.*

In the history of Myanmar/Burma, Theravāda Buddhism has been tied to *Burmanization*, a form of ethnic hegemony that dates back to anticolonial struggles against the British.[2] Buddhism has functioned as the de facto national religion through which the Burman/Bamar majority "institutionalized discrimination against other religious groups" and ethnic minorities.[3] In the twenty-first century, Myanmar Buddhism is tied to ethnonationalistic "paranoia"[4] and Islamophobic "terror"[5] in ways that differ radically from stereotypes of the pacifist Buddhist or serene Oriental monk ubiquitous in US popular culture.[6] Yet because of Burma's history as a transnational trading port, British colonialism, and American missionization, there are also significant Islamic, Hindu, Christian, Indo-Aryan, South Asian, Chinese, and European influences, and Indigenous, diasporic, and multiethnic communities who reside there with long, multi-generational histories.

Tâm Thâm Tịnh: *My family emigrated from Việt Nam and went first to France before immigrating to the US. Similar to your Sino background, we are part Cantonese from both sides. Because of patriarchy, my paternal Cantonese grandmother was not sent to Chinese school and did not know how to read and write in Chinese, unlike her brother who identified as Chinese from Việt Nam. My family identifies as Vietnamese with Chinese background. My father and paternal grandmother are Buddhist: My grandmother is an active practitioner and my father is religious in name only. My mother is Catholic, and her mother was Buddhist and occasionally served as a medium for local village spirits (thần). I was taught that all religions teach us to be a good/humane person (Đạo làm người), so that's all we needed to be.*

Growing up, I was exposed to yummy vegetarian food in Buddhist cere-monies and fatalistic and superstitious Buddhism. The latter was not appealing to me, especially in its justification of restrictive gender roles. I didn't care for the judgmental monotheism of my mother's Catholicism either and oscillated between agnosticism and atheism.

Although my immediate family and I were lucky to not have to escape by boat or via the jungle, we adapted to the US with a refugee/war mentality. Some of my half-uncles and aunt did escape by boat. My younger siblings have little memory of the war, so they didn't develop this refugee mental-ity; whereas, I, for a long time, felt the need to be prepared to escape any situation. This alertness to fight or flee also came from growing up in a violent family and neighborhood where we had to fight off local kids who constantly harassed us. It was not until near the end of graduate school that I realized my unconscious behaviors when entering a room: looking for an exit and sizing people up to see if I could take them, should I have to fight them. One humorous example of my refugee impulse was when I was a teaching assistant for a professor who weight-lifts at the muscle beach in Venice (California). His bicep was bigger than my face, and yet, I was illogically assessing how I could fight him.

Thanda Aung: *That readiness to fight or flee reminds me of what author Thi Bui calls the "Refugee Reflex."*[7] *I don't have memories of Burma from my infancy, but I've witnessed versions of this response to traumatic upheaval and the push factors of (forced) migration in my own family. In her graphic memoir* The Best We Could Do, *Bui names this hypervigilant orientation as part of her cultural legacy: "This—not any particular piece of Vietnamese culture — is my inheritance, the inexplicable need and extraordinary ability to run when the shit hits the fan."*[8]

Both sets of my grandparents left China in the early twentieth century and settled in British Burma. My mother grew up in Rangoon, the colonial capital, and my father in Pathein/Bassein, the port capital of the western Ayeyarwady region. My mother was educated in a British Catholic high school run by Irish nuns, while my father attended local Burmese and Chinese schools until the pre-medical program enabled his move to Rangoon. My parents and I, and most of our extended family, migrated to the United States after postcolonial xenophobia made being Chinese (*tayoke* in Burmese) a danger and liability. Thanks to the US Immigration and Nationality Act of 1965, I grew up on Tovaangar, amid citrus groves at the suburban base of Yoát/Joat ("snowy mountain" in Tongva), where Asian Americans were few compared to white Euro-Americans, Chicanos, and Latinos.[9]

When asked "What are you?" I struggled to describe my place of birth: a relatively isolated Southeast Asian nation that recognizes more than one hundred and thirty "ethnic nationalities" (*taingyintha*) and eight "major national ethnic races," while also enforcing tiered racialized citizenship— effectively denying political rights and equal social status to people of Chinese, Indian, Tamil, or Muslim ancestry, regardless of their place of birth.[10] Although immigrants from Burma/Myanmar were relatively few in the 1970s, my family could still access diasporic communities who spoke either the same languages (Burmese, English) or similar Chinese dialects (Toisanese/Taishanese or Cantonese) at restaurants, homes, Buddhist home-temples, and Christian churches.

My father's two sisters illustrate the interreligious intimacies and spiritual diversity within the Myanmar and Chinese diasporas: Each followed a different religious path in the US. First Aunt and her children became devout evangelical Christians after their migration from Burma and resettlement in the United States were assisted by an international Christian network and Chinese American churches that offered free child care. Second Aunt married into a Sino-Burmese family with many Mahāyāna Buddhist practitioners who are vegetarian. For the past two decades, she has been a dedicated member of the Tzu-Chi (Compassionate Relief) Foundation where she regularly volunteers. Founded by the female Dharma Master Cheng Yen in Taiwan in 1966, Tzu-Chi is now an international charity organization that practices engaged Buddhism, philanthropy, and crisis relief; it has various centers and clinics in southern California and throughout the world.[11]

At the Catholic elementary school I attended, Irish American clergy-teachers convinced my immigrant parents to baptize me and my sisters, so we could "fit in better" with our peers. I attended Catholic Mass every morning before school. Like other Californian students, I studied the Spanish missions in fourth grade and labored (unsuccessfully) to make adobe bricks from local mud as one of my homework assignments. My most notable achievement at age ten was winning a cash prize from the Daughters of the American Revolution for writing a poem celebrating my religious conversion. It was my first American lesson about how assimilation and Christianity are braided together with racial capitalism.

Because my parents' colonial education made them fluent in English and my father was able to work as a surgeon in the US, my upbringing was fairly privileged. I was obsessed with dictionaries and the two sets of encyclopedias in our home. I also learned Latin in junior high from the school principal, who was also a former CIA agent. My Christian and Latin literacy served me well in terms of intellectual capital, social mobility, and later academic pursuits.

Could you share more about your educational journey and your path?

Tâm Thâm Tịnh: *My parents are not educated folks. We lived in a housing project with other poor Mexican immigrant families. This poor upbringing informed my take on my professorship as a job rather than a career. There was no real elite family reputation to protect or regain.*

I came to my first sense of agency in college when I was first introduced to Asian American studies. That was when I adopted a Vietnamese American woman identity in lieu of a Vietnamese immigrant girl. I came out in graduate school and claimed another identity as a queer person.

Learning about the social construction of inequality was liberating for me when I was surrounded by explanations of karma (*nghiệp*). When I learned about the social construction of inequality, I happily tossed out karma as an explanation for patriarchal gender roles. I was a young, anticolonial, neo-Marxist who thought religion was the opiate of the masses, especially with a White Jesus.

Having a liberatory education empowered me to create my own future, and I wanted to share my knowledge with others, my students. I had little attachment to my identity as a career scholar. My choice of education as a path out of poverty and violence was a practical matter.

Shortly after I started my university teaching job, I started experiencing PTSD. Luckily, I discovered mindfulness breathing, sitting, and walking to calm my emotions so that I can continue to function.

Reflecting on my pursuit of higher education, I was seeking "truth" and thought gaining knowledge via obtaining a PhD was the way. But I have now realized in my struggle with PTSD that what I was seeking was "wisdom," and not just knowledge. Because of Plum Village's mindfulness practices, I have been able to manage my PTSD and depression better.

Thanda Aung: *Your description of learning about social construction, inequality, patriarchy, and power resonates really strongly with my own consciousness-raising through women's studies, queer studies, and ethnic studies—which is not surprising, considering we went to the same institutions at the same time! I didn't pursue higher education out of practicality; my parents expected me to be a medical doctor or scientist for the sake of* *economic security and mobility. After discovering activism and intersectionality, I thought teaching might be a better path for me to be of service and to assist others and perhaps work toward transformative justice. So I opted out of medical school to pursue an interdisciplinary doctorate in the humanities.*

Could you talk more about how Buddhism helped you cope with PTSD?

Tâm Thâm Tịnh: *Shortly after 9/11 and the US beginning its endless wars against terrorists, I had flashbacks of the war in Việt Nam. I couldn't stop crying when reading news about the war in Iraq. Loud noises like firecrackers, firework shooting, and Taiko drumming would scare me into needing to go and hide. Depression beset me a few times when family circumstances set off a more familial PTSD. This situation was also made worse by memories of neighborhood and domestic violence. Weekly therapy sessions to deal with childhood repressed feelings and war memories were not sufficient. I couldn't talk about current events in class because I couldn't recompose myself when discussing the news with my students. I became angrier at reports of the ongoing slaughter. Soon, my anger consumed me, and I became toxic and lost a good friendship.*

When I was struggling with PTSD, I instinctually sought out a spirituality: attending a Tibetan Buddhist meeting, a Hindu gathering, and a Quaker meeting. A friend suggested that we attend a People of Color Retreat at Deer Park Monastery in 2005. At that time, I had only heard of Zen Master Thích Nhất Hạnh's poem about a rose in my pocket and a gatha about dishwashing.[12]

Thích Nhất Hạnh's engaged Buddhism helped me learn different ways to take care of my PTSD. At that first retreat, I learned two powerful mantras: "No mud, no lotus" and "Pain is inevitable, but suffering is optional." I had a hard time accepting the first Noble Truth and suffered from the equity/equality complex—with my internal record playing, "but it shouldn't be that way." At the time, I pondered how we could have a Buddhist version of liberation theology so that it does not become so individualistically centered in the quest for peace. Back then, I thought we needed mass mobilization with Buddhists to bring forth equity in the world.

At Deer Park, I finally understood what monastics had said about needing to practice peace within oneself first. At one Dharma talk on "beginning anew," a monk shared his childhood traumas and how practicing breathing and walking meditation helped him to calm his emotions and not react with violence or fear. I walked out of the meditation hall with his story about bombs dropping, and I was reminded of grenades exploding and M16s firing when I was hiding under the table with my siblings. Strong emotions surged through my body, and I felt the need to run up Mt. Yến Tự and yell and scream.[13] I started weeping uncontrollably. My breathing became erratic; I thought I was going to hyperventilate. Then, I thought, maybe I should practice the walking meditation that the monk had shared. "Breathing in, I know that I am breathing in. Breathing out, I know that I am breathing out. One step forward. In deeply; out slowly. Another step forward. Breathing in, I am taking care of the child within me. Breathing out, I am cradling my pain like a baby. Another small step forward. Breathing in, I recognize the fear and confusion of the child within. Breathing out, I assure the child that we are safe now and I am taking care of her. Another step. Focusing on my in-breath and out-breath, I soothe my fear and pain." Within a minute, I was able to calm my emotions. It was amazing!

Since then, I have learned to take refuge in my own breathing and my every step. I learned to appreciate walking meditation, then hiking, and, now, nature has become my refuge. With each struggle, I learned to better handle my sadness, brokenness, and fear. I hike to heal. It is my self-care practice.

Thanda Aung: *I'm not formally trained in Buddhist studies nor a dedicated practitioner, but I am deeply grateful for its therapeutic potential. My immigrant mother has no interest in self-care, psychologists, or talk therapy, but I can testify to Buddhism's salvational power in her life.*

My maternal family bears the scars of intergenerational trauma, many stemming from deep wounds of moral injury enacted by my maternal grandfather, whom I do not remember. My mother's childhood was relatively economically privileged, yet still filled with anxiety and tension.

Oral histories represent my mother's father as an almost textbook example of toxic patriarchy. Grandfather was a successful businessman but not a great husband: He gambled, was not monogamous, and was openly ethnically biased. Cousins have circulated anecdotes about his temper and punishing beatings. Because my grandmother was neither educated nor wealthy, her unhappiness and paucity of options drove her to consider not only suicide but also infanticide. We all have heard and knew the story of how Poa Poa set out to drown herself and her young children during a particularly low point in her marriage, only to be stopped and saved by a random woman passing by who chose to speak to and comfort her. My feminist education helped me to situate my grandmother's moment of desperation within a much longer, transnational cycle of female resistance to the violent and dehumanizing conditions of heteropatriarchy: infanticidal mothers from Medea to Margaret Garner, La Llorona, and Sethe of *Beloved*.[14]

My mother has always wrestled with her own demons (hungry ghosts?) of depression and despair, especially when she became a widow almost twenty-five years ago and was forced to negotiate US life without the "security" and "protection" of a male patriarch or male spouse. Unmoored by my father's death and heartbroken with grief, my mother found solace in meditation and new purpose and community within Burmese Buddhist diasporic communities at local home-temples (*pongyi kyaung*).

It's good that I didn't kill my father.

This sentence came out of my mother last year while we were driving together in the car. After a few moments of silence, my mother shared the following talk-story. My mother's parents fought frequently. As the oldest child and a favored daughter, my mother was sometimes sent by her mother to ask her father for money after these fights so my grandmother could purchase groceries to feed the family of seven. My mother also revealed that her father kept a gun in the house, and that she would look at it during these times of intense parental conflict. She considered killing her father on more than one occasion. "But," she explained calmly, "it's good that I didn't kill my father. Because Buddha says you can't reach enlightenment if you kill a parent."

While I concurred that it was good that my mother had not committed patricide, this unexpected revelation reminded me of Ohlone-Costanoan Esselen scholar Deborah Miranda. Her memoir *Bad Indians* offers a searing exploration of religious violence and gendered trauma within California Native and Latin@/x communities and also shares myriad forms of Indigenous re-clamation, re-memory, and survivance. Miranda also describes an abusive father. When Miranda was fifteen, she also contemplated killing her father with his gun.[15] While Miranda situates her father as a legacy of the Catholic mission system, Spanish colonialism, and US racism, my grandfather seems to be a portrait of Chinese settler affluence and heteropatriarchal privilege in Southeast Asia.

Buddhism was a lifeline that pulled my widowed mother back from her own suicidal ideation and tendency toward crippling grief and fatalism. After my father's death, my mother became a devout Theravadin Buddhist. She practices Vipassana meditation regularly in her prayer room at home (see Figures 1a and 1b). She used to be known by a British/English name, but has since adopted a new Burmese moniker and donates significant time, labor, and material resources to support local pongyi kyaung (monasteries) and to feed or care for monks from Myanmar who live in or travel through California. She also travels to pongyi kyaung in other parts of the United States and attends meditation retreats in Myanmar and other parts of Asia, when possible.

My mother's Catholic education has been eclipsed by deep concerns about karma, reincarnation, freedom from samsara (the cycle of dukkha/suffering), merit-making, and enlightenment. Burmese Theravāda Buddhism, however, diverges sharply from the engaged Zen Buddhism of Thích Nhất Hạnh; its practice and community energies are more "inwardly" directed toward caring for the sangha, cultivating merit, and seeking enlightenment for oneself. Like other Southeast Asian practitioners, self-described Buddhists from Burma/Myanmar might also consult with shamans/spirit mediums or fortune tellers or rely on esoteric rituals related to animism, divination, and astrology.[16]

Image 1a: Central Buddha altar at Thanda Aung's mother's house. Image 1b: Guanyin altar at same house, situated on the left of altar pictured in 1a.

Let's shift topics and talk about dynamics we've experienced and witnessed within academia over the past two decades, and how Buddhism might factor in there.

Tâm Thâm Tịnh: *When I decided to become an acting chair of the Asian American Studies department, I had no clue that emotional intelligence was a job requirement. I thought the job needed organizational skills to meet bureaucratic deadlines. As acting chair, I handled complaints and resolved conflicts from many sources: faculty, students, and staff. It was shocking. I learned things I wished I didn't know about my colleagues. That temporary responsibility nearly burned me out, especially because it was only my second semester as tenured faculty.*

My PTSD intensified when I joined CSUN United for Peace and Justice, an antiwar coalition of faculty, staff, and students who organized teach-ins and peace rallies. The group had different views about wars, classism, and racism. We clashed and eventually broke apart. Some more privileged white faculty saw attention to race and racism as "false consciousness"—as opposed to a form of class consciousness that could be a primary tool of liberation—and they also claimed the purpose of socialism was to make everyone "rich" or middle-class. Faculty of color saw race/racism as integral to social organization and that the intersection of race, class, gender, and sexuality could not be ranked in order of importance. I witnessed people's selfishness, deceptions, and fearfulness, and I became disenchanted with academia.

Thích Nhất Hạnh explained that antiwar groups fall apart because we don't practice peace with each other and yet demanded peace in the world. This irony resonated deeply for me and aptly described CSUN United for Peace and Justice. In Ocean of Peace, the Deer Park meditation hall, the significance of "practicing peace with oneself" finally sank in when I considered the violent communication that we had had in CSUN United for Peace and Justice meetings and email exchanges. We wanted peace in the world, but we did not practice peace with each other.

Learning about impermanence was also comforting because it means suffering and pain are not everlasting. Suffering is pain × resistance. A Buddhist lens that conceptualizes inherited trauma and the transmission of negative energy helped me to be proactive in creating conditions for my mind to thrive, instead of being thwarted or encumbered by second and third arrows.[17]

In short, the most practical lesson I received from Thích Nhất Hạnh was to see my pain as a baby crying and to tend and calm the crying baby with gentleness so that I don't become my emotions or repress my pain.

I almost left academia to become a Buddhist nun when I realized that my truth-seeking was not for knowledge but for wisdom. The heterosexism and heteronormative beliefs and practices of some of the monastics made me realize such a sangha cannot be my place of refuge, given that I am a queer person and an LGBTIQ+ advocate. I am also sex-positive, and an ascetic, sex-repressive, or celibate life just did not appeal to me.

I miss Sư Ông/Thầy.[18] He's the father I wish I had and a grandfather I never had. Due to wars, I never met my grandfathers. Both my parents lost their fathers when they were young. Thầy's forty-nine-day memorial was a very touching and beautiful ceremony that made me feel interbeing through the monastics.[19] They are Thầy's ambassadors. We all are our ancestors' ambassadors. Thầy had taught me valuable lessons about how to live mindfully in the present moment and to not let regrets and fear or worries block me from enjoying the preciousness of life and our interbeing. A kind and wise male role model, Thầy was someone I didn't know I needed.

I remind myself to choose a joyful moment each day. There is a Trịnh Công Sơn song that fits perfectly to practicing joy each day, and sometimes each moment. For example, I am grateful and joyful that I don't have a toothache and can enjoy a bite of this sweet carrot that helps me to taste its vibrant orange color.

Thanda Aung: *How interesting that you thought of leaving academia for a renunciate or monastic path. I seriously considered becoming a Catholic nun: "marrying" Jesus, living a life of service and simplicity. Like you, I eventually found Catholic gender hierarchies too patriarchal and restrictive and decided that was not the best path for me.*

Then I discovered feminist exegesis and critiques of heteropatriarchy and imperialist control of sexuality and gendering. Professors of African, Latina/mestiza, and Asian descent introduced me to Edward Said's analytic of Orientalism as well as the transformative potential of ethnic studies, critical race theory, postcolonial studies, and the inspirational work of Women of Color theorists and organic intellectuals. Buddhist studies, however, seemed an alienating realm in which the white and Asian male intelligentsia of area studies and Asian studies enacted gatekeeping through white supremacy, the textual bias of Orientalist scholars, and an androcentric focus on male monastics and male-authored scholarship. Starting in the 1990s, Asian American scholars of religion, such as Jane Naomi Iwamura, Sharon A. Suh, Carolyn Chen, Joseph Cheah, Kwok Pui-Lan, and David Yoo, offered different approaches to and more nuanced methods for analyzing the intersection of lived spirituality and race. They, along with many others, inaugurated the intellectual community of Asian Pacific American Religions Research Initiative (APARRI). For me, APARRI scholarship has been deeply influential: illuminating how one can better research Asian American religions and articulate embodied intersectionality and racialized religious communities.

In contrast to your "pragmatic Buddhism" (which some might call a kind of "modernist" orientation—one distanced from the supernatural, superstition, and rituals), my interests in Buddhism are more comparative and perhaps intellectual: embracing the fungibility of rituals and religion. I would describe myself as "Catholic-educated and Buddhist-adjacent" since my mother and aunts are devoted practitioners and involved in local Buddhist temples, organizations, and communities, but my formal US education is decidedly Christian-oriented (remember how our college's seal and motto heralded it as a "Tribute to Christian Civilization"?). As an Asian American comparativist, I'm intrigued by interconnections and variations among different immigrants, racialized citizens, diaspora, and those who are called "heritage" or "cradle Buddhists." I'm intrigued with how rituals enable one to connect with ancestors and the invisible, supernatural, or divine, and how storytelling operates in the context of faith, identity formation, cultural imaginaries, collectivity, and world-building.[20]

One example of this is Guan Yin 觀音, a beloved icon whom my mother called our Chinese "godmother of mercy." Predating crosses and rosaries, there were always Guan Yin statues and representations in my family's home. Avalokiteśvara, the Sanskrit name for this benevolent bodhisattva, was originally depicted in India as a male creator god. In China, this Buddhist figure was "indigenized," feminized, and popularized over a millennium as Guanyin (Perceiver of Sounds) or Kuan-shih-yin (Perceiver of the World's Sounds).[21] Scholars such as Chün-fang Yü and Yuhang Li have analyzed this gendered transformation. In *Becoming Guanyin*, Li explores how lay Buddhist women in late imperial China created "a bodily connection with the divine" through Guanyin and artistic production: "the processes of self-, object-, and world-making."[22] My feminist interest fixates on Avalokiteśvara's androgyny, fluidity, and plurality. The deity is known by many names and forms: e.g., Guanyin/Kuan Yin in China, Kwan Yin Medaw in Burma, Kannon in Japan, Gwaneum or Gwanse-eum in Korea, Karunamaya in Nepal, Lokesvara and Chenrezig in Tibet, and Quan Thế Âm in Việt Nam. Many turn to Guan Yin as a merciful embodiment of compassion and wisdom. Known as the "Divine Mother" who witnesses human suffering, Guan Yin's overlap with the Catholic Virgin Mary as a feminized deification of maternal care is not surprising.[23] Patrick Cheng claims this Buddhist icon as "a mirror of the queer Asian Christ" and "a mirror of the queer experience" because of the deity's gender fluidity, sexuality, and queer compassion.[24] Avalokiteśvara/Guan Yin can morph "into countless forms to help those in need," and each transformation "comes with the tools needed to help," explains Nhi Yến Đỗ Trần.[25] Kay Larson asserts that "the bodhisattva of compassion shows us how to model new ways of acting that enable us to skillfully help other beings."[26]

In the Disney+ series *American Born Chinese*, Michelle Yeoh plays the Chinese Goddess of Compassion. Wise, compassionate, and humorous, she takes multiple forms. I particularly appreciate how she is able to skillfully fight without anger or a desire to hurt others, even when they act out or break rules.

Screenshot of Michelle Yeoh as Guanyin in "Rockstar Status," episode 3 of American Born Chinese (Disney+, 2023).

Circling back to earlier topics, I also second your caution with romanticizing the sangha (and its sedimented heteronormativity) and share your disenchantment with academia after more than two decades. The revolutionary work of women of color theorist-teachers, visionary artists, and storytellers originally inspired me to pursue a PhD, but teaching and working "in the trenches" of intellectual institutions has taught me that even supposedly liberal academics, "progressive" colleagues, and even self-proclaimed "feminists" can and will do harm—plagiarize, steal, exploit, lie, and take advantage—through words and actions. Internalized forms of violence and oppression—sexism, racism, ableism, transphobia, and homophobia—still operate within and through academia, even despite Covid-times, illustrating that we *can* do things differently, with more care and compassion. But now, it's increasingly back to the capitalist grind, accompanied by a disheartening backlash against education and DEI programs—specifically targeting immigrant students, workers, and communities; ethnic studies and gender studies; gender-expansive and queer representations; or *anything* that encourages critical thinking or cultural literacy.

What I find more promising is how Asian American Buddhists are creating new rituals, telling new stories, and skillfully world-building in the name of reducing collective suffering, addressing our racial karma, and working toward healing, repair, and transformative justice. In addition to Chenxing Han's important book *Be the Refuge*, another Asian American Buddhist example that I find deeply inspiring is May We Gather, organized by Duncan Ryūken Williams, Funie Hsu, and Chenxing Han. Along with thousands of others under Covid-related stay-at-home orders, I watched the 2021 May We Gather event online, and was happy to be able to participate in the second ritual gathering in March 2024. The public pilgrimage in Antioch, California, where my friend's son Angelo Quinto was killed by unchecked police violence, was deeply touching. My friends—Angelo's mother, sister, and stepfather—drew comfort in the multiracial gathering and the hybridized Asian American ritual event that braided together Buddhist and Taoist rituals of repair and transformative justice practices.[27] Taking seriously the first bodhisattva vow, "Beings are numberless; we vow to save them all," the May We Gather organizers invited Buddhists to manifest freedom together through public rituals of mourning and memorialization. I would suggest that May We Gather moves us toward collective liberatory Buddhist community-building, an endeavor that is grounded in local place and history but also anchored in the present and justice.[28] The May We Gather rituals not only honored Asian American ancestors by calling out the names of those killed unjustly by racial or religious animus, but they also sought to cultivate belonging, healing, interdependence, and liberation for all beings—across ethnic, racial, socioeconomic, and ideological differences and divides.[29] I was particularly pleased and inspired that the 2024 ritual in Antioch centered the voices and work of female and nonbinary Buddhist teachers of different races and ethnic backgrounds.[30]

Perhaps you could close out our conversation by sharing about your practice, priorities, and challenges?

Tâm Thâm Tịnh: *My new colleagues revived my interests in academia again. I became a two-year-term department chair (for six years) after being inspired by my two more progressive colleagues and their students. In my second term, however, I did face pushback from other colleagues on how our resources should be spent. I pushed too hard, and they pushed back. In the end, I left feeling betrayed, and my work was undermined by the next chair.*

I moved on to fight a bigger battle at the CSU (system)-level as Ethnic Studies (ES) was being gutted by new policies from the central Chancellor's Office. Along with more progressive colleagues and our students, we organized and fought back against Executive Orders 1100R and 1110 that were neoliberal attempts to push out our students. Our successful campaign led to our campus being the only one saved from being cut from General Education Section F.[31]

Faculty and students organized and successfully pushed for the passing of AB 1460 to make Ethnic Studies a graduation requirement in the California

State University system. Unfortunately, folks made deals with the Chancellor's Office that ultimately whitewashed the Ethnic Studies graduation requirement. Big personalities wanted to be worshiped instead of working to ensure Ethnic Studies–designated courses are actually taught from an ES perspective. Within our own campus, egos and personal selfishness began to rear their ugly heads as different folks who were never part of previous struggles to expand the curriculum swooped in to receive the rewards of reassigned time. Instead of using AB 1460 to uplift existing programs and create new programs that are helping or would help our more vulnerable students and faculty, those people tended to posture with little actual effective work. This is how we reproduce the master's house and tools in academia: keeping each other under surveillance and making each "prove our worth" in order to receive funding from AB 1460. It was devastating to be gaslit by people I thought were my comrades.

I have not found academia as a place of refuge and liberation. While there are still many wonderful colleagues at CSUN, I am exhausted from dealing with opportunists and manipulators. I am leaving academia because my mental health is more important. As I was exploring retirement options earlier this year, my father had a stroke and my mother's dementia has gotten worse. I was planning to retire early to help take care of them and to build my own refuge in nature. My family's class position constrains me to be able to care for my family and to also be an academic. Academia's ableist reward system makes it difficult to self-care and to provide parental care while dealing with my own debilitating PTSD that resulted from a history of structural, cultural, and familial violence.

My practical Buddhist practice suggests that I prioritize self-care and transplant myself from a malnourishing environment of passion-exploitation to a more nurturing garden of my making. This is practicing compassion for myself and learning to practice detached compassion for others. I guess you can say I am evolving spiritually: from being detached from my emotions in order to survive turbulent earlier years, to learning compassion for self and others, to now practicing detached compassion or equanimity for self and others.

Detached Compassion, Family, and Collective Liberation

Thanda Aung: *As we finish up our conversation, I suggest that we recap some of our past conversations about filial debt, family care, collective liberation, and your therapist's recent advice to you about your parents.*

Tâm Thâm Tịnh: *My dad had a stroke last year and is still recovering with limited mobility, so it's very costly for twenty-four-hour care. I have thought of retiring early, but I have to reconsider that because how am I going to contribute to care for my parents? There's also my mother whose dementia is getting worse and needs home-boarding care. I have all these worries about my parents, so I think now I will have to work longer. My father has so much sorrow and anger, and then there's my mother's dementia, her judgmental perspective, and vulnerability to conspiracy theories (e.g., Epoch Times).[32] I need to get away so that I can have a more peaceful mindset. But having them as constant stimuli, it's not good for me.*

My therapist asked me, "Why are you living their lives? What about your own life? Because you have no boundaries here. It should not be at your expense." I responded, "I don't want to regret not trying to help when I can."

She pushed me to rethink the situation. "You're supporting patriarchy. It's not really your duty. It's patriarchy."

Yes, I am a feminist in the sense that I don't care for the patriarchy. I don't like those stupid gender roles, but I do not agree that my filial duties support patriarchy. Even if it's not my father, if someone in front of me is in need of help, I would help, because it's about compassion.

Why would I not help if I can? I'm quoting the Dalai Lama—paraphrasing what the reporter said about what the Dalai Lama said—which is that Buddhism is about helping others when you can, and when you cannot, refrain from hurting others. So that's what I'm doing. I'm a practitioner. I don't know too much about Buddhist ideology. Dharma. But that's it.

My therapist then asked, "What about detached compassion?" She said, because I have no boundaries, "You need detached compassion."

I responded: "Yes, equanimity is important. I sometimes get overwhelmed, because my parents' lives become interwoven with mine, and I get really stressed out. And that's all I think about."

I talked about my PTSD earlier and how Buddhist practice had helped me with that. I'm wondering, how is it gonna help me now? Can the previous practice help me to deal with this present moment of chaos on my father's side, and the deterioration of my mom? How is that helpful now? I need to walk and breathe. Do my walking meditation at least, so that I can get in touch with my breath again, and remember how important it is to have equanimity in this kind of stressful situation.

I was thinking about this practice of compassion. I feel like there's not enough of it right now in the world. We could use more interconnectedness and interbeing.

Thanda Aung: *No, there definitely is not enough compassion nor a widespread sense of interconnectedness. I agree that's something that is deeply needed. Remember how you brought up the deep need for collective liberation earlier? I think this moment definitely calls for some form of liberation theology that is more about collective compassion as opposed to vengeful nationalism or calls for imperialist war and violence. I fear the prevalence of a binaristic ideology: that either you're on my side, or you're the wrong kind of human—which then justifies exploitation, expulsion, or death.*

Right now, so many are antagonistic and so adamant and unyielding in what they believe. Most folks do not seem really interested in building bridges and are not interested in coming to a consensus or finding ways to build community across differences.

Tâm Thâm Tịnh: *I've been thinking about how Buddhism has helped me. I was talking about the past, but I wasn't thinking about the present moment. What my therapist advised about detached compassion makes sense. That's how the monks are able to survive. And there was that compassion fatigue study. You have to be detached otherwise you will drown in the pain.*

Thanda Aung: *It's so hard. Family responsibilities can be overwhelming to the point where it is nearly impossible to get any sense of your own center, or something outside of your particular family vortex of irrationality, demands, and intensity. I know that feeling too well.*

In past conversations, we have talked about the long history of violence in your father's family—how male heirs/young boys had been murdered to steal their wealth and inheritance—and in your own nuclear family. There is a long history of violence in Southeast Asia and in Việt Nam that many families had to live through. We've talked about how your father has internalized some of that violence, paranoia, desire for revenge, tendency to harm, and so on.

But I also think, like the Buddha, that you spent most of your life trying to find a different path, to break these cycles of suffering. I think you've sought to cultivate your own detachment, equanimity, and compassion. Sometimes, one has to cultivate detachment—because you can't "save" other people or live their lives for them when they are caught in cycles of toxicity or suffering. If one cannot help, sometimes all one can do is just walk away and hope to reduce harm.

Tâm Thâm Tịnh: *I feel more detached compassion with my nieces. I helped all of them, but I'm also okay with letting go. With my parents, it is a little bit different. I've been raised to feel that I owe them. They gave life to me; they sacrificed. So I must sacrifice too.*

Thanda Aung: *I understand the sometimes-crippling sense of filial debt and family responsibility, which is a strong theme in Asian American literature and scholarship. I internalized the same expectation that I would reciprocate the care, labor, and sacrifices of my immigrant parents when they got older. Elder care is a serious financial and social issue for our generation, which is known as the sandwich generation, since many are caring for both dependent children and increasingly frail elders.[33] Although neither you nor I have biological children of our own, we've talked at some length about how much Auntie-care we've put into helping to raise our nieces and nephews, especially those who are disabled or have higher levels of need and require more support.*

I still want to encourage you in thinking about detached compassion and self-kindness or self-compassion because I don't often take that advice myself.

I don't publish as much as is expected for a faculty member at a Research-1 university because I'm often busy taking care of everybody else. Your therapist would probably say that I also struggle with boundaries.

I'm not good at an individualist orientation either: the mindset that I'm going to do only my own research, ignore everybody else's needs, and do no service or minimum service. I spend a lot of time trying to be of service. That's how my immigrant anxiety and imposter syndrome shows up. My "stalled" professional rank reflects this cycle, focusing more time and labor on collective compassion and service over pursuing individual research opportunities or upward mobility.

Tâm Thâm Tịnh: *It's hard. Before, I was trying to run away from other family issues. And now I'm back and engaged. But then I have no boundaries.*

I don't know if it's insight, or is it practicing "no self"? There are short moments where I'm connected, in the zone, acting out of compassion for our interbeing. No separation. Then all is good. Other times, when there's chaos, then I only feel duty and resentment.

On Facebook, I saw a picture that one of the monks shared of two novices shaving their heads. It made me remember when I had thought that would be a more peaceful route to go. I've been thinking about going down to Deer Park and going to my local sangha.

Thanda Aung: *Oh, yes, the Buddhist route of becoming a renunciate or nun.*

Tâm Thâm Tịnh: *Yeah, the idea of centering practice—in a community that is collectively trying to practice peace.*

9
—

BEING WITH THE BODY IN A BODY

SYD YANG

How might eating disorder recovery be a feminist endeavor?

What might the bodhisattvas have to teach about an embodiment of liberation?

How might the physical body be the raft that will take me to the Other Shore?

Remembering the Body

In my late twenties I interviewed for a position at the Women's Foundation of California and the executive director at the time asked me at the end of the third interview, "Are you a feminist?" I was taken aback. I was interviewing for a position that would include leading a young women's program for a women's rights organization and it seemed like an obvious question that didn't need to be asked.

"Yes, and. Yes I am a feminist and yes, I believe that feminism is so much more than women. I do not believe that 'woman' is a monolithic term and I am a feminist in that I will fight for all bodies and genders to thrive outside of a patriarchal lens." This absolutely included trans women and women of color who do not see themselves or their rights reflected in Western-centric feminism. Once I accepted the position, I would quickly learn the ways that I perceived feminism differed from more essentialist Second Wave values held by many within the organization at the time. The existence of different versions or understandings of feminism punctuated for me how lived experience, not just theory, was critical in shaping a collective future.

In the twenty years since I left that job I have often wondered how I might answer that question were I to be asked again. Am I a feminist? I'm no longer sure this is an adequate course of inquiry. In the past two decades, my understanding of feminism has evolved and shifted dramatically as my contemplation on gender has led me to recognize both feminine and masculine as two sides of the same coin—not separate, definitely not opposites. As I move more intentionally and visibly through the world in a physical embodiment that is defined as trans masculine and nonbinary—that is, not a woman—my conceptualization of feminism further complicates my response to whether or not I am a feminist. I am not even sure I could define "woman" at this point in my life—additionally, I believe this is the wrong question to be asking.[1]

What then is feminism? Can feminism exist beyond the body? Can a feminist ethos exist outside of the binary of man and woman, masculine and feminine? I believe it can, though in many Buddhist spaces I encounter, I continue to discover that my existence as a trans, nonbinary being collides with a feminism rooted in gender-essentialist interpretations of the Dharma. Fear of and prejudice against the female body absolutely exists within sutra (which makes sense given the bias of those writing and giving the teachings), however, is not mettā offered for all beings, regardless of gender? Consider the stories of the Dragon Girl in the Lotus Sutra and Uppalavanna—well-known tales of women attaining enlightenment.[2] These are stories that affirm the assertion that all beings (in variously gendered bodies) are able to attain enlightenment.

If enlightenment is attainable for all bodies, then to limit feminism to bodies assigned female at birth or to be constrained to a binary notion of gender confines it to a reductionist understanding of lived experience. For me, it has been through a committed practice of sitting at the feet of trans women that my understanding of feminism has grown. Julia Serano writes in her book *Whipping Girl: A Transsexual Woman on Sexism and the Scapegoating of Femininity* that "In trans women's eyes, I see a wisdom that can only come from having to fight for your right to be recognized as female, a raw strength that only comes from unabashedly asserting your right to be feminine in an inhospitable world."[3] As someone who has ruthlessly engaged in self-harm practices in the hopes of denying my own body—to distance myself from a felt discomfort of perceived femininity, disembodying through eating disorders, substance use, and excessive physical exercise as ways to disconnect from a body assigned female at birth—Serano's words have the tender ability to always help me reset. What am I rejecting when I turn away from my own body, my femininity? Is it learned social and cultural disdain for the woman or is it perhaps something different altogether? What might be the spiritual practices that will help me discern?

My eating disorder tiptoed into my life before I was ten years old, a gentle shoulder tap that turned me toward a path that would lead to full-blown bulimia by my mid-teens. I found relief in throwing up. I touched into intoxicating self-empowerment through restriction. I convinced myself that I could quiet the desperate screams of powerlessness in my mind the more and more I could control both my eating and my hunger.

In the conservative evangelical Christian community I was raised in, I was taught that the body was sin, that the body was to be denied, and that my body was inherently wrong. Especially *my* body—a body assigned female at birth and a body that rejected being a girl. My body was too large, too loud, too defiant, too queer, and too masculine. Even before I hit my pre-teen years, I had become consciously aware of how unacceptable my existence was to my parents, to the church, and to many others in the worlds beyond these two—even if none of this made sense to me. Outside of my family of origin, I was subjected to persistent bullying that fixated on my body as too Asian, too awkward, and too smart. To control and contort my own body became the safest way forward. Head down, become more feminine, please others, erase desire, be smaller—in all the ways. My physical body became the site of my increasing suffering. I consumed the belief that if I could effectively deny the body, my suffering would reduce. To dissociate from the body was to get free. For many years I operated from this belief, engaging in more and more self-harm behaviors to "succeed."

Internally, I pushed back at authority and I peeled back the worn edges of patriarchal power. In wanting to fit in and to figure out what spaces wanted me, I somehow became too threatening and too challenging to others. As a child, I didn't understand the intricacies of social conformity as a tool for quieting dissent. At my core, I understood that I existed; that was all. The dissonance between the internal and external felt like a sensory nightmare most of the time. My eating disorder helped to quiet the noise and reduce the pain.

What is an eating disorder but a way that a body learns how to survive in a world obsessed with controlling and constraining bodies and desire? I believe that my eating disorder was the appropriate response at the time to systemic oppression, settler colonialism, and white and Christian supremacy for a queer, trans/nonbinary Asian American body.[4] Gloria Lucas of Nalgona Positivity Pride, through her critical advocacy and community research on eating disorders, speaks to the ways historical trauma and colonial violence have made BIPOC bodies nonconsensual sites of conflict. Her analyses of power and bodies has been instrumental in my own understanding of liberation and eating disorder recovery. What might become true once that response was no longer viable, no longer the best choice—no longer the choice I wanted to make?

Trauma and addiction are the best liars. This is well known in recovery spaces. My unresolved addictions and unacknowledged complex PTSD reinforced my delusions and shackled me to the illusion that I could only get free by destroying myself—a flawed understanding of liberation that was alive within me when I connected to Buddhism in my early twenties. If my body was the cause of my suffering, I should focus on other things. Focus on the mind, focus on touching into the spaciousness between thoughts, and most importantly, get still. The body is there to sit on the cushion, nothing more. Or, so I thought. In those early years of reclaiming Buddhism as both an ancestral and personal spiritual practice, I was determined for it to help me transcend my gender discomfort and my disdain for living in a body. Mindfulness would set me free—right? I had bought into the narrative that a mindfulness practice ensured a stress-free life.

Seated now in the present moment, I can confidently say this: Mindfulness, as a stand-alone practice, has not saved me. It has, however, guided me into a sustained and compassionate recovery in which I am learning to set down the compulsions to self-harm and disengage from my own existence. It has and continues to teach me to seek out the middle way. It has invited me into the spacious possibility of liberation for all beings, for all genders, for all bodies. The intersection of mindfulness practice and being in recovery for an eating disorder reminds me daily of the Four Noble Truths, and of the Bodhisattva Vows that I have taken.

First Noble Truth: Suffering is. (dukha)
First Bodhisattva Vow: Beings are numberless; I vow to free them.

Second Noble Truth: Suffering has a cause. (samudaya)
Second Bodhisattva Vow: Delusions are inexhaustible; I vow to end them.

Third Noble Truth: Suffering can end. (nirodha)
Third Bodhisattva Vow: Dharma Gates are boundless; I vow to enter them.

Forth Noble Truth: There is a way out of Suffering. (marga)
Forth Bodhisattva Vow: The Buddha Way is attainable; I vow to attain it.

A mindfulness-based recovery roots me into an ontology of interconnected and living systems as the only path forward that makes sense.[5] For me, this touches into the core of how I now define the feminist endeavor—to enhance the conditions for all bodies to exist, thrive and self-determine.

Embodying the Bodhisattva

The bodhisattvas have held my fascination since I first stood before a giant marble statue of Quan Yin, at Tianxiang in Taroko National Park in Taiwan. I must have been in my mid-twenties. It was the first time I had encountered an embodiment of the goddess of this size. Acutely aware of my insignificance in all manner of things, I stood before her, staring boldly up into the face of One who could peer into my heart and know my fears. Was I good enough to bow to Her? Was I Asian enough? My body hovered in that space between knowing and not knowing, lost within a pernicious interrogation of my "enoughness" until that moment when my shame convinced me to walk away, the untaken bow still vibrating in my limbs.

Each bow I take now before the bodhisattvas carries within it a phantom tremor of that day. To bow, for me, is to affirm an existence that is enough— even in its periodic experience of not-enoughness. To bow is to invite my whole body into devotion and into practice. Each bow also invites me to examine how my Buddhist practice and relationship to Dharma may also be unraveling my attachments to gender and to the idea of the body. Can a feminist ethos that affirms all embodiments be found in the experience of nonduality and *prajnaparamita*? What becomes possible when I touch into how this body that I reside in, in this lifetime, that is neither man nor woman, is an emanation of the Buddha? Are not the bodhisattvas fundamentally trans in the ways so many shapeshift gender and navigate androgyny across history and culture? What does it even mean to live in a body?

In mid-2019 I found myself in San Francisco for work and at that time was voraciously reading *Fearing the Black Body* by Sabrina Strings.[6] The social and historical discourse on race and Black women's bodies in the US and Europe prodded my mind to wonder how bodies and body shapes had been considered in Asian history. How did the imprint of colonialism shift the expectation of bodies in that part of the world? What were the belief systems in play that constrained or allowed bodies to be round or strong, or within or outside of gender, before the Western colonizers arrived? As I read, I became more and more convinced that a key to finding ease in my own body resided in this history.

Also during this time I was imperfectly moving through a painful divorce that poked at my familiar practices of self-harm and body dissociation. My sense of self had been torn apart, deconstructed down to its quantum parts. There was nothing left of who I knew myself to be—except for my hatred of the body itself. I clung tightly to that old belief that my body was the source of my suffering.

As I trudged through the muddy fields of body-based trauma, I wondered how I might disrupt the flow of self-critique and the seemingly inarguable non-desirability of my own body—the softness of my belly, the roundness of my face, the fullness of my chest—when I remembered that I was in San Francisco. I canceled my meetings for the rest of the day and took myself to the Museum of Asian Art.

I wandered that afternoon through rooms and galleries. I peered into subtle brush strokes of mountainous landscapes and the soft lines that traced intimate shapes of women's bodies. I circumambulated figurines of demons and bejeweled objects severed from their original seating places in temple shrines. I found myself entranced as I gazed in awe upon statues of the Buddha and a myriad of other deities. And, I bowed easily before the embodiments attributed to both Avalokiteśvara and Quan Yin. It was in these practices that I began to see myself reflected back at me. Within each artistic expression the sacred presence of my ancestors reminded me that I belonged.

That day I found myself coming back again and again to a Chinese wooden sculpture of a seated Quan Yin/Avalokiteśvara from the Song dynasty, drawn in by its rounded and soft features, its open posture and ambiguously gendered body. Gazing up at this physical expression of the Bodhisattva—the softness of their belly, the roundness of their face, the fullness of their chest—I realized I was peering into my own image reflected back at me. There were no faults or mistakes in who I was. All the pieces fit.

Bowing before Quan Yin in the gallery that day, I could hear a voice rising from within me: "What if my body—this body—is the path to liberation? What if being fully in this body, in all of its gender fluidity, its queer desire, and its complex histories of harm is how I will get free?" The words began to repeat in a cadence that expanded my breath and opened up my heart. Moving from a tentative whisper to a thundering roar within my head, an unexpected smile pierced through the grief mask I had been wearing for so long. What if? What if I had gotten it wrong all these years? What if my body was not the suffering I needed to escape? What if, instead, this body was the path, the Way itself?

Later that year I would be sitting on my cushion, repeating the Bodhisattva Vows three times as I began my morning sit. Repeating the vows three times to open and close my practice was something I had adopted at this time, as a way to more fully enter into the vows that I had taken a few months earlier. On the third recitation, I encountered the sublime transcendence of a nonhuman being with me in the room. There, seated next to me was Avalokiteśvara, their posture mirroring mine. As I continued to recite, they placed two of their thousand hands on my body, one at my heart and the second cradling my belly. Holding me with the gentle confidence of immortality, they whispered into my ear: "This is the way. This body. This is your path. Remember this."

Contemplation on a Body in a Body

In my Dharma study, I am frequently drawn to the Sattipathana Sutta in the Pali Canon. In this sutta, the Buddha speaks of the four foundations of mindfulness that, when practiced, are for the "purification of beings, for the overcoming of sorrow and lamentation, for the destruction of suffering and grief, for reaching the right path, for the attainment of Nibbana."[7] The first of these four is the contemplation on the body in a body. This contemplation focuses on the body as a composite of many parts, each of which functions to sustain life, and yet will inevitably decompose and dissolve back into the earth after death. The existence of the body is one of impermanence, an admonition to not get stuck in the illusion of beauty and bodily aesthetics. Sitting with this practice—of contemplating on a body in a body—has become a core practice for me. It invites me to consider the body as a Dharma gate, one I am asked to enter and walk through in this lifetime. For much of the time I have been alive in this body I have wrestled with a complicated relationship to the wholeness of my body. I have spent so many years dissociating from this body, trying to escape this embodiment, that I don't even remember much of my childhood, or my younger years. Encounters with my body often felt unsafe or unpredictable. To bring careful attention to the physical form would also mean that I might have to accept this body—for what it is and what it isn't. Inviting the body to be simply a contemplation, releasing it of obligation to be anything other than what it is, has been transformative.

Within the eating disorder and body image advocacy arena, there is a concept called *body acceptance*. This term promotes the idea that one can learn to accept and appreciate their body even when dissatisfied with its various parts. More broadly, body acceptance proclaims that all bodies are good bodies, even in all the ways they conform or not to social and cultural norms (for example: gender, race, age, size), in all the ways they meet or resist expectations (of ourselves and of others), and in all the ways they engage ability and disability. There is an implied judgement of goodness within this idea of acceptance, and the other side of body acceptance is body shame, especially if and when one chooses to change the body. Body acceptance in this regard feels limited and constrained.

I have struggled with this idea of body acceptance given this perceived judgment of good versus bad within it. I do not believe that one's experience of the physical body is able to exist outside of social, cultural, and political contexts. On the surface, I think that body acceptance sounds like a good idea; however, I have found little within the secular discourse around it that moves the needle to dismantle the cultural myths of beauty, attractiveness, and thinness. What might become if I paired this idea of body acceptance with a Buddhist framework of acceptance?

On my refrigerator door there is a small piece of paper with handwritten words in fading green ink. It reads: "If I were to accept what is, then what?" A Dharma teacher once offered me this question at the end of a meditation. It has become a mantra practice for me in the many years since. Paired with the contemplation of a body in a body as presented in the Sattipathana Sutta, I have discovered a way toward body acceptance, on my terms. To accept my body, I didn't have to disavow it or push it aside. I simply had to sit with it, judgements and all.

What am I accepting? Bodies are never fixed. The dance between acceptance, shame, suffering, and curiosity follows a never-ending cadence within me. There are so many conscious and unconscious belief systems I have carried within me about bodies. In returning to my cushion and to my breath I discovered that there is wonder beneath the grasping to know. This is the beginning of acceptance. My partner asked me the other day if there was a reason I didn't write more about the suffering I am now encountering as my body ages: more persistent injuries that keep me from running the distances and frequencies I long for, increasing aches and pains throughout my body, evolutions in body shape and size, and seemingly insatiable fatigue. I'm not sure I have an answer other than noticing the ways I am still conditioned to disavow my body from time to time.

Accepting what is while contemplating on a body in a body, therefore, is an ongoing endeavor of humility and care.

What then? Allowing wonder to guide me, I became more curious about the Dharma of transgressive bodies. Was I allowed to accept this body of mine that so many deem as transgressive, as wrong, as imperfect or even offensive? Did acceptance mean I was not allowed to change this body (by accessing gender-affirming surgeries and medical care) or get to explore pleasure and body-based practices that may also be outside the norm but may move me toward more alignment? Within that question posted on my refrigerator door lies a second step: "What then?" Acceptance, in a Buddhist context, also invites in space for action. I accept, now what? I can choose differently and I can invite in change to what is. Acceptance creates new possibilities. These lines of inquiry eventually morphed into an examination of which practices might best help me access the spaciousness of being in a body.[8]

The more I sit with and inhabit this body, the more I am able to touch into compassionate awareness of the moment. There is a knowing that arises out of the body that to be with impermanence is to be with all things, all the time. This body is neither good nor bad. It simply is. It is ever evolving as my breath, it is as mysterious as the creatures who thrive within the deepest parts of the sea, and it is as magically elusive as a shooting star. It is all of these things, and more. It is all of these things, and none of them at the same time. Sitting with my body as the path, as the way of the Bodhisattva, I have come to experience the body as *sunyata* (emptiness).

> *Listen, Sariputra,*
> *This Body itself is Emptiness*
> *And Emptiness itself is this Body.*
> *This Body is not other than Emptiness*
> *And Emptiness is not other than this Body.*[9]

The Body as Emptiness

I have found that when encountering suffering, there comes a point when my mind asks, "Is this really what we are going to keep doing? What if life doesn't have to be this hard?" I find there is often a choice to how much into the suffering I can or need to go. Do I wallow? Sometimes and for a period of time, perhaps. Or, do I acknowledge the pain and allow the suffering to reside alongside me as I move through my day? More often, yes, I choose this. It is then, in these moments of setting down my attachment to my suffering, when my body touches into the mystery of sunyata. Everything gets quiet, my questions fall away, and my breath becomes the breath of the entire world. These are also the moments when, seated on my cushion or breathing with the trees in my favorite neighborhood park, I know that everything is and is not, at the same time. This knowing and practice has risen out of my study of the Heart Sutra (*Prajnaparamitahrdaya*—the Heart of the Perfection of the Wisdom Sutra), which is a sacred text I turn to frequently when my body-suffering takes up too much space.

When I first encountered the Heart Sutra, I naively believed it would be a simple text to understand in a similar way that I assumed that entering into recovery for an eating disorder would be an easy task. I didn't realize at the time that I would be committing to a life-long (lifetimes-long, even) relationship with prajnaparamita nor did I realize that recovery is a life-long practice, not a single moment. In the same way, being with the body is a relational, ever-evolving practice of care.

For years I focused on this one line in the Heart Sutra: "This Body itself is Emptiness." In an attempt to embody this teaching, I kept sitting, and then would sit some more. My lungs kept breathing, and then would breathe some more. "Be the emptiness, let go of this body." That was the refrain I repeated to myself in my mind. That was how I understood the teaching at the time. What was so complicated about surrendering to the unknowable nature of impermanence? I discovered that I often didn't want to accept the unacceptable— that I am no longer able-bodied and that I still desire the aesthetics of youth and long to fit in with contemporary beauty ideals. The harder I tried, the more discomfort rose up within me. My suffering was growing, not diminishing, as I expected it would. This realization stunned me. Doing and trying *not* to suffer created the conditions for more suffering. What was I missing?

I returned to the Heart Sutra and in my recitation I let my breath anchor me into a body that is ever moving and always shifting. I set down my own knowing and let my breath guide me. Gently I placed my hands over my heart in *gassho mudra* and there I noticed it again: the kind presence of one of the hands of Avalokiteśvara resting on my chest. "Notice the repetition," They said. "The meaning you seek is just beyond the words."

> *Listen, Sariputra,*
> *This Body itself is Emptiness*
> *And Emptiness itself is this Body.*
> *This Body is not other than Emptiness*
> *And Emptiness is not other than this Body.*[10]

What if the practice is not to push the body away but rather, to lean into being in a body? What would happen if I took this step? I was surprised and challenged to notice how much actual desire to not exist in a body continued to be alive within me. I still wanted to escape embodiment, to transcend this physical plane. This is perhaps why I succeeded so well at living with an eating disorder, engaging in substance use/abuse, and over-exercising. Dissociating had become a skillfulness that kept me stuck in a closed loop of suffering. But, emptiness is not transcendence. It is *being-ness*, or what I have come to refer to as *being-with-ness*.

I need my body. I am not my body, however; the body has become the path that is both teacher and teaching, for me. As I lean into being in a body, so much more becomes possible. In learning to be with this body, the suffering has not disappeared, but my relationship to it has profoundly shifted. In those moments when the suffering seems to be too great, I now place a hand on my heart and return to my breath. "Be here with me," I whisper to myself. "The Body is not other than Emptiness. Emptiness is not other than the Body. Keep breathing. Keep going." This body is becoming the raft itself—the raft that will carry me (and perhaps others) to the Other Shore.

I am reminded here of the story of Yasodhara, the wife of the Buddha. Even after all she endured in her life—that of being abandoned by her husband Siddhartha (without even a goodbye), and later losing her son and social reputation—she continued to seek out and reach toward enlightenment. The Buddhist texts may focus more on male protagonists and the attainment of nirvana for male bodies given who wrote them, however the Dharma is much larger than what was written down. Her suffering and her gender/her body did not prevent her from getting free. She lived this and she knew this. Upon her death she declared, "I am my own refuge."[11] I hear in this an affirmation of her body as the path—as both teacher and teaching. She did not shy away from her embodied realities.

Eating disorder recovery has been about coming back in/to my body. It is sustained through a continual remembering that I have a body and that this body is worth caring for. That this body is worth loving, regardless of its transgressiveness or gender, regardless of sexuality, regardless of age. My recovery is an endeavor that invites me into a deeper and kinder embodiment that roots into a Dharma-based feminism that honors the liberation of all bodies, all lived/living experience, and all ways of being-with oneself and (in) the world.

Living in a body is complicated. Living into the Dharma in a body, is not. I know now that I can experience my body as a reflection of the Bodhisattva, and as an embodiment of Dharma. Leaning more into the sensations and feelings of the physical body is how I stay in my recovery. Staying with my body—learning to trust it, walk with it, be in practice with it, let it be my teacher—is how I am touching into prajnaparamita and how I am living the Bodhisattva Vows. I must be in my body to no longer be a body.

10

—

ASIAN AMERICAN FEMINIST BUDDHIST RAGE, TRAUMA, AND SELF-LOVE

SHARON A. SUH

Twice-divorced. Oops, I did it again. In *Living a Feminist Life*, Sara Ahmed writes, "Feminism begins with sensation: with a sense of things," and it is usually a sense of when things have gone awry.[1] Feminism is therefore, "sensational" in its refusal to be ignored, in its demand to be seen, and it is imperative that we trust when our senses have been triggered. It is, as Ahmed notes, a "sensitive return to the injustices of the world."[2] Noticing and sensing with and through the body are integral to an Asian American feminist Buddhist approach to recovering the felt sensation of our bodies, which may have been lost in response to multiple assaults to our well-being. This embodied approach to mindfulness and meditation is, therefore, an inherently political strategy for individual and collective liberation.

Since its publication in 2017, I have adhered to *Living a Feminist Life* as my north star, as an antidote to my mind's habitual tendency to rationalize or minimize what does not feel right in my gut. More and more I find myself resonating with the popular adage, "trust your gut," for it knows things and it won't lie to you; it will usually tell you things that your brain doesn't want to hear. When my second marriage was ending, my gut had been speaking to me for years in a language that I had yet to understand—the language of trauma whose grammar and syntax spoke to me through an elevated heart rate, breathlessness, and chest tightness. *Leave the second marriage. Who cares if you will be twice-divorced? Who says you are a failure? You have nothing to be ashamed of. Just leave.* My body registered cues that my mind was unable and perhaps unwilling to see—I had entered into a second marriage with a white man who was becoming increasingly emotionally abusive with lies, threats of taking his own life when he didn't get what he wanted from me, and button-pushing critiques of me being a selfish woman.

Anger, disappointment, rage, or despair should have been the appropriate responses to such behaviors, but instead, I retreated into the well-worn path of silence and dissociation that I had learned as a coping mechanism growing up with my mentally ill first-generation Korean immigrant mother. This practice of ignoring the increasingly loud murmurs of my body was not just a survival mechanism learned in the home, though; it was also a learned strategy for being Asian American in a white supremacist capitalist patriarchy. I have returned to *Living a Feminist Life* several times over the past eight years since its publication; I treat it as a lifeline and operating manual for honing my feminist sense-ability and as a rebuff to a heightened sense of precarity that has rendered Asian Americans ever more suspect during the Covid-19 pandemic and after the reelection of a president hell-bent on making America white again.

When I began learning to trust the signs of my body through careful noticing and paying attention with mindfulness practices, I realized just how much I have been swallowing my anger and rage at unjust systems. My nervous system had been telling me for years that I wasn't in right relationship with so many hallowed institutions—including traditional academia, where my studies of Buddhism, race, and gender were considered less-intellectual pursuits than textual translation and marriage.

A few short months after meeting my now ex-husband in 2016, I began experiencing symptoms of a racing heart, chest tightness, throat constriction, and acid reflux. I was sent to several doctors for bloodwork to test my thyroid, I breathed into a spirometer to test my lung capacity, I was hooked up to an ECG machine, and I wore a halter monitor. The tests were all negative or inconclusive; there didn't seem to be anything physically wrong with me. And yet not one of my health practitioners inquired if I was emotionally okay or under psychological duress. This phenomenon occurs all the time. Asian American women are often dismissed and unseen, for we embody the Model Minority myth, which says it is unlikely that I, an Asian American woman, would be suffering from trauma, stress, and anxiety. The Model Minority myth constructs Asian Americans as hardworking and apolitical, a trope that discourages vocal resistance and erases the struggles of those who do not conform to this stereotype. And yet, as my social-worker friend remarked over lunch, "Isn't it telling that no one bothered to ask you if you were emotionally okay? As a clinician, I see this all the time—Asian American women are the Model Minority and no one even considers that what was happening was a panic attack and symptoms of anxiety." She gives me a knowing look, rolls her eyes, and remarks, "They never bother to ask because they don't think it's possible. Asian Americans seem to have no emotional life; it's all work, work, work with the same stoic faces over and over again."

I was hiding from the truth of my own anxiety because I didn't want to be seen as a twice-divorced failure of an Asian American woman. It didn't help that I cleaved to silence as a life-long survival strategy of self-protection, but my body was keeping score, and silence proved itself a failed coping mechanism. To learn to breathe deeply again, I eventually found refuge in mindfulness techniques that taught me how to decipher and trust my body's cues and to acknowledge that it was okay that I was angry, and that I had a healthy dose of rage that I no longer needed to suppress, be ashamed of, or deny. Learning to accept these outlaw emotions has become a transformative act of self-care and a catalyst for what I call an *Asian American feminist Buddhist ethic of self-love.*

In *Rage Becomes Her: The Power of Women's Anger,* Soraya Chemaly explores the gendered nature of anger where men's anger is validated as a sign of power inspired by the pursuit of justice and women's anger is dismissed as out of control, irrational, and pathological. Reading Chemaly's fascinating work helped me see how I too had been glossing over my rage for decades. In America's racial imaginary, it was and remains unacceptable, unbecoming, and out of character for a second-generation, educated, and professional Asian American woman like me to become undone and push back. Chemaly explains:

> We go out of our way to look "rational" and "calm." We minimize our anger, calling it frustration, impatience, exasperation, or irritation, words that don't convey the intrinsic social and public demand that *anger* does. We learn to contain our selves: our voices, hair, clothes, and most importantly, speech. Anger is usually about saying "no" in a world where women are conditioned to say almost anything but "no."[3]

When I first encountered Chemaly's text, I experienced both chagrin and relief. The silence that muted my rage was not something to be ashamed of, for it was a learned response in a world where women's anger is deflected and becomes an indictment of her shortcomings rather than an indictment of the system that mutes her rage in the first place. I had been habituated to eat my feelings of rage, and it was no longer digestible. Staying in my second marriage, which had become untenable, rendered my gut a minefield; I could no longer ignore the signs of my body and suppress my anger because doing so had begun to compromise my health. My esophagus felt like it was perpetually ingesting toxic battery acid that threatened to burn a hole through it and my stomach filled with knots of dread and anxiety. The dyspeptic sensations in my stomach would turn on a dime into nausea. My heart was often aflutter but not in any romantic kind of way. The physiological impact of denying my anger and rage was undeniable. Chemaly explains, "By the time a woman reaches midlife, the most significant predictors of her general health are her levels of stress and where she ranks in terms of keeping her anger in."[4]

To get a handle on my health, I needed to get back into my body and actually familiarize myself with what anger and rage felt like, for I had spent a lifetime denying its presence. As a professor of Buddhism, I had already been acquainted with one of the most cited Buddhist texts on mindfulness, known as the *Sattipatthana* (Foundation of Mindfulness). In this mindfulness manual, the Buddha encourages practitioners to draw our awareness to the four foundations of the body, feelings, mind, and mental qualities. Although practicing with the four foundations of mindfulness is profound, I found that neutrally observing my body felt like another kind of silencing. I wanted instead to identify, feel, and learn how to skillfully express outlaw emotions like anger. I wanted to cultivate body literacy that would liberate my rage so that I could wield it toward liberation.

In 2018, I began my certification as a Mindful Eating–Conscious Living teacher at Great Vow Monastery in Oregon. There I was introduced to one of the most powerful mindfulness techniques, "Linking Emotions with Physical Sensations in the Body," that taught me how emotions create chemical reactions in the body. This brief practice taught me how to reattune myself to the crucial messages that my body had been sending me my whole life that fear had taught me to ignore. My Zen teacher guided my training cohort through a seated meditation that encouraged us to gently focus on the felt-sensations of breathing. We dropped back into our bodies and sat in gentle awareness as our natural breathing stimulated our parasympathetic nervous systems. The peacefulness of the meditation space, the calm voice of our teacher, and our own rhythmic breathing did not prepare me for the heart of the meditation practice that soon followed.

Our teacher guided us through the practice by reminding us that our bodies have their own wisdom that is different from yet connected to our minds. She reminded us that our emotions could be felt in our bodies if we took the time to listen deeply to them with nonjudgmental attention. She counseled us to bring a kindly attention to whatever our bodies were feeling so that we could learn to take better care of ourselves and attend to our emotions without suppressing or ignoring them. Then she drops a line that I will always take heed to remember—"For every emotion that we experience, there is a chemical reaction in the body that manifests as a physical sensation. If we can become aware of these physical sensations, we may be able to know what we are feeling and then take better care of ourselves."

The Zen priest then invited us to "allow a scene or incident to come to mind that made you mildly angry—not the five-hundred-pound weight of anger, but the five-pound weight of anger." We were prompted to "visualize, see, hear yourself perhaps standing in line too long, being cut off in traffic, or arguing with someone. Fully imagine this incident, as if you were there. Be in the experience. Now, bringing your attention to your body, noticing where in your body you experience anger. Where do you feel anger? Noticing as best you can the physical sensations of anger."

I was immediately drawn to a tightness in my chest and a constriction in my throat. My heart rate began to elevate as I remembered when my ex-husband lied to me about applying for jobs after he got laid off and how he began to blame me and shame me for being greedy for asking him to contribute to our grocery bills.

The anger that welled in my body through this recollection mimicked the bodily sensations that had me visiting countless doctors in search of the source of my breathlessness. I suddenly realized that the physical sensations I felt by just invoking this memory presented themselves in the same way as they did when my body was reacting to the anger and rage I was suppressing in order to remain calm during these oft repeated situations with my ex-husband. I was beginning to learn to read the signs of my body and, more important, to no longer override what my body had been telling me for years—I was not in the right relationship, and I needed to get out. It took being abandoned in Mexico while on a vacation, having zero contact for ten days, being ghosted, and finally being accused of trying to passively kill my husband by somehow getting him to kill himself that I finally listened to what my burning gut had been yelling for the past three years—leave.

My teacher led us through a similar exercise to notice the felt-sensations of sadness in our bodies, which to me felt like a dull heaviness as my body closed in on itself. We concluded this embodied meditation practice by invoking a memory that brought us joy as we explored what joy felt like and where we could identify it in our bodies. While the meditation itself only lasted for ten minutes, its impact on me has been profound; I am now more attuned and inclined to listen to the murmurs of my body and can register its reactions to external events. I no longer refuse to listen to what I am feeling in the moment so that I can care for my anger rather than ignore or suppress it. Acknowledging the presence of anger and rage has become a fruitful practice because it reminds me that while my mind may be used to overriding, second-guessing, or even gaslighting my emotions, my body will not lie to me.

In *Anger: Wisdom for Cooling the Flames*, Thích Nhất Hạnh invites us to acknowledge and embrace our anger so that it doesn't burn us up. Likening this acceptance of our anger to a mother's care for her child, he writes, "As practitioners, we do exactly like this. We hold our baby of anger in mindfulness so that we get relief. We continue the practice of mindful breathing and mindful walking, as a lullaby for our anger."[5] Nhất Hạnh's instructions to tenderly hold our anger rather than pretending it does not exist are based on the Buddha's teaching to accept reality as it is and to be with our current experience. Nhất Hạnh reminds us, "The Buddha never advised us to suppress our anger. He taught us to go back to ourselves and take good care of it."[6] Anger, as the Buddha taught, is part of us and we have to take good care of our anger so that we "recognize it as it is, embrace it, and smile."[7] Anger is not something to be afraid of, or ashamed of; instead, it is to be acknowledged—something to be grateful for as a signal that something is amiss and awry.

My nervous system had been been prodding me for years, telling me that I was in a toxic, imbalanced relationship. I never wanted to be the sole financial support for my spouse who was capable of working. I didn't want to be with a man who insisted that I create a work chart with stickers for rewards for chores done or buy multiple sets of dish gloves in different colors so that he wouldn't be bored doing the dishes. My body has been priming me to run, to flee, to make haste, and to choose myself, but I didn't listen. I was a car with the parking brake on while my nervous system kept its foot on the gas pedal.

In *Minor Feelings: An Asian American Reckoning*, Cathy Park Hong draws attention to our "minor feelings," or the discontent we are forced to swallow despite the prevailing assumptions that Asian Americans are the Model Minority. It is the hallmark of American racism. Hong explains:

> Minor feelings occur when American optimism is enforced upon you, which contradicts your own racialized reality, thereby creating a static of cognitive dissonance. You are told, "Things are so much better," while you think, Things are the same. You are told, "Asian Americans are so successful," while you feel like a failure.[8]

Living and succeeding as an Asian American woman means being gaslit all along the way by the greatest myth of all—the myth of our resilience, ingenuity, frugalness, and dedication to family. Any complaint we make is used against us; I experienced this in my faulty marriage all along. I was blamed for being a greedy woman and a feminist imposter who only claimed to be a self-sufficient single mother, someone who, underneath it all, only wanted to milk my husband for money.

Practicing mindfulness and listening to my body with deep hearing and compassion, I realized that I was not experiencing a physical health crisis; it was a marriage crisis. I was suffering from an acute case of not listening to what my senses were telling me. Every time my body tightened and revved up my heart, she was demanding to be heard because she knew what I had been afraid of admitting out loud—I needed out. It took me almost three years to muster up the courage to leave this unhealthy marriage, and I am still recovering from the imprint of these past traumas on my body. I continue to work diligently to allow myself to acknowledge that the harms of the marriage were not indicative of something lacking in me, despite what patriarchy wanted me to think, and I have come further along the path to cultivating an Asian American feminist Buddhist ethic of self-love. This ethic of self-love compels me to embrace myself as I am and to refuse to reside in a reservoir of shame for breaking from the hallowed institution of marriage yet again. In the context of Asian American feminist Buddhist practice, rage often emerges as a response to systemic injustice and the silencing of our experiences. Rather than viewing rage as something pathological and something to be suppressed or transcended, perhaps we can see it as a vital sign—an embodied message signaling that boundaries have been crossed and harm has occurred. Allowing ourselves to feel and acknowledge this rage without judgment opens the door to radical self-love. Honoring rage as a valid and necessary emotion becomes an act of deep care for ourselves, reclaiming our agency and dignity in the face of systems that seek to erase or minimize us.

The Asian American Female Rage I Didn't Know I Needed

Asian American women don't often get the chance to be emotionally messy in the public eye. Most of the time we are seen as quiet, head-down, get-through-the-work, and the suffer-in-silence types. Rarely are we given the airtime to flip our lids when something enrages us. And I'm not just talking about the kind of meltdowns attributed to white cisgendered women whose ne'er-ceasing racist anti-Black violence has become so widely recognized as par for the course that they are referred to by the infamous sobriquet "Karen." There's the Central Park dog-walker Karen who screams hysterically into the phone to the police about the mere presence of a Black man near her, his mere existence a perceived threat to her safety. There's the Karen who blocks two men of color from trying to get into their own garage as they wave their keycard in front of her. There's the rich Karen who calls the cops on the Black man trying to get into his own apartment. There's the old Karen shouting racial slurs at the young Asian American woman attempting to exercise in a public park. There are so many more incidents like this that they have created an archetype of the racist white woman crying wolf over perceived threats of violence, usually by Black men, so many that "to be a Karen" has morphed into a caricature that can blind us to the actual violence meted out by their false claims of victimhood. Many of us would prefer to hide ourselves behind the laughter that these images elicit as a sign of our indignation, akin to putting up Black Lives Matter signs on our front lawns as if to say, "we're one of the good ones."

What fascinates, repulses, and infuriates me simultaneously about the Karens' behavior is the safety and privilege these women reflect in their bold-faced racist violence. They can vocalize, embody, and enact their racist rage without provocation and without fear of serious repercussions; they do not fear death when they unleash the racist monsters within them. Instead, they are protected from the violence they mete out on bodies of color by claiming self-defense, by invoking the fragility of their white femaleness that relies upon tears as a symbol of authentic fear, and by and large, they are let off the hook. White women like Patricia McCloskey can stand upon their fancy lawns in St. Louis casually aiming handguns at peaceful protestors with the same ease that they loosely grasped their martini glass at yesterday's evening soiree. Hell, Patricia could even aim a gun in public with barely any consequences. Her outrage and violent threat against Black Lives Matter protestors merely resulted in a $2,000 fine, a guilty plea to second-degree harassment, and a presidential pardon.

White supremacist culture has created the image of the angry white woman embodying her indignation with every phone call to the police, every power stance she takes in front of cars trying to get into their rightful parking spots, every finger wag against people of color for simply existing, and this troubling history of white womanhood weaponizing their fragility goes way back. But today it has become a meme, an image, and an icon of the Karen with the bad hair, the talk-to-the-manager mom, the anti-vaxxer mom refusing to wear a mask, insinuating her fancy sweat-suited self into restaurants, bars, and shops. As a meme, Karen becomes the protective force that we can invoke against our own racism, so long as we remember to roll our eyes and repost the latest iteration of her bad behavior.

Though I loathe and disavow the kinds of violence and rage expressed by these white women, I have to say that I sometimes fantasize about what it would be like to feel so entitled and privileged that I could push myself into spaces where I am not welcome. I do not harbor any desires to call the police and play victim to some concocted fear, but I do wonder what it must feel like to act without fear of serious consequence. Now again, don't get me wrong, I don't want to unleash hell on some unsuspecting innocent person out in public. I fantasize more about mustering up the entitlement and fearless privilege of no longer remaining silent about all the microaggressive violence meted out on smaller playing fields like the workplace, the grocery store, or city streets.

And this is why Ali Wong's unhinged character Amy Lau in the Netflix series *Beef* left such a delicious taste in my mouth. The show opens with Daniel Cho (played by Steven Yeun) attempting to return a pile of hibachi grills that he has purchased in an attempt to kill himself through carbon monoxide poisoning. Frustrated that he can't find his store receipt, he tosses the grills back into his car, and pulls out of the hardware parking lot only to stop a hair short of hitting a pristine white Mercedes SUV. We do not yet see her face, but Amy Lau immediately hits her horn as if it is screaming out all of her pent-up collected frustrations. We only know the driver is actually a woman when she hits the gas and sticks her middle finger defiantly out the window. Amy and Daniel engage in a high-speed road rage chase through suburban California, neither willing to relent, and the scene ends gloriously with Lau speeding her car in reverse to crash into Cho's truck. She stops short of bashing into Cho's car but leaves him emotionally damaged nonetheless. Amy Lau has come undone and it is glorious. She is unapologetic, fearless, and completely out of control for all of us to witness. The incident goes viral after it is captured on security camera, and Amy Lau becomes the embodiment of Asian American female rage that I have longed to see on screen—not because I endorse violence, but because I have wanted to see angry, vengeful, loving, tired, bored, desirous Asian American female subjects on screen, and here she is, behind the wheel.

Watching Wong's performance on the heels of Michelle Yeoh's 2023 Oscar-winning multidimensional character in the metaverse in *Everything, Everywhere, All at Once* is like the anger-filled icing on the cake. Yeoh's portrayal of Evelyn Quan existing in simultaneous universes as an exhausted immigrant laundromat owner estranged from her daughter, a kung-fu master turned famous actress, and a hotdog-fingered wife in a same-sex multiracial relationship offered us an opportunity to see an Asian woman in all the complexities and messiness of everyday life. We are not all the calm, docile, gentle Buddhists that many white practitioners have made us out to be. While viewers got to see parts of themselves in each of the universes that contain parts of Evelyn Quan, in *Beef*, we do not have to travel to other worlds to glimpse the parts of ourselves we haven't yet seen on screen. Instead, we get the satisfaction of watching Amy Lau do and undo it all as a mother, wife, entrepreneur, and road-rager gone off the deep end.

I admit somewhat sheepishly that I am quite joyful of these images on screen despite the Buddha's encouragement to refrain from harmful acts of rage. Like many of my Asian American friends, I was glued to the screen, binge-watching to my heart's content as an Asian American woman comes undone. It was such a rare moment of Asian American female rage that even Amy's humorously New Age Buddhist husband finds her reactions unintelligible. We remain the Model Minority, constructed in the public eye as selfless, self-sacrificing, family-oriented, economically privileged, perpetual foreigners who, unlike the Karens, are not supposed to get angry (we are Buddhists after all!), or at least we're not supposed to show our anger, our indignation, and our irritation at the limits and limitations of whiteness. When Asian women do express opinions and defy the submissive lotus-flower stereotypes constructed by whiteness, they are usually punished, cast as dragon ladies, and scapegoated as the downfall of men—but not Amy Lau.

In America's racial imaginary, Asian American women are not allowed to be real women with genuine feelings of hurt, rage, and pain; instead, we are to continue to be calm, amenable, docile sexual objects. Our agency and subjectivity are rendered invisible when we become inconvenient and emotionally excessive, or we become hypervisible as perpetual foreigners and embodiments of contagion and fear; we have been a necessary evil in the American imagination—cheap labor to fulfill the fantasies of American exceptionalism yet dispensable when convenient.

Beef's Amy Lau is the angry Asian American female character I didn't know I was waiting for. She is not "one of the good ones." She craves money, success, a non-vanilla sex life, and revenge, no matter the cost. She's pushed to the edge, pissed off, doubts her mothering skills, barely contains her disdain for her mother-in-law, screams and seethes into the phone, and embodies the rage I have always fantasized about unleashing. She's not taking the racism and sexism peppered throughout the series, with her husband's claims that she comes across as cold and unhinged and her future boss's fetishization of her as a fount of Buddhist calm. She is not a Karen, but an Amy, whose time has come to join the ranks of the out-of-control woman. As a Buddhist vegan, I was ready to consume more *Beef*. Sadly though, at the time of writing this essay, it seems that Amy Lau's rage is no longer to be consumed in the show's next season.

Since the emergence of Covid-19, Asian and Asian Americans have become ever more visible in the public eye as the scapegoats for the virus itself. Racially motivated attacks in shopping centers, buses, and even broad daylight have become the norm as more and more Asian and Asian American women have been beaten, slashed, and killed. The equation of Asian and Asian American bodies with illness, disease, and plague is nothing new. In 1899 Chinese American bodies were blamed for the bubonic plague outbreaks and Chinatowns were quarantined. In the 1940s, Asian bodies were blamed for tuberculosis, and the racial stereotypes of Chinese immigrants as the Yellow Peril still invoked fear and hysteria as Japanese Americans were incarcerated during WWII. While not explicitly associated with physical contagion, the incarcerated Japanese Americans were envisioned as a symbolic viral threat to the nation-state. In 2003, mass hysteria and anti-Chinese rhetoric reared its head around SARS, or what comedian Margaret Cho brilliantly referred to as "Severe Asian Racism Syndrome." And most recently, it is Covid-19, or what the recently reelected Trump referred to as the "Kung flu," used to stir up the ever-present anti-Asian racism that has persisted in the United States since the 1860s when Asian bodies were labeled as pollutants sullying the image of a pristine white American West. Our hypervisibility is deeply tied to the ever-evolving racial politics of this country desperate to forever skew white despite what the demographers prognosticate.

We are a projected image and a fantasy. We come into view only when it serves white supremacy, but we are served up as the counter-example, the false proof of America's narrative of hard work and industriousness as the key ingredients for economic and social success. We serve as the visual model in America's myopic vision of itself as a land of plenty and, like many minoritized communities in this country, we are experiencing ever-increasing levels of race-based trauma, which I do not see changing in this latest reiteration of "democracy" with the reelection of Trump. Cathy Park Hong reminds us, "In the popular imagination, Asian Americans inhabit a vague purgatorial status: not white enough nor Black enough; distrusted by African Americans, ignored by whites, unless we're being used by whites to keep the Black man down."[9]

In the illogical logic of white supremacy, Asian Americans have become collateral damage, which has become ever more apparent in the aftermath of the pandemic that barely registers the impact of race-based violence against Asians and Asian Americans. Min Jin Lee's tweet following the 2021 Atlanta shooting of eight victims (six were Asian American women) summarizes the collective trauma created by hypervisibility and hyperinvisibility. She laments, "Our bodies are not designed to absorb and process this much violence, loss, and grief."[10] How many Asian American women need to be shot in spas, pushed into oncoming subways, beaten in broad daylight, and followed and murdered in front of their own apartments before we will have the adequate support to be safe?

Like all minoritized people, Asian Americans have become habituated to the daily effects of oppression and violence in public and private spaces that often compromise our integrity. This habituation comes at a cost. In *Restorative Yoga for Ethnic and Race-Based Stress and Trauma*, Gail Parker notes that "Racial stress is a cumulative experience that is often magnified by lack of opportunity to recover before the next experience, causing it to be chronic."[11] Racism carries physiological and psychological effects that cause lasting scars that render our bodies vulnerable. By practicing embodied mindfulness through restorative yoga and trauma-informed yoga, I have learned to experience pockets of parasympathetic rest by slowing my heart rate, metabolic rate, and breath. Through restorative yoga practices, where my body relearns radical rest, I can lower my blood pressure, slow my brain waves, and allow myself to recover before the next trigger. Reading my body's cues through mindfulness techniques that remind me to deeply listen to its felt sensations and to know when anger, fear, or sadness are present has made a world of difference. But this deep listening also required a move toward intentional care for my body so that it could learn how to rest and come back to a sense of safety. Restorative yoga's emphasis on radical rest, where my body is effortlessly supported on cushions, bolsters, and blocks, has also been a powerful antidote to the hustle culture that makes our worthiness contingent upon how much we are doing.

A practice that invites me back into my body as a haven and refuge has been a profound act of positive self-regard and self-love that many Asian Americans are still uncomfortable acknowledging. But learning to care for the self and explicitly cultivate self-love are not shameful selfish acts. They are survival skills that also help us thrive.

Learning to practice self-care and self-love has meant deeply listening to the anger and rage that I have suppressed for fear of retaliation for as long as I can remember. It means trusting my gut when it tells me that I am in an unhealthy and emotionally abusive relationship. It means loving myself enough to walk away from my second marriage of just shy of three years to become a twice-divorced woman. It means forgiving myself with compassion, allowing myself to say, "Oops, I did it again," and no longer remaining in a relationship out of fear of what others will say. An Asian American feminist

Buddhist ethic of self-love also means being willing to break from shame culture, stigmatization, and the Model Minority stereotype in order to experience liberation. It also means being a willful single mother in my fifth decade who is willing to wade through the fear, delusion, and anxiety that can come from choosing to be alone.

My Asian American feminist Buddhist ethic of self-love also means that I embrace myself as a bad Buddhist who skips meditation practice often, who sometimes spends hours zoning out on Netflix, who doom scrolls, and who has an affinity for fashionable boots, jackets, and handbags. In *All About Love: New Visions*, bell hooks articulates a self-love that is a process of self-recovery based in truth-seeing and telling. She writes, "When we see ourselves as we truly are and accept ourselves, we build the necessary foundation for self-love."[11] But, she counsels, we cannot do this alone. For hooks, love is "the action we take on behalf of our own or another's spiritual growth," and when we see love as "a combination of trust, commitment, care, respect, knowledge, and responsibility," we can learn to direct this love to ourselves.[12] In other words, the ability to cultivate self-love is dependent on our capacity to love others in a generative, capacious, healthy manner. For this Asian American feminist, Buddhism is about liberating ourselves from systems of domination and cycles of trauma that requires a deliberate and thoughtful process of self-care and self-love. Self-care and self-love are not the result of self-conceit or excessive self-centeredness, which Asian American families and Western Buddhists so readily proclaim. They are the result of an ethics of care that requires abandoning our cultural propensity to self-silence, practicing techniques that keep us from dissociating from our wise bodies, acknowledging our anger and rage, and affirming our inherent worth and value. An Asian American feminist Buddhist ethics of self-love is therefore foundational to collective healing and liberation.

CONCLUSION

While guided by the spirit of the feminist killjoy, this book is also motivated by love, a topic undertheorized in Asian American cultures because it is often equated with loyalty, whose foundation is often about power and domination. In *All About Love: New Visions,* bell hooks explains that love cannot exist in dominator culture which is premised on power relationships. That is, love and domination are mutually exclusive. Love is a verb and a process that involves both self-love and the connection of the self to the other in a perpetual drawing toward the other. I am inspired to conclude this volume by foregrounding love and self-love because many of us were not explicitly taught to love ourselves in our own families and in our own communities. Instead, we often mistook love for obligation. The Asian American notions of love that are given voice tend toward proxies of expressing true love. In fact, many of us joke and balk at using the words "I love you" in Asian and Asian American cultures, as if the phrase itself were a misguided and frivolous energy. How many of us lament that we did not hear the words "I love you" from our parents' mouths; instead, love was expressed through feeding us and stories of self-sacrifice. But, if, as hooks writes, love is a verb *and* an action, and love can end domination, why are Asian Americans so afraid to talk about it and express it verbally? Talking about love is, after all, a speech act, and yet in Asian American cultures, it is a word we so rarely expect to hear from our parents. But, if we cannot expect to hear the words "I love you" from those who raise us, how can we be expected to cultivate it for ourselves?

As Asian American feminist Buddhists, can we love ourselves as fiercely as we love others? Is there an Asian American feminist Buddhist ethic of love that is not duty-bound, not based on expectations and accusations of gratitude and ingratitude? What does it mean to love the self deeply, and how do we begin to have these potent and healing conversations in our own minds, hearts, families, and communities? What kinds of love are we talking about when we are not talking about love? What is an Asian American Buddhist ethic of love? Is it just *mettā* (lovingkindness) and *karunā* (compassion)or is there something more? Do Confucian values of filial piety and duty blunt our ability to love outside of the scripts of affinity, obligation? Is love really about obligation to the other? Is obligation really liberatory?

hooks suggests that we often misconstrue love by experiencing it through the lens of woundedness or loss, but perhaps Buddhist teachings can help us transform this sense of loss by bearing witness to our brokenheartedness and encouraging us to cultivate self-love. hooks's meditation on love recognizes that we may not have been raised in a loving way and that we are perhaps unfamiliar with a love that is unconditional, non-transactional, and liberatory. Yet, as the authors in this anthology attest, Buddhism and the Buddhadharma have the power to liberate us from our traumatic experiences and our mis-translations of love as something we are obligated to give to others through our own self-sacrifice. The Buddhadharma can, in fact, teach us to love our Asian American selves, despite our cultural hesitance to focus on self-love. The desire for self-love is a spiritual impulse for healing and resilience and becomes the training ground and seat of liberation.

In the ever-emergent sangha woven together throughout this book, self-love is not an indulgence or a private act of self-care, but the essential ground from which our collective liberation arises. In a culture that demands our erasure and extracts our compliance and our silence, practicing self-love as Asian American feminist Buddhists is an act of resistance and reclamation. It is the radical turning toward ourselves internally and toward community with our bodies, our rage, our joy, our imperfect humanity, with tenderness and compassion, that inspires this Asian American feminist Buddhist killjoy spirit. This act of deep care of the self and other-as-self is not a rejection of Buddhist understandings of no self; rather, it is a clarification and adaptation reminding us that the self is relational, contingent, and fluid. To practice self-love from an Asian American feminist Buddhist perspective is to honor our embodied experience as worthy of attention and deep care. An Asian Ameri-can feminist Buddhist ethic of self-love embodies the practice of non-harming of self and other and is a refusal to participate in our own diminishment and continued invisibility. In this way, self-love is not only compatible with the Buddhist path but a necessary ground for awakening. It is how we cultivate the resilience and tenderness to show up for ourselves and for others in this ever-evolving and ever-more-needed collective struggle for liberation.

NOTES

Introduction

1 adrienne maree brown, *Emergent Strategy: Shaping Change, Changing Worlds* (AK Press, 2017), 3.

2 brown, *Emergent Strategy*, 9.

3 brown, *Emergent Strategy*, 13.

4 bell hooks, *Feminist Theory: From Margin to Center* (South End Press, 1984), 31.

5 George Yancey, *On Race: 34 Conversations in a Time of Crisis* (New York: Oxford University Press, 2017), 15.

6 bell hooks, *remembered rapture: the writer at work* (Henry Holt and Company, 1999), 7.

7 Roxane Gay, *Bad Feminist: Essays* (Harper Perennial, 2014), xi.

8 Gay, *Bad Feminist*, xi.

9 Gay, *Bad Feminist*, xii.

10 Sara Ahmed, *The Feminist Killjoy Handbook: The Radical Potential of Getting in the Way* (Penguin Random House, 2023), 16.

11 Ahmed, *Feminist Killjoy Handbook*, 20.

12 Ahmed, *Feminist Killjoy Handbook*, 18.

13 Ahmed, *Feminist Killjoy Handbook*, 38.

14 Ahmed, *Feminist Killjoy Handbook*, 268.

15 Ahmed, *Feminist Killjoy Handbook*, 137.

Chapter 1 (Han)

1 Special thanks to Trent Walker for editorial acumen, and for the *Karaṇīyamet-ta-sutta* translation.

2 Grace M. Cho, *Haunting the Korean Diaspora: Shame, Secrecy, and the Forgotten War* (University of Minnesota Press, 2008), 1.

3 Maxine Hong Kingston, *The Woman Warrior: Memoirs of a Girlhood Among Ghosts* (1975; Vintage International, 1989), 3.

4 James Baldwin, *Notes of a Native Son*, revised ed. (1955; Beacon Press, 2012), 103.

5 Daniel Kwan and Daniel Scheinert (dir.), *Everything Everywhere All At Once* (A24, 2022).

6 Cho, *Haunting the Korean Diaspora*, 2.

7 Grace M. Cho, *Tastes like War: A Memoir* (The Feminist Press at the City University of New York, 2021), 13.

8 Cho, *Tastes like War*, 70–71.

9 r/AsianParentStories, www.reddit.com/r/AsianParentStories/.

10 "Asking for Mother's Forgiveness," in *Until Nirvana's Time: Buddhist Songs from Cambodia*, Trent Walker (Shambhala, 2022), 83–84.

11 "Filial Debts," in Walker, *Until Nirvana's Time*, 81–82.

12 "Recollection of the Virtue of Parents" (AN I 62), in *The Numerical Discourses of the Buddha: A Translation of the Aṅguttara Nikāya*, trans. Bhikkhu Bodhi (Wisdom Publications, 2012), 153.

13 Billy Collins, "The Lanyard," *The Poetry Foundation*, 2005, www.poetryfoundation.org/poems/50975/the-lanyard.

14 Putsata Reang, *Ma and Me: A Memoir* (MCD Farrar, Straus and Giroux, 2022).

15 The phrase "price of rice and milk" is from Grégory Kourilsky, "Filial Piety: Shades of Difference across Theravādin Traditions," in *Routledge Handbook of Theravāda Buddhism*, eds. Stephen C. Berkwitz and Ashley Thompson (Routledge, 2022), 164.

16 "Discourse on Maternal Debts," from Trent Walker, "Liquid Language: The Art of Bitextual Sermons in Middle Cambodia," *Journal of Indian Philosophy* 50, no. 4 (September 2022): 719.

17 "Struggling with the Teaching of Karmic Debt Toward One's Parents," r/Buddhism (2023), www.reddit.com/r/Buddhism/comments/13n1llv/struggling_with_the_teaching_of_karmic_debt/.

18 Reiko Ohnuma, "Debt to the Mother: A Neglected Aspect of the Founding of the Buddhist Nuns' Order," *Journal of the American Academy of Religion* 74, no. 4 (2006): 882.

19 Ohnuma, "Debt to the Mother," 879–880.

20 Ohnuma, "Debt to the Mother," 886.

21 Ohnuma, "Debt to the Mother," 890.

22 Ohnuma, "Debt to the Mother," 891.

23 "Struggling with the Teaching of Karmic Debt."

24 Sam [erin Khuê Ninh], *Ask a Model Minority Suicide* (blog), *Hyphen,* https://hyphenmagazine.com/contributors/ask-model-minority-suicide.

25 erin Khuê Ninh, *Ingratitude: The Debt-Bound Daughter in Asian American Literature* (New York University Press, 2011).

26 erin Khuê Ninh, *Passing for Perfect: College Impostors and Other Model Minorities* (Temple University Press, 2021).

27 Sam [erin Khuê Ninh], "Ask a Model Minority Suicide: Hello," *Ask a Model Minority Suicide* (blog), *Hyphen,* November 11, 2010. https://hyphenmagazine.com/blog/2010/11/ask-model-minority-suicide-hello.

28 Kingston, *Woman Warrior,* 45.

29 "Struggling with the Teaching of Karmic Debt."

30 Kingston, *Woman Warrior,* 29.

31 Erik W. Davis, "Kinship Beyond Death: Ambiguous Relations and Autonomous Children in Cambodian Buddhism," *Contemporary Buddhism* 16, no. 1 (January 2, 2015): 3.

32 Thích Nhất Hạnh, "A Rose for Your Pocket," *Thich Nhat Hanh Foundation: Planting Seeds of Compassion,* November 9, 2018 (originally published in 1962), https://thichnhathanhfoundation.org/blog/2018/5/9/a-rose-for-your-pocket.

33 Reang, *Ma and Me,* 12.

34 Putsata Reang, "At Sea, and Seeking a Safe Harbor," *New York Times,* July 15, 2016, www.nytimes.com/2016/07/17/fashion/modern-love-bisexuality-cambodia.html.

35 Trent Walker, "Voicing Gratitude in Verse: Genre, Affect, and Orality in Buddhist Poems on Filial Piety from Central and Northeast Thailand," paper delivered at the Debt and the Family Across Buddhist Communities panel, Buddhism Unit, American Academy of Religion, San Antonio, November 2023).

36 Bhikkhu Sujato, "Sedakasutta (SN 47.19)," SuttaCentral, accessed August 28, 2024, https://suttacentral.net/sn47.19/en/sujato.

37 Tsering Wangmo Dhompa, *Coming Home to Tibet: A Memoir of Love, Loss, and Belonging* (Shambhala, 2016), 212.

38 Dhompa, *Coming Home to Tibet,* 213.

Chapter 2 (Hsu/Chhî)

1 A+ Po (phonetically "ah po") is the Taiwanese Hailu Hakka romanization for maternal grandmother. In addition to Taiwanese Hakka, I also use Taiwanese Hokkien and Mandarin in this chapter.

Chapter 3 (Iwamura)

1 See Gwendolyn Gillson, "Traversing the Nenbutsu: The Power of Ritual in Contemporary Japanese Buddhism," *Japanese Journal of Religious Studies* 46, no. 1 (2019): 31+; and Rev. Yozo Taniyama and Carl B. Becker, "Religious Care by Zen Buddhist Monks: A Response to Criticism of 'Funeral Buddhism,'" *Journal of Religion & Spirituality in Social Work: Social Thought* 33, no. 1 (2014): 51–52.

2 Ken Tanaka, *Parents Sharing the Nembutsu Teachings with Their Young Children* (San Francisco: Buddhist Churches of America, 1995), 20.

3 Dennis Klass, "Continuing Bonds in the Resolution of Grief in Japan and North America," *American Behavioral Scientist* 44, no. 5 (2001): 752–53; Paula Arai, *Bringing Zen Home: The Healing Heart of Japanese Women's Rituals* (University of Hawai'i Press, 2011); Gillson, "Traversing the Nenbutsu."

4 Arai, *Bringing Zen Home*, 81.

5 "Carol Gilligan," interview, Ethics of Care: Sharing Views on Good Care, June 21, 2011, https://ethicsofcare.org/carol-gilligan/. For further reference, see Carol Gilligan, *In a Different Voice: Psychological Theory and Women's Development* (Harvard University Press, 1982); and Nel Noddings, *Caring: A Feminine Approach to Ethics and Moral Education* (University of California Press, 1984).

6 "Carol Gilligan," interview.

7 *Mattōshō* 7 and 18, *Shinran chosaku zenshū,*. ed. Kaneko Daiei (Hozokan, 1964), 590, 608, quoted in Jacqueline I. Stone, "Shinran's Rejection of Deathbed Rites," in *Chūsei bunka to Jōdo Shinshū* 中世文化と浄土真宗, ed. Imai Masaharu Sensei Koki Kinen Ronbunshū Henshū Iinkai 今井雅晴先生古稀記念論文集編集委員会 (Shibunkaku, 2012), 602.

8 Ken Yamada, "Deathbed Rituals and Jodo Shinshu," Higashi Honganji USA, January 17, 2023, https://higashihonganjiusa.org/2023/01/17/deathbed-rituals-and-shinran/.

9 John W. Traphagan, *The Practice of Concern: Ritual, Well-Being, and Aging in Rural Japan* (Carolina Academic Press, 2004), 81. See also Dennis Klass, "Continuing Bonds in the Resolution of Grief in Japan and North America," *American Behavioral Scientist* 44, no. 5 (2001): 749–50.

10 The 2023 Pew Research Center Survey, "Religion Among Asian Americans," reports that although only 19 percent of Japanese Americans identify as Buddhists, 62 percent "express some connection with Buddhism." Pew Research Center,

"Religion Among Asian Americans," *Pew Research Center*, October 11, 2023, www.pewresearch.org/religion/2023/10/11/religion-among-asian-americans/.

11 Traphagan, *The Practice of Concern*, 81.

Chapter 4 (Tillakaratne)

1 See Sara Ahmed, *Strange Encounters: Embodied Others in Post-Coloniality* (Routledge, 2000).

2 See "Reimagining Diaspora Dharma: Asian American Buddhists Shaping Identities and Creating Communities," Asian American Buddhist Working Group, Summer 2023, https://web.archive.org/web/20240508171754/https://drive.google.com/file/d/1_zyk1BIzTl6g7q8vrANoDL9iLghWM5t8/view.

3 Sara Ahmed, Claudia Castañeda, Anne-Marie Fortier, and Mimi Sheller, *Uprootings/Regroundings: Questions of Home and Migration* (Berg, 2003), 9.

4 Jack Halberstam, *The Queer Art of Failure* (Duke University Press, 2011), 9.

5 Mihiri Tillakaratne, "Feelin' Diasporic: Embodied Memory in Sri Lankan America" (PhD diss., UC Berkeley, 2023).

6 See Purnima Mankekar, *Unsettling India: Affect, Temporality, Transnationality* (Duke University Press, 2015), 89–90.

7 Mihiri Tillakaratne, "Feelin' Diasporic," 103.

8 See Mihiri Tillakaratne and Arisika Razak, "Embodying Loving-Kindness with Arisika Razak," *Lion's Roar* (podcast), Episode 129, June 1, 2024, www.lionsroar.com/podcast/129-arisika-razak-loving-kindness/.

9 Kareem Khubchandani, "Critical Aunty Studies: An Auntroduction," *Text and Performance Quarterly* 42, no. 3 (June 2022): 221–45.

10 Mihiri Tillakaratne, "Spilling the Tea: Aunty Discipline and the Queer Diasporic Child in D'Lo's To T, or Not To T?," *South Asia: Journal of South Asian Studies* 46, no. 1 (2023): 152–69, https://doi.org/10.1080/00856401.2023.2162238.

11 See Patricia J. Sotirin and Laura L. Ellingson, *Where the Aunts Are: Family, Feminism, and Kinship in Popular Culture* (Baylor University Press, 2013).

12 Khubchandani, "Critical Aunty Studies," 221–45.

13 See Layla F. Saad, *Me and White Supremacy: Combat Racism, Change the World, and Become a Good Ancestor* (Sourcebooks, 2020). See also Layla F. Saad, *Good Ancestor* (podcast), accessed March 23, 2025, http://laylafsaad.com/good-ancestor-podcast.

14 Tillakaratne, "Spilling the Tea," 11.

15 See Lee Edelman, *No Future: Queer Theory and the Death Drive* (Duke University Press, 2004).

16 See Mai-Linh K. Hong, Chrissy Yee Lau, and Preeti Sharma, *The Auntie Sewing Squad Guide to Mask Making, Radical Care, and Racial Justice* (University of California Press, 2021).

17 Sara Ahmed, *What's the Use? On the Uses of Use* (Duke University Press, 2019), 228.

18 Laura Nichols, "Social Desire Paths: A New Theoretical Concept to Increase the Usability of Social Research in Society," *Theory and Society* 43, no. 6 (2014): 658.

19 Naomi Smith and Peter Walters, "Desire Lines and Defensive Architecture in Modern Urban Environments," *Urban Studies* 55, no. 4 (October 2017): 2987.

20 Laura Nichols, "Social Desire Paths: An Applied Sociology of Interests," *Social Currents* 1, no. 2 (2014): 168.

21 Monisha Das Gupta, *Unruly Immigrants: Rights, Activism, and Transnational South Asian Politics in the United States* (Duke University Press, 2006), 61.

22 See Mihiri Tillakaratne, "I'm the Aunty Now!," *Lion's Roar*, March 4, 2024, 19–22.

23 See Nalika Gajaweera, "Buddhadharma: Reclaiming Our So-Called 'Cultural Baggage,'" Center for Religion and Civic Culture, University of Southern California, December 3, 2021.

24 Nichols, "Social Desire Paths: Applied Sociology of Interests," 168; Laura Nichols, "Social Desire Paths: A New Theoretical Concept to Increase the Usability of Social Science Research in Society," *Theory and Society* 43, no. 6 (November 2014): 658.

25 Smith and Walters, "Desire Lines and Defensive Architecture," 2987.

26 Rachel Fendler, "Desire Paths: A Reflection with Preservice Students in the Eventful Space of Learning," *Studies in Art Education* 60, no. 4 (2019): 275–86, www.doi.org/10.1080/00393541.2019.1669132, 279-280.

27 Smith and Walters, "Desire Lines and Defensive Architecture," 2991.

28 Bhante Walpola Piyananda, *Sharing Buddhism in the Western World* (Metta From Us, 2018), 39.

29 Piyananda, *Sharing Buddhism*, 46.

30 Fendler, "Desire Paths," 277.

31 Fendler, "Desire Paths," 279.

32 Fendler, "Desire Paths," 279.

Chapter 7 (Kasumi)

1 Douglas Eby, "Alchemy of Art: How Creative Expression Transforms Pain,"
   Creativity Portal Author Series, January 24, 2006, www.creativity-portal.com
   /bc/douglas.eby/alchemy.art.html.

2 The terms *catharsis* and *cathartic* originate from the Greek word *kathairein*,
   which means "to cleanse" or "to purge." Initially, *catharsis* entered the English
   language as a medical term related to the purging of the body, particularly
   the bowels, of unwanted substances. Correspondingly, the adjective *cathartic*
   described this process of physical cleansing. Over time, these terms evolved to be
   used metaphorically, referring to releasing emotional tension and attaining spiritual purification. www.merriam-webster.com/dictionary/cathartic.

3 Vivian Manning-Schaffel, "Why Art Can Offer Us Catharsis and Healing," *Shonda-
   land*, December 30, 2021, www.vivianmanningschaffel.com/blog/2021/12/30
   /why-art-can-offer-us-catharsis-and-healing.

4 Zara Abrams, "The Facts About Abortion and Mental Health," *American Psychological Association* 53, no. 6 (2022): 40.

5 Naomi Kasumi, "Personal Diary," 1998. Unpublished.

6 Eby, "Alchemy of Art."

7 Roxanne Chinook, "Healing & Art," accessed March 25, 2025, https://talent
   develop.com/healing.html.

8 Gary L. Chamberlain, "Learning from the Japanese (Pro-Life Rituals in Buddhism an Shinto)," *America Magazine: The Jesuit Review of Faith and Culture* 171,
   no. 7 (September 17, 1994): 14–16.

9 Tony Law and Peggy Orenstein, "Mourning My Miscarriage: When the Author's
   Pregnancy Ended in Japan, Thousands of Miles from Home, She Discovered a
   Culture Willing to Acknowledge Her Loss," *New York Times Magazine*, April 21,
   2002, 38.

10 Law and Orenstein, "Mourning My Miscarriage," 40.

11 Law and Orenstein, "Mourning My Miscarriage," 40.

12 William R. LaFleur, *Liquid Life: Abortion and Buddhism in Japan* (Princeton
   University Press, 1992).

13 LaFleur, *Liquid Life*.

14 Tazeen Ahmad, "Religious Trends in Japan—Non-Religious in a Religious Culture," *The Review of Religions*, April 21, 2014, www.reviewofreligions.org/10609
   /religious-trends-in-japan-non-religious-in-a-religious-culture-2/.

Chapter 8

1 I use Burma and Myanmar interchangeably, although I prefer Burmese and Burma and reserve Myanmar to refer to the post-1989 nation-state and more recent diaspora (immigrants and refugees who were born or migrated after 1989). "In the Burmese language, 'Myanmar' is simply the more formal version of 'Burma.' The country's name was changed only in English. It was linguistic sleight-of-hand," Kim Tong-Hyung, "Myanmar, Burma and Why the Different Names Matter," Associated Press/PBS News, Feb 3, 2021. www.pbs.org /newshour/world/myanmar-burma-and-why-the-different-names-matter.

2 Since 1962, postcolonial Burma/Myanmar has been ruled primarily by a series of corrupt militarized dictatorships, which have instituted xenophobic, genocidal campaigns displacing Christian, animist, and Islamic populations within the nation. Asia Centre reports, "Burmanisation is a system whereby Bamar-dominated governments and junta regimes force members of ethnic minority groups in Myanmar to relinquish their ethnic identities such as culture, language and religion and, instead, adopt the dominant Bamar culture." Asia Centre, "Burmanisation and Buddhisation: Accelerating the Decline of Religious Rights in Myanmar," Asia Centre, June 2023, 1, https://asiacentre.org/wp -content/uploads/Burmanisation-and-Buddhisation-Accelerating-the-Decline -of-Religious-Rights-in-Myanmar.pdf. "The promotion of Burmanisation and Buddhisation to ensure the dominance of the Bamar culture and Buddhist religion, respectively, are not new policies and have been used widely by past governments. However, the application of these policies post-coup as a response to the junta-defined national security and terrorism threats has had severe con-sequences for ethno-religious minorities," James Gomez, "Acknowledgements" in "Burmanisation and Buddhisation." Lian H. Sakhong, "The Dynamics of Sixty Years of Ethnic Armed Conflict in Burma" (Analysis Paper No. 1), Burma Center for Ethnic Studies: Peace and Reconciliation, January 2012, www.burmalibrary .org/docs13/BCES-AP-01-dynamics(en).pdf.

3 David Moe describes Buddhist nationalism in Myanmar as *lumyo-gyi wada*, or the "domination of the majority race"; he explains its ethnoreligious dimensions: "leaders promoted Burmese as the national language at the expense of ethnic minority languages, nationalized Buddhism as the state religion, and privileged the Bamar majority Buddhists." Angela Lu Fulton, "The Christians Living Under Buddhist Nationalism" (Interview with David Moe), *Christianity Today*, October 29, 2024, www.christianitytoday.com/2024/10

/myanmar-christian-ethnic-minority-church-buddhist-nationalism/; Khen Suan Khai, "A Threatened Identity in Chinland of Burma/Myanmar: A Glimpse of Freedom of Religion and Belief," in *Myanmar's Changing Political Landscape*, eds. Makiko Takeda and Chosein Yamahata (Springer, 2023), https://doi.org /10.1007/978-981-19-9357-2_5.

4 Khen Suan Khai, "Threatened Identity," 2023.

5 Hannah Beech, "The Face of Buddhist Terror," *Time*, July 1, 2013, https://time .com/archive/6643742/the-face-of-buddhist-terror/. The cover of *Time* magazine and Beech's titular story, which circulated in Europe, Asia, and the Middle East, spotlighted Ashin Wirathu, a Burmese Buddhist monk who cofounded the "Organisation for the Protection of Race, Religion, and Belief," translated as "the Patriotic Association of Myanmar," and commonly abbreviated as "MaBaTha." Wirathu has been a leader in the anti-Muslim nationalist movement in Myanmar known as "969." Journalist Hannah Beech characterized the ultranationalist monk as "the Burmese bin Laden."

6 Jane Naomi Iwamura, *Virtual Orientalism: Asian Religions and American Popular Culture* (Oxford University Press, 2011); and Sharon A. Suh, *Silver Screen Buddha: Buddhism in Asian and Western Film* (Bloomsbury Publishing, 2015).

7 Thi Bui, *The Best We Could Do: An Illustrated Memoir* (Abrams ComicArts, 2018), 305.

8 Bui, *The Best We Could Do*, 305.

9 The Immigration and Nationality Act of 1965, or the Hart-Celler Act, established an immigration policy that overturned national-origin quotas that favored Western and Northern Europe and focused on attracting skilled workers to the US and reuniting immigrant families. Settler-colonial mapping refers to the mountain as "Mt. Baldy," the town as "Upland," and the area is known colloquially as "the Inland Empire" (also IE or "Inlandia"). Tovaangar is the world of the Tongva, the original peoples of Greater Los Angeles; Tongva settlements extended from Palos Verdes to San Bernardino, from Saddleback Mountain to the San Fernando Valley. Sean Greene and Thomas Curwen, "Mapping the Tongva Villages of L.A.'s Past," *Los Angeles Times*, May 9, 2019, www.latimes.com /projects/la-me-tongva-map/.

10 National races include Bama/Bamar/Burman, Karen (Kayin), Chin, Shan, Kachin, Kayah, Mon, and Rakhine. Those of Chinese and Indian ancestry who may have been living in Burma since the British colonial period and the Muslim population known as the Rohingya are excluded as "non-indigenous" populations; are considered outsiders, foreign, or latecomers; and are thus restricted

from full citizenship within Myanmar. Since 1982, there has been a "tiered system with differential eligibility, rights, and application procedures" restricting citizenship on the basis of birth, ethnicity, and religion, which "severely eroded citizenship rights of those deemed non-indigenous to Myanmar, particularly those with Chinese or South Asian forebears, creating a special legal position for 'natives.'" See Elizabeth L. Rhoads, "Citizenship Denied, Deferred and Assumed: A Legal History of Racialized Citizenship in Myanmar," *Citizenship Studies* 27, no. 1 (2022): 38–58, https://doi.org/doi:10.1080/13621025.2022.2137468.

11   Tzu Chi is "devoted to spreading Great Love in the fields of Charity, Medicine, Education, and Culture. It later expanded its work to International Relief, Bone Marrow Donation, Environmental Protection, and Community Volunteerism. Today, Tzu Chi has volunteers in 68 countries and regions, and has provided aid in more than 136 countries and regions." Tzu Chi Foundation, "History," accessed Sept 30, 2024, https://global.tzuchi.org/history.

12   "Gathas are short verses which we can recite during our daily activities to help us dwell in mindfulness." Thích Nhất Hạnh, *Present Moment Wonderful Moment: Mindfulness Verses for Daily Living* (Parallax Press, 2006), 1. See also Thích Nhất Hạnh, "Memories from the Root Temple: Washing Dishes," Plum Village, November 13, 2018, https://plumvillage.org/articles/memories-from -the-root-temple-washing-dishes.

13   Known as the cradle of Truc Lam Zen Sect, Mt. Yến Tự (Yen Tu Mountain) is a celebrated historical site for the development of Buddhism in Northeastern Việt Nam since the fourteenth century.

14   Euripides dramatized the myth of Medea in ancient Greece. Margaret Garner was a pregnant African American woman who ran from enslavement in 1856 with her husband and four children. When captured, she had murdered one of her children, wounded the others, and attempted suicide rather than return to the brutality of enslavement. Listed in the 1850 Slave Census as an "unnamed mulatto" and property in Kentucky, Garner's story was embraced by nineteenth-century abolitionists; Frances Ellen Watkins wrote about her in the poem "The Slave Mother: A Tale of the Ohio." Toni Morrison's novel *Beloved* (1987) brought twentieth-century awareness of Garner and the history of enslaved African American women/mothers. See Angela Davis, "Racism, Birth Control, and Reproductive Rights," in *Women, Race, & Class* (1981; Knopf Doubleday, 2011), 21, 29, 205. Also, Steven Weisenburger, *Modern Medea: A Family Story of Slavery and Child Murder from the Old South* (Hill and Wang, 1998). For more about La

Llorona, the Aztec deity Cihuacōātl ("Snake-woman," associated with motherhood, fertility, infanticide, and the earth), and their significance in Chicana borderlands storytelling, see Jacqueline Doyle, "Haunting the Borderlands: La Llorona in Sandra Cisneros's 'Woman Hollering Creek,'" *Frontiers: A Journal of Women Studies* 16, no. 1 (1996): 53–70, https://doi.org/10.2307/3346922.

15 Deborah A. Miranda, "IV. Unsheathed," in *Bad Indians: A Tribal Memoir* (Heyday, 2013), 113.

16 While the monastics may eschew and refute supernatural elements as not "really" part of Buddhism, temple altars and lay practitioners from Burma/Myanmar may endorse and pursue multiple practices simultaneously. See Tamara C. Ho, "Transgender, Transgression, and Translation: A Cartography of *Nat Kadaws*: Notes on Gender and Sexuality within the Spirit Cult of Burma," *Discourse* 31, no. 3 (2009): 273–317, https://dx.doi.org/10.1353/dis.2009.a402310.

17 See Plum Village App, "Pain, Despair, and The Second Arrow | Thich Nhat Hanh," YouTube, Jan 27, 2021, www.youtube.com/watch?v=MlLvjFPtFXw.

18 Followers refer to Thích Nhất Hạnh as Thầy ("master; teacher"); any Vietnamese monk in the Mahāyāna tradition can be addressed as "Thầy."

19 During the weekend of March 12, 2022, there were global commemorative gatherings for a forty-nine-day ceremony honoring Thích Nhất Hạnh. Members of the international Plum Village sangha and communities of Engaged Buddhism convened and memorialized Thầy both in-person and online via Zoom.

20 Chenxing Han outlines how "the dominant story of Buddhism in America" is that of "two distinct and mutually isolated brands of Buddhism": *convert Buddhism*, which tends to refer to overwhelmingly white, upper-middle-class practitioners, focused on individualistic meditation, rationality, psychology, and modernist interpretations, and *heritage Buddhism*, which was originally called "ethnic" or "immigrant," often represented as "traditional," tied to immigrant communities, with devotional rituals, superstition, chanting, bowing, and merit-making activities. Han's interviews with Asian American Buddhists challenge this "two Buddhism" typology and separation. Chenxing Han, *Be the Refuge: Raising the Voices of Asian American Buddhists* (North Atlantic Books, 2021), 10.

21 Yuhang Li, *Becoming Guanyin: Artistic Devotion of Buddhist Women in Late Imperial China* (Columbia University Press, 2020), 1. Li writes that Guanyin became the most popular female deity by the Ming (1358–1644) and Qing (1644–1911) periods.

22 Li, *Becoming Guanyin*, 1–2.

23 1600s Catholics in Edo-era Japan (Kakure Kirishitan) concealed their Christianity by "disguising" statues of Mary as Kannon/Avalokiteśvara or hiding these statues within other Buddha statues; these syncretic forms are now known as "Maria Kannon" (マリア観音) or "Buddhist Madonnas." A variant of Guan Yin called Songzi, developed during the Ming dynasty (sixteenth to eighteenth centuries), emphasizes the deity's child-giving capacity and is depicted as a female figure holding a child on her hip or lap.

24 Patrick Cheng, "Kuan Yin: Espejo del Cristo queer asiático," *Religión e Incidencia Pública* 1 (2013): 135–54, www.patrickcheng.net/uploads/7/0/3/7/7037096 /kuan_yin_espejo_cristo.pdf.

25 Nhi Yến Đỗ Trần, *Budding Lotus in the West: Buddhism from an Immigrant's Feminist Perspective* (Broadleaf Books, 2024), 193, https://doi.org/10.2307 /jj.10819608.

26 "Avalokiteshvara responds to an infinitude of circumstances by acquiring new qualities, putting on new robes, and accepting new names." Kay Larson, "Who Is Avalokiteshvara?," *Lion's Roar*, November 2, 2018, www.lionsroar.com/who -is-avalokiteshvara/.

27 Chenxing Han, *Be the Refuge: Raising the Voices of Asian American Buddhists* (North Atlantic Books, 2021); May We Gather, "49 Days Ceremony: A National Buddhist Memorial Ceremony for Asian American Ancestors, accessed October 1, 2024, www.maywegather.org/49-days; Matt Naham, "'This Is What We Do to Keep Them Calm': Settlement Ends Suit Alleging Police Knee-on-Neck Restraint Caused Death of Navy Veteran in Crisis Just Months After George Floyd's Murder," *Law and Crime*, May 17, 2024, https://lawandcrime.com /lawsuit/this-is-what-we-do-to-keep-them-calm-settlement-ends-suit-alleging -police-knee-on-neck-restraint-caused-death-of-navy-veteran-in-crisis-just -months-after-george-floyds-murder/. The 2024 May We Gather ceremony included dharma talks, a peace pilgrimage, "circumambulating Antioch's former Chinatown, . . . [then] a Daoist memorial ritual and an offering of Tibetan blessing scarves at a monument marking the 'Birthplace of Antioch.'" The gathering concluded with a community reception sharing food. Mihiri Tillakaratne, "'May We Gather' Buddhist memorial and pilgrimage honors Asian American ancestors," *Lion's Roar*, March 21, 2024, www.lionsroar.com/may-we-gather-2024/.

28 The first ritual occurred in Los Angeles at a previously vandalized Buddhist temple in Little Tokyo; the second ritual took place in Antioch, California, and honored Filipino American veteran Angelo Quinto Collins (who was killed by

the local police) and others lost to racial animus. See Tillakaratne, "'May We Gather.'"

29 May We Gather 2021 convened followers from every major school of Buddhism "for what is believed to be the first time since the tradition was founded 2,500 years ago." Teresa Watanabe, "Rare Gathering of World's Vast Schools of Buddhism Offers Healing Against Racial Hate," *Los Angeles Times*, May 8, 2021, www.latimes.com/california/story/2021-05-08/rare-gathering-of-worlds-vast -schools-of-buddhism-offers-healing-against-racial-hate. Duncan Williams stated, "Today we join together to repair the racial karma of this nation, because our destinies and freedoms are intertwined." Elizabeth Dias, "Repairing Generations of Trauma, Repairing Generations of Trauma, One Lotus Flower at a Time," *New York Times*, May 5, 2021, www.nytimes.com/2021/05/05/us/asian-american -attacks-buddhism.html.

30 The 2024 ceremony "featured Buddhist leaders representing Chinese, Indian, Japanese, Khmer, Korean, Lao, Sri Lankan, Taiwanese, Thai, Tibetan, and Vietnamese Buddhist traditions, chanting and conducting rituals in multiple languages. Buddhist women leaders gave dharma talks on loving kindness, spiritual kinship, the sublime attitudes, interconnection, caste equity, compassion and collective healing, and paths to enlightenment." Tillakaratne, "'May We Gather.'"

31 The CSU system has a set of General Education (GE) course requirements that all students must pass before moving on to upper division courses in their majors and/or minors. There used to be sixty units of requirements in different categories: Basic Skills (Section A) including math, speech, writing, and critical reasoning; Natural and Physical Sciences (Section B); Arts and Humanities (Section C); Social Sciences (Section D); and Lifelong Learning (Section E). At CSUN in the 1980s, faculty from Ethnic Studies and History worked together with others across the campus to create another requirement: Comparative Cultural Studies (Section F) that included courses in Ethnic Studies, Gender and Women's Studies, Music, Anthropology, and so on. Executive Order 1100R was going to cut down and streamline GE requirements to hasten graduation and increase the four-year graduation percentage. This would have eliminated Section F; CSUN faculty, students, and staff fought and won for CSUN to keep our Section F requirement.

32 *The Epoch Times* is "one of the country's most successful and influential conservative news organizations," reports NBC News. Based in New York, *The Epoch Times* has financial and organizational ties to the Falun Gong spiritual movement.

Started by Li Hongzhi, a Chinese messianic leader who claims supernatural powers (e.g., levitation, walking through walls, seeing the future), Falun Gong (aka Falun Dafa) incorporates Buddhist and Taoist elements, personal development practices, and other beliefs. In 1999, the Chinese Communist Party banned Falun Gong as a "heretical organization," leading to widespread persecution and human rights abuses. Falun Gong practitioners established *The Epoch Times* in 2000 as a free propaganda Chinese newsletter; it expanded and became a global media outlet around 2020. The Associated Press reports that *The Epoch Times* "has become politically conservative over the years and has embraced both former President Donald Trump and various conspiracy theories." Brandy Zadrozny, "How the Conspiracy-Fueled Epoch Times Went Mainstream and Made Millions," NBC News, October 13, 2023, www.nbcnews.com/news/us-news/epoch-times-falun-gong-growth-rcna111373; Associated Press, "Epoch Times CFO Is Arrested and Accused of Role in $67M Multinational Money Laundering Scheme," *AP News*, June 3, 2024, https://apnews.com/article/epoch-times-cfo-indictment-money-laundering-caad358778bb6b73e32e9f989f3b9665.

33 According to the Pew Research Center in 2021, about a quarter of US adults (23 percent) have a parent aged sixty-five or older, and are either raising at least one child younger than 18 or providing financial support to an adult child. This number of people "sandwiched" in between care responsibilities for both younger and older family members was expected to increase in subsequent years. See also Grace J. Yoo and Barbara W. Kim, *Caring Across Generations: The Linked Lives of Korean American Families* (New York University Press, 2014).

Chapter 9 (Yang)

1 Julia Serano, "What Is a Woman? (A Response)," *Switch Hitter*, September 27, 2023, https://juliaserano.substack.com/p/what-is-a-woman-a-response.

2 The Dragon Girl is a tale of the eight-year-old daughter of the Dragon King who, upon hearing the Buddha teach, attained instantaneous enlightenment much to the shock of Sariputra:

At that time in the saha world to the bodhisattvas, voice-hearers, gods, dragons and others of the eight kinds of guardians, human and non-human beings all from a distance saw the dragon girl become a Buddha and preach the law to all the human and heavenly beings in the assembly at that time. Their hearts were filled with great joy and all from a distance paid reverent obeisance. Immeasurable living beings, hearing the Law, understood it and were able to reach the level of no regression. Immeasurable living beings received prophecies that they would gain the away. The Spotless World quaked and trembled in six different ways. Three thousand living beings of the saha world remained on the level of no regression. Three thousand living beings conceived a desire for bodhi and received prophecies of enlightenment. Bodhisattva Wisdom Accumulated, Sariputra and all the other members of the assembly silently believed and accepted these things. ("The Lotus Sutra," in Devadatta, ch. 12, trans. Burton Watson, accessed March 26, 2025, https://nichiren.info/buddhism/lotussutra/text/chap12.html.)

In an encounter with Mara, Uppalavanna is able to see clearly, her consciousness piercing through the illusion of the "Evil One" without fear, who then leaves, disappointed and dismayed.

I am the master of my own mind

The bases of power are well developed;

I am freed from every kind of bondage,

Therefore I don't fear you, friend.

Then Mara the Evil One, realizing, "The bhikkhuni Uppalavanna knows me," sad and disappointed, disappeared right there. (Upanayanas Sutta, SN 5.5, trans. Bikkhu Bodhi, accessed March 26, 2025, www.accesstoinsight.org/tipitaka/sn/sn05/sn05.005.bodh.html)

3 Julia Serano, *Whipping Girl: A Transsexual Woman on Sexism and the Scapegoating of Femininity* (Seal Press, 2007).

4 Gloria Lucas. "How Does Settler Colonialism Connect to Eating Disorders?" Nalgona Positivity Pride, July 25, 2024, https://nalgonapositivitypride.squarespace.com/npp-blog/how-does-settler-colonialism-connect-to-eating-disorders. This article explores the multifaceted impacts of settler colonialism on Indigenous communities, particularly focusing on how these effects contribute to the development and perpetuation of eating disorders.

5 I refer to an ontology of living systems here that is defined through a lens offered by Bayo Akomolafe in his writing. This understanding of the world is akin to my lived experience of dependent origination.

In an essay entitled "Do Our Bodies Matter?" Akomolafe shares:

Our modern tendency to parse the world into fixed categories, into boundaried sectors and fields, often blinds us to the significance of a world that is entangled—and not merely entangled in the sense of having predetermined, pre-relational properties, but in the queer sense popularized by Karen Barad, a theoretical particle physicist who coined the word "intra-action" (as opposed to inter-action) to show how ongoing relationships, not discrete "things," are what the world is made of. As such, Ebola is not a virus per se, but a "phenomenon"— and to understand it, we must study how it materializes from a particular configuration of humans, the non-human world, national boundaries, scientific discourse, the media, technology and more.

Once you can wrap your thoughts around this (that there are no individual "things," and that everything is intra-connected to everything else), it becomes easier to see why health is a political-economic-spiritual-epistemological-ontological issue, and why addressing today's escalating tally of reported sicknesses means paying close attention to the discourse of development, to the myriad ways we have divorced ourselves from "nature," to the way work culture is framed, to the way knowledge is produced and reproduced, to the masculinities that exert themselves in form of economic progress and growth, and to the ways our bodies, ironically, do not matter. (Bayo Akomolafe, "Do Our Bodies Matter? Revisiting Health as Entanglement with the Nonhuman World," *Bayo Akomolafe*, accessed March 26, 2025, www.bayoakomolafe.net/post/do-our-bodies-matter.)

6 Sabrina Strings, *Fearing the Black Body: The Racial Origins of Fat Phobia* (New York University Press, 2019).

7 "Satipatthana Sutta: The Foundations of Mindfulness," trans. Nyanasatta Thera, accessed March 26, 2025, www.accesstoinsight.org/tipitaka/mn/mn.010.nysa.html.

8 Lama Rod Owens speaks of spaciousness as liberation in his book *Love and Rage*. He teaches that it is in the experience of spaciousness that one is able to touch into liberation. Lama Rod Owens, *Love and Rage: The Path of Liberation through Anger* (North Atlantic Books, 2020).

9 Thích Nhất Hạnh, *The Other Shore: A New Translation of the Heart Sutra with Commentaries* (Palm Leaves Press, 2017), 37.

10 Nhất Hạnh, *The Other Shore*.

11 Jacqueline Kramer, "Yasodhara and Siddhartha: The Enlightenment of Buddha's Wife," *Turning Wheel: A Journal of the Buddhist Peace Fellowship* (Summer 2010): 10–13.

Chapter 10 (Suh)

1 Sara Ahmed, *Living a Feminist Life* (Duke University Press, 2017), 21.

2 Ahmed, *Living a Feminist Life*, 20.

3   Soraya Chemaly, *Rage Becomes Her: The Power of Women's Anger* (Atria Books, 2018), xxiii–xxiv.

4   Chemaly, *Rage Becomes Her*, 63.

5   Thích Nhất Hạnh, *Anger: Wisdom for Cooling the Flames* (Riverhead, 2001), 33.

6   Nhất Hạnh, *Anger*, 32.

7   Nhất Hạnh, *Anger*, 55.

8   Cathy Park Hong, *Minor Feelings: An Asian American Reckoning* (One World, 2021), 36.

9   Hong, *Minor Feelings*, 9.

10 Min Jin Lee, "Our bodies are not designed to absorb and process this much violence, loss, and grief," X, May 24, 2022.

11 Gail Parker, *Restorative Yoga for Ethnic and Race-Based Stress and Trauma* (Singing Dragon, 2020), 37.

11 bell hooks, *All About Love: New Visions* (William Morrow, 2018), 53.

12 hooks, *All About Love*, 54.

INDEX

CONTRIBUTORS

Chenxing Han (she/her) is the author of *Be the Refuge* (2021); *one long listening* (2023); and over twenty articles and book chapters for both academic and mainstream audiences. She is a regular contributor to *Lion's Roar* and *Tricycle* magazines and a frequent speaker and workshop leader at schools, universities, and Buddhist communities across the nation. She has received fellowships from Hedgebrook, Hemera Foundation, the Lenz Foundation, and elsewhere. Chenxing holds a BA from Stanford University, an MA in Buddhist Studies from the Graduate Theological Union, and a certificate in Buddhist chaplaincy from the Institute of Buddhist Studies in Berkeley, California.

Funie Hsu/Chhî (she/they) is a transdisciplinary scholar and associate professor of American studies at San Jose State University. She was raised in, and continues to practice, the Taiwanese Humanistic Buddhist tradition and is a co-organizer of May We Gather: A National Buddhist Memorial for Asian American Ancestors.

Jane Naomi Iwamura is chief academic officer and professor of religious studies at University of the West. Her publications include *Virtual Orientalism: Asian Religions and Popular Culture* and the co-edited volume, *Revealing the Sacred in Asian and Pacific America*. She has also written on Japanese American lived religion. She was raised in the Jodo Shin Buddhist tradition.

Mihiri Tillakaratne is an associate editor at *Lion's Roar*, where she focuses on Asian American Buddhist issues. She has a PhD in ethnic studies and gender, women, and sexuality from UC Berkeley, where her dissertation explored how the tensions between body, diaspora, and time take on contradictory meanings affecting Sri Lankan American identities.

Mushim Patricia Ikeda, sacrae theologiae doctor, honoris causa, is a Buddhist teacher, writer, poet and justice activist based in Oakland, California, whose most recent publication is a series of poems on the Heart Sutra in *Cascadian Zen, Volume One* (Watershed Press 2023). She is featured in the 2008 documentary, *Between the Lines: Asian American Women's Poetry*, which offers rare interviews with over 15 major Asian Pacific American women poets, and in the 2005 documentary, *Acting on Faith: Women's New Religious Activism in America.*

Nalika Gajaweera (she/her) is a research anthropologist at the USC Center for Religion and Civic Culture. Her specializations are in the anthropology of Buddhism and its intersections with race, ethnicity, and nationalism in the US and Sri Lanka. She is a Sri Lankan American of Sinhalese Buddhist heritage living in Los Angeles, CA. Her work has been published in popular presses such as *Buddhadharma, Jamhoor* magazine, and *Arrow Journal,* and in peer-reviewed academic publications such as *Journal of Global Buddhism* and *Anthropology Today.*

Naomi Kasumi is a Seattle-based artist, scholar, educator, and designer born in Kyoto, Japan. In 1995 she moved to the US, where she earned an MFA in visual design at the University of Oregon. In 2003 she established the Digital Design Program in the Department of Fine Arts at Seattle University. Recurring themes in Kasumi's research and art include "presence and absence," "memory/memorial," and "loss and healing." Kasumi's work includes a variety of media—some ephemeral, some permanent. Kasumi's main work, focused on a memorial series, employs a ritualistic process of repetitive creative actions in which she makes handmade objects spontaneously and obsessively and represents a therapeutic healing process.

Tâm Thâm Tịnh is a professor of Asian American studies at California State University, Northridge. She co-edited and contributed to the publication of a queer Vietnamese bilingual magazine called *O-Moi Zine* (2005), the second-ever publication about queer Vietnamese women and trans men; her essay "O-Moi" was published in *Many Bridges, One River: Organizing for Justice in Vietnamese American Communities* (2017). She also co-edited *Embodiments of Asian/American Sexualities* (2009, with Sean Metzger).

Thanda Aung is associate professor of gender and sexuality studies at UC Riverside, a co-producer of the *Transformative Hope* video series (2022, with Russell Jeung), and serves on the managing board of the Asian Pacific American Religions Research Initiative (APARRI). She is the author of *Romancing Human Rights: Gender, Intimacy, and Power between Burma and the West* (2015), and her interdisciplinary research has been published in various journals such as *Journal of Feminist Studies of Religion, PMLA,* and *Amerasia,* and in edited collections in Asian American studies.

Rev. Syd Yang, MDiv (they/them) is a mixed race/Taiwanese-American queer trans/nonbinary lay Buddhist minister and spiritual counselor who engages decolonial possibilities for shared liberation through their practice, Blue Jaguar Healing Arts. Syd is also a certified Movement Chaplain through Faith Matters Network. Syd's work finds its resonance in the stories we each hold at the intersection of memory, body, sexuality, and mental health. Syd works primarily with queer and trans BIPOC individuals, and regularly leads workshops and facilitates community-based practice spaces for well-being and healing justice, with a specific focus on grief, healing ancestral trauma, sexuality and spirituality, body liberation, and recovery. Some of their recent writing can be found in *Lion's Roar (Bodhi Leaves), Q+A: Voices of Queer Asian America, ColorBloq Journal, Chrysanthemum: Voices of the Taiwanese Diaspora,* and *Bloody Hell! Adventures in Menopause from Around the World.*

Sharon A. Suh, PhD holds the Patricia Wismer Professor of Gender and Diversity Studies chair at Seattle University. She is professor of Buddhism at Seattle University and author of *Being Buddhist in a Christian World: Gender and Community in a Korean American Temple* (University of Washington Press, 2004), *Silver Screen Buddha: Buddhism in Asian and Western Film* (Bloomsbury Press, 2015), and *Occupy This Body: A Buddhist Memoir* (Sumeru Press, 2019). She is current president of Sakyadhita International Association of Buddhist Women and certified teacher of Mindful Eating-Conscious Living through the UCSD Center for Mindfulness, with extensive training in trauma-informed yoga.

ABOUT
NORTH ATLANTIC BOOKS

North Atlantic Books (NAB) is an independent, nonprofit publisher committed to a bold exploration of the relationships between mind, body, spirit, and nature. Founded in 1974, NAB aims to nurture a holistic view of the arts, sciences, humanities, and healing. To make a donation or to learn more about our books, authors, events, and newsletter, please visit www.northatlanticbooks.com.